Blood Stories

BLOOD STORIES

Menarche and the Politics of the Female Body in Contemporary U. S. Society

Janet Lee
and
Jennifer Sasser-Coen

ROUTLEDGE
New York and London

Published in 1996 by
Routledge
29 West 35th Street
New York, NY 10001

Published in Great Britain by
Routledge
11 New Fetter Lane
London EC4P 4EE

Printed in the United States of America on acid-free paper.

The following cartoons are reprinted with permission from the artists and the publications in which they first appeared: 1.1: Piro, Stepanie H. 1993. The curse. In *Men! Ha!,* 61. Bela Cynwyd, PA: Laugh Lines Press; 3.1 Stevens, Noreen. 1994. The egg: One from the memoirs. *Sojourner: The Women's Forum* 20 (11): 3; 3.2 Bourke, Linda. 1984. Swiss army tampon. *Sojourner: The Women's Forum* 20 (11): 3; 3.3 Piccolo, Rina. 1994. Without warning, the wings on her panty-shield started flapping furiously. *Stand back, I think I'm gonna laugh,* 33. Bela Cynwyd, PA: Laugh Lines Press; 3.4 Piccolo, Rina. 1994. At 40 second intervals, Becky checks for the little string. *Stand back, I think I'm gonna laugh,* 86. Bela Cynwyd, PA: Laugh Lines Press; 4.1 Hollander, Nicole. 1994. On days when women are in charge of heaven. In *The best of contemporary women's humor,* ed. Roz Warren, 32. Freedom, CA: Crossing Press; 5.1 Katz, Lori, and Meyer, Barbara. 1995. Queen for a day jewelry. In *101 super uses for tampon applicators: A parody.* El Segundo, CA: High Stress Press; 7.1 Goodman, Janis. 1992. I said pass a crampon. *The best contemporary women's humor,* ed. Roz Warren, 30. Freedom, CA: Crossing Press.

Library of Congress Cataloging-in-Publication Data
Lee, Janet, 1954–
Blood stories: menarche and the politics of the female body in contemporary U.S. Society / Janet Lee and Jennifer Sasser-Coen.
p. cm.
Includes bibliographical references and index.
ISBN 0-415-91546-5. — ISBN 0-415-91547-3 (pbk.)
1. Menarche. 2. Menstruation. 3. Body, Human—Social aspects. 4. Body, Human—Political aspects. I. Sasser-Coen, Jennifer, 1966–. II. Title.
GN484.38.L44 1996
612.6'62—dc20 96-26910
CIP

Contents

Acknowledgments

Most important and special thanks go to all the women who shared their memories of menarche with us. Their knowledge and insights have been crucial in giving direction and energy to this project. Thanks go to Jan Hare and other Oregon State University Extension faculty and staff for their help in recruiting older women for the study. We also want to thank the great team of research assistants for their assistance with interviewing, especially Alida Benthin, Sindy Mau, Monica Molina, and Tamara Shaub. Heartfelt thanks to Kathy Jones for the many hours spent transcribing the narratives and to Linda Hahn for her clerical and computing support. Thanks also to several anonymous reviewers for their important feedback at several crucial stages of this project's development. We appreciate the funding support from the Oregon Council for the Humanities and from the Center for the Humanities and the Research Office at Oregon State University.

Many colleagues offered friendship and support as well as important feedback on our writing. Thanks to Oregon State University Women's Writing Group members for their encouragement and tireless comments on many drafts, especially to Mina Carson, Lori Cramer, Lisa Ede, Hillary Egna, Joan Gross, Nancy Rosenberger, and, last but certainly not least, Rebecca Warner, a long-time friend of Janet's who helped nourish the ideas in this book. We also thank and truly appreciate those other feminist friends and colleagues with whom we have shared the joys of feminist thinking and action and who have helped spark our creativity as writers, in particular Cynthia Adams, Vicki Collins, Deltra Ferguson, Cheryl Glenn, Anita Helle, Patti Lather, Annie Popkin, Lani Roberts, Karen Seccombe, and Barbara Paige. Jennifer also thanks the members of her doctoral committee, particularly her mentor Clara C. Pratt and her comrades Jennifer Viviano and Wendy Willis.

This project flourished in part because of the trust and encouragement we have had for each other as authors. We also have cherished the support of our families—especially the strong women in our mother lines: grandmothers Jewell and Edith, mothers Lettie and Susan, and aunts Martha and Elsie. For their love for and confidence in us we thank Gary Barnes and Jean-David Coen, as well as Liam Slusser,

Fiona Lee, and Edyth Lee-Barnes. In the spirit of hope we dedicate this book to our children, borrowing the words of Frigga Haug, that we may work toward a "politics of the body which enables us to live a life of resistance, to perceive in different ways, to forge new connections, and not subjugate our lives" (1987: 283).

Portions of this book have been previously published. "Menarche and the (hetero)sexualization of the female body" was published in 1994 in *Gender and Society* 8(3): 343–362, and we have an article in press, "Memories of menarche: Older women remember their first menstrual period" in the *Journal of Aging Studies* 10(2), forthcoming in 1996. We gratefully acknowledge the cartoonists whose humor enriched this book as well as our moods during this process. Special thanks to Roz Warren for her help with the cartoons.

Introduction

Menarche and Body Politics

Autumn, 1968

I am fourteen years old and the youngest of two children growing up in a working-class family in the north of England. I have discovered brownish-red stuff in my underwear and am realising this is the "visitor" that my mother has told me about. A year or so earlier she gave me a matter-of-fact lecture on reproduction and I tried to understand the different terms. I didn't really make the connection to sex; I had vague ideas about how that worked, and had learned that it was to be avoided at all costs. Our sex education at school consisted of a chapter of a book on rabbit reproduction, basically how rabbits "did it," completely out of the blue since the book or the topic wasn't tied to any other curricula. I can remember at the time thinking how odd it was that we should be told to read this, no questions, no tests, no discussion. At fourteen I'm one of the last to start among my friends. Actually, I don't know that for sure; we have never really talked about it—periods or sex. I just know somehow. I feel ambivalent; ready to take on this challenge, these changes, yet anxious about what it all implies. While the whole topic is relatively hush hush, and my developing body must be covered appropriately and protected from the advances and glances of boys, I know that my worth in life is to attract these very same boys. A bit of a dilemma.

We are at my grandma's house and I am wearing a dress my mother has made me. It has yellow, orange, and green flowers on it, a scoop neck, long sleeves and a drop waist. I remember this dress distinctly—I liked it a lot, yet always felt stiff and awkward when I wore it. I wonder now why I was wearing it that day when I already felt uncomfortable having started my period for the first time. I think it's a Sunday since we are visiting Grandma and I am not at school. The sky is grey and overcast and there is a chill in the air. Except for the brightly coloured dress, in my memory this incident is grey and gloomy. My grandma and mother are whispering in the kitchen, loud enough for me to overhear that they are talking about me. I feel embarrassed and wish this were not happening to me. My brother wants me to go out and play cricket with him, but I only wanted to stay curled up in the chair, nursing my cramps and feeling tired. I remember the chair and its location in the living room as if it were only yesterday. Looking back I wonder if my brother knew what was going on. I'm not sure; I don't remember being overly concerned about that, although I do remember learning later, as if by osmosis, because I have no memory of actually being told this, on no condition should I let my brother see my sanitary towels (British English for pads). I should conceal all evidence of menstruation from him. Perhaps I was too preoccupied with myself and my own feelings to care at that moment.

I have a huge sanitary towel with a belt and learn how to put it on and dispose of it properly. It feels like a mattress between my legs and I immediately start plotting how to avoid having to wear this thing. My passion is horses and I think about how such a large bulky thing will feel between my legs when I ride, restricting my movements. I also play field hockey in high school; my position is left wing—the one who has to be the fastest sprinter on the field. I love the feeling of flying down the field, dribbling the ball and whacking it back to the centre forward. We wear short grey wrap-around skirts; I remember Kathleen P. losing her skirt in the middle of a game and being glad it wasn't me—especially me with this mattress between my legs. I remember I often stuffed toilet paper in my underwear to avoid having to wear all the menstrual rigmarole and, since my periods were mostly light, this seemed to work quite well. I don't remember much else about that Sunday except that my Grandmother tells me I shouldn't be thinking about washing my hair if I am menstruating, and I do get up eventually and join my brother in playing cricket. It feels good to be moving. Maybe this means things won't change too drastically after all.

Fortunately, and to my delight, I don't have another period for seven or eight months and feel I've been given a reprieve from impending woman-

hood. When I do menstruate again it is a humiliating experience. I am staying overnight at a friend's home and bleed all over the bed, staining the sheets and making an awful mess. The friend's stern aunt asks me if I need any "products" and that makes me even more uncomfortable. I am terribly embarrassed and wash the sheets out by hand in the kitchen, wishing more than anything that this was not happening to me.

As I grow older I start to take control; a friend shows me how to use a tampon and my periods continue light and pain-free enough that for the most part I don't notice them too much. I learn to trust my body and appreciate its strength. I continue to work with horses, riding and mucking out stables, carrying bales of straw on my back and learning how to fix fences. Other than wishing I could lose a few pounds, I continue to feel okay about my body. I like it most of the time; it's strong, healthy and I especially like the way it usually doesn't let me down. My tendency as I age is to be in my head too much, but fortunately my body seems to follow along okay—jl.

Autumn, 1979

I am "the new girl." I am twelve years old and I have just started seventh grade at a new school, in a new town, in a new state. My parents just moved us north, to Oregon from California, so that my deaf brother can go to a special school. My dad hasn't found a job yet, and we don't have a house of our own to live in. For now, we are staying an hour away from where I go to middle school, with some elderly, distant cousins and their elderly, chain-smoking friends in a big, odd house on a busy street. Because I am new and because I look and dress strange and because I don't even live in the town where I go to school, I haven't any friends. No friends, that is, except for the brown-eyed boy who helps my dad and me push our run-down '57 Chevy truck each time it stalls in front of the school. Just in case all of this isn't disruptive and humiliating enough for me, this is the same time my body decides to thrust me into womanhood.

It is the beginning of gym class and I am in the girl's locker room getting ready to "dress down." I always put my gym clothes on in the privacy of one of the toilet stalls, rather than suffer the humiliation of displaying my body before the other girls in the locker room. As I am undressing I have noticed a clay colored smear on my pants, and then my panties, and I start to panic because I am unprepared, because I have no friends, because I don't know the gym teacher well enough to ask him for help, because now I am officially a "young lady." And then, because there is nothing else I can do, I sit down on the toilet and weep.

At some point, the very toughest girl in the eighth grade asks me through a crack in the stall door if I am okay. I tell her that I've just had my period for the first time and I don't know what to do. I let her come into the toilet stall and she begins to instruct me on how to insert a tampon into my vagina. Through my tears I inform her that my parents will not allow me to use a tampon until after I am married. I can tell she thinks I'm weirder than weird. I start stuffing toilet paper between my legs. The tough girl says that toilet paper is not what you're supposed to use. She gets a sanitary napkin from the machine in the locker room and passes it to me under the stall door. I open the brown card-board box and find a huge white pad and two safety pins. This pad is much thicker than the kind my mother uses and I don't recall being told anything about safety pins! She tells me to pin the pad on to my panties. My panties are a mess, and I try to wipe off some of the stuff with the toilet paper. I hate the thought of going through the rest of the day with a pad the size of a shoe, attached to my bloody panties with sharp safety pins, pressed into my crotch. Even more, I hate the thought of trying to run up-and-down the basketball court in my tight, little red gym shorts with this totally obvious pad bulging from between my legs. Well, at least if I have an accident the blood won't show on my red shorts.

I don't remember anything else about this day. I don't recall telling my mother that I had started menstruating. I do remember having very heavy bleedings—with bad cramps and break-outs—every month thereafter and even now. And I will never forget the mortifying experiences I had during high school. I often bled through my sanitary pads and onto my clothing. Sometimes I would discover blood pooling on my chair at the end of a class. I would have no way to get home to change my clothing—I wasn't allowed to ride in friends' cars and my parents were unavailable—so I would stand in the main hall with my back against a wall and wait until a friend passed by from whom I could borrow a jacket or sweater to tie around my waste and hide my accident. I also remember being asked if I was "on the rag" whenever I got sad or angry or impatient. By my Junior year in high school I decided I could no longer live under such conditions every month and so I developed some strategies to take care of myself. I used tampons, without my parents knowledge, while at school; my friends and I developed code words to use when talking about our periods ("Beelzebub," a name for the devil, meant "please look at my bottom and tell me if you see any blood"); if a menstrual disaster occurred, I found a friend to sneak me home so I could clean up and change clothing. It was not until I was in college, living on my own, free from the craziness of my family that I began to reacquaint my self with my body and the things it does. Only in the past few years have I ceased thinking of my body as an "it" and my monthly bleeding as something disgusting and humiliating. Often now I recapture the bliss of my girlhood and live fully and freely in my body. I'm still working on a polite response when someone asks me if I am "on the rag." I have found life with a female body to be problematic and often painful. At the same time, I have found self-determined and conscious embodiment to be a source of joy, power, and passion—jsc.

We begin with ourselves because this is where all projects begin. Our experiences of menarche and our bodily histories provide the backdrop for our intellectual journies; they are the lenses through which we interpret the politics of the body and they have guided our interpretations of other women's stories. Despite our difference in age (Janet is forty-two, Jennifer is twenty-nine), we are both of white European or European-American descent and grew up in working-class homes. We are both married: Jennifer has a new baby daughter Isobel Monique, and Janet has a son Liam and two daughters Fiona and Edyth. We also have both come to our interest in the politics of the body through our academic and practical entanglements with feminism and feminist praxis, as well as through our experiences as women growing up in misogynous societies. We work at Oregon State University: Jennifer is a Research Associate in Adult Development and Aging, and Janet is an Associate Professor and Director of Women Studies.

Our own biographies and stories of menarche resonate with those of the women in this book. The issues we recount are also contained in the voices and words of the women who shared their memories of menarche with us. These themes are about contamination and concealment, about the embarrassments, shame and fear of discovery, of teasing, of showing, and of staining. All involve the disciplinary practices associated with femininity, the use of specific products, and restrictions on body and behavior. These stories are also about alienation and sexualization, lack and transformation of power, ambivalences about changing bodies, relationships between menarche and subsequent perceptions and experiences of menstruation and the menopause. They are also about changing relationships with mothers and fathers, girlfriends and boys, other family members and strangers, and about struggles to resist the disciplinary practices of menarche.

We explore menarche as a central aspect of body politics, loaded with the ambivalence associated with being a woman in Western society. We also explore the issues of sexuality and sexualization, looking at these phenomena in terms of how, through menarche, the body is invested with certain properties and inserted into regimes of truth, knowledge and power. Yet what does it mean to experience such a crucial signifier of womanhood in a society that devalues women, especially when this devaluation occurs through cultural scripts associated with the body? Overwhelmingly, messages associated with menarche in a wide range of cultural and historical contexts are ones of ambivalence (Buckley and Gottlieb 1988; Delaney, Lupton and Toth 1988; Golub 1983, 1992; Lander 1988). Even those women who reflect with positive thoughts and memories upon their first blood experience also articulate its negative and shameful aspects (Hays, 1987; Jackson, 1992;

Koff, Rierdan and Jacobson 1981; Martin 1987; Weideger 1976; Whisnant and Zegans 1975). To talk of menstruation in contemporary Western culture is to articulate its secretive, emotionally-laden, and shame-filled dimensions (Thorne 1993).

Over time and across cultures, women have been associated with the body, and with blood and flesh. Their bodies have been despised, tolerated, and exalted depending upon the immediate context and prevailing politics. Male desires and policies have been scripted onto the female body at the same time that "woman" has been overdetermined and overrepresented in contemporary art, social science, and politics, not to mention scientific and medical discourses. Given this context, menstruation and menarche, the onset of women's monthly bleeding, have particular significance as illustrations of the ways bodily events take on cultural codings, that is to say, how social institutions shape the knowledges and practices surrounding menstruation and frame menarche as an important event.

Given that "womanhood" is conflated with biology and sexuality in contemporary Western societies, it is at menarche that girls start to produce themselves as women, reproducing gender in compliance with and in resistance to patterns of domination. Our goal for this book is to explore the forms of knowledge and practices that surround menarche and that help to produce women as embodied, sexualized beings. Through these processes, girls' bodies are trained and moulded in the context of prevailing systems of power, and girls receive important lessons about female blood and feminine bodies, women's place and desire. Using excerpts from oral and written narratives, we explore the regulatory forms of knowledge and concrete disciplinary practices that affect women, focusing on the internalization of these discourses and the reproduction of oppressive gendered social relations. We also discuss ways that women have resisted such practices. In this way, we analyze the role played by menarche in the reproduction of gender and the implications of menarche for life course development.

A prevailing fear among feminist scholars has been that, by studying uniquely female processes such as menstruation, one might indirectly perpetuate the essentialist ideology which defines women as sex objects and reproducers, and which sees women as being at the mercy of their biology. The women's stories presented here raise questions concerning the ways dominant socio-cultural constructions of gendered biological processes affect women's experiences of menarche as well as their menstrual histories over the life course. We are not positing an essentialist or determinist approach to the female life course, or to women's experiences generally, based soley on the female body. At the same time, however, we must remember that development is *embodied*, and our understanding of how women go through the life course can only be clarified and deepened by listening to women's stories surrounding their bodily selves (see Lee 1994; Martin 1987; Sasser-Coen 1991, 1996; Ussher 1989). We emphasize that in collecting and analyzing these stories, we are attending to the processes that position subjects and produce their "experiences." In this sense this project is concerned with the contributions of discourses, languages and practices surrounding menstruation to the ongoing production of the body as a cultural entity. We hope to provide a clearer picture of the social construction and representation of menarche or first period in contemporary Western industrial societies, and to explore cultural models that attempt to proscribe such a bodily event by sharing the voices of women who have spoken and written about their experiences of menarche.

"Discourses" involve the ways in which women and women's bodies are spoken and written about, and, more fundamentally, what these words and attributions reveal about the cultural metaphors that shape dominant "realities." The discourses surrounding menarche are intimately wound up with the politics of the female body. As Jane Ussher tells us, they have been used "to confine women, to define women as dangerous and deviant, and to exclude them from a role in society equal to that enjoyed by men" (1989: 133). In this sense, "discourse" refers to the patterns and workings of power surrounding certain issues, or as McNay suggests, "discursive formation is to be understood as an amalgam of the material practices and forms of knowledge linked together in a non-contingent relation" (1992: 27). In other words, the material and the nonmaterial get linked together in a concrete theory of discourse. Discourses involve the interplay of power within, through, and between assumptions, beliefs, practices, ways of talking about phenomena and ways of behaving. A discourse can also be seen as a "system of meaning," or, as Gavey puts it, "a way of constituting meaning which is specific to particular groups, cultures, and historical periods and is always changing" (1989: 46). Patterns of concrete, everyday behavior, the disciplinary practices of femininity, and the language, words and gestures used to describe women's bodies create the discourses of the body politic and structure our thinking, communicating, and acting. Cultural discourses of the body and its menstrual secretions and cycles represent the point where power relations are manifest in their most concrete form.

Discourses also reflect the underlying assumptions and metaphors which constitute different epistemological systems. Thus, for example, in the context of social scientific thinking and researching, specific discourses are revealed by both the questions which are asked and the methods which are used to construct and interpret answers (Harding 1991; Maguire 1987; Morgan 1983). While discourses vary in their mainstream legitimacy and authority, all systems of meaning provide only a partial truth—a "possible knowledge"—and a temporary one at that (Clifford 1983). Dominant social scientific discourses, at present and historically, at best provide incomplete descriptions of women's lives, and at worst ignore or misconstrue the complexity and diversity of women's life course experiences.

While women's bodies are produced discursively within misogynist societies, women's everyday experiences in negotiating adolescence, and life with a female body generally, are concrete. Women internalize and maintain such negative discourses, but also actively resist them through appropriation and/or integration of more positive discourses of the body. While women are always located in a particular configuration of the everyday, and, as Dorothy Smith reminds us, "the standpoint of women never leaves the actual" (1992: 91), it is important to emphasize that this "actual" does involve the negotiation of subject positions through discourse, of positions from which women as subjects emerge. Women's thoughts and behaviors are grounded in these particular discursive spaces; at the same time, women's agency to comply with and resist such discourses is recognized. Attention to this discursive formation does not remove agency from the human subject; instead, it problematizes human behavior and emphasizes how individuals negotiate identities and subject positions. Narratives of women's memories of menarche highlight this interactive nature of discourse and agency; when women remember their first menses, their memories are framed by many competing discourses. Women become subjects by sifting through and making meaning of their experiences.

We are interested in the ways individuals work themselves into socio-sexual structures that constrain and mould their lives. Since it is important to see women's bodies as sites of struggle that involve both compliance and resistance to normalizing discourses, we use "working themselves into" various scripts to mean the ways women maintain as well as resist such narratives. This project explores these social relations of menarche as they are concretely lived by diverse groups of women, providing a glimpse into the ways women construct themselves in relation to the practices and norms of menstruation. We wish to share stories of the body, to give voice and affirmation to individual women at the same time as we identify menarche as a crucial site for critical cultural production. Telling, writing and analyzing the stories of menarche are steps toward deconstructing the negative discourses that surround menstruation, and contribute to the historical study of the patterned nature of women's sexual and reproductive selves.

Our project is in part about "identity" and the construction of embodied subjectivity. These concepts are necessary in order to grapple with human agency and recognize the rights of marginalized peoples to be subjects in their own right, yet problematic because of their association with static and unified notions of the self. We emphasize that for us "identity" is in constant formation as individuals work through their own biographies in particular historical and socio-political locations, modifying these constructions as they negotiate various cultural and discursive contexts. In this sense, to indulge in such an empirical analysis is to work with a relatively stable notion of the subject. However, since the "self" is inherently unstable and multiple, any unitary and fixed notion of the subject and "identity" is problematic. As a result, to avoid the untenable position of not being able to say much about anything, we negotiate between our empiricist tendencies and our poststructualist theoretical leanings to emphasize a changing notion of identity that recognizes material and discursive contexts within which individuals are constituted and constitute themselves. For this project, these contexts concern the multiple meanings of female bodies, blood and sexuality, and the everyday practices associated with the menstruating body. "This text is framed by Western discourses that stress the essential and embodied nature of gender identity, and its focus on menarche does tend to imply an overprivileging of gender based upon sexual difference. However, we hope to contribute to a dialogue that problematizes issues of sex/gender difference generally and that moves us in the direction of understanding experience as a form of embodied subjectivity" (Moore 1994).

Our work also concerns the notion of "bodily histories" (Sasser-Coen 1996) and the personal and sociocultural discourses which shape them. By "bodily histories" we mean the psychosocial experiences of going through one's life course, within specific historical and sociocultural spaces, with a particular body. The bodily histories of women over the life course provide important insights into how menarche as a maturational event—and menstruation as an ongoing process—is shaped by the contexts in which they take place, and into the ways in which the menarcheal experience impacts menstrual history, body-image, and gender development. If we are to challenge mainstream discourses about women's life-span development, diverse voices must join the ongoing project of constructing knowledge. Specifically, individual women must name what is true to them as women who are embodied. By gathering bodily histories of both separation and wholeness, of alienation and embodiment, we can start to reshape and transform language, thinking, and ultimately "reality," informing theories of life-span development concerning the specific developments of women.

Chapter 1, "Bodies and Blood," explores the association of women with the body, the wide-ranging cultural expressions of such associations in mythologies and institutions, and the social practices that sustain them. We outline theoretical discussions on the body, explore the politics of body issues, and provide an overview of scholarship on menstruation and menarche. In terms of menstruating bodies, we emphasize that women are caught up in practices that sustain relations of domination, frequently receiving pleasure from the management of such activities—or if not pleasure, certainly embarrassment should these practices not be followed. Menstrual blood invokes strong reactions, and its significance for female embodiment is great.

In chapter 2, "Re-membering Firstblood," we focus on methodological issues and theoretical and practical implications of feminist personal narrative work. We describe our sample of women's voices, as well as how we conducted the research generally. We will also share one oral history transcript, edited, but almost in its entirety, that illustrates some themes that run through all women's stories. It provides a grounding for the other chapters, which tend to use shorter excerpts from multiple transcripts.

Within Western industrialized societies, medical discourses of the body—with their accomplices, the discourses of hygiene—have worked together to frame the female body and its bloody discharges as problematic and potentially pathological. This underscores the message that women's bodies and genitals (coded in terms of sexuality) must be closely monitored lest they get out of hand, and certainly must be attended to lest they smell or offend. Chapter 3, "Contamination and Concealment," explores the politics of menstrual taboo and pollution in more detail, emphasizing how these are played out at menarche in the everyday lives of women, from the ways women receive information and the products they use, to the practices that maintain notions of pollution and enforce concealment. This chapter explores the everyday disciplinary menstrual practices and the various regimes of "truth" that support them—practices coded as normative femininity that regulate the female body and ultimately reproduce gender.

It is primarily through the body that women are inserted into the hierarchical ordering of the sexual. Menarche represents the entrance into embodied womanhood in a society where women are framed by their reproduction and devalued, in part, also through sexualized cultural scripts attached to the body. These scripts, while never completely dormant during childhood, tend to be activated at menarche; young women's developing bodies represent their sexualization in a misogynous culture. Chapter 4, "(Hetero)Sexualization," explores these issues, illustrating objectification and sexualization. In this chapter we discuss the language that women use to describe menarche and explore the processes whereby girls learn to look at and judge themselves in accordance with societal standards of contemporary femininity.

Experiencing menarche involves negotiating the web of relationships that accompany this adolescent journey. Chapter 5, "Intricate

Relationships," explores how mothers and women's relationships with their mothers are prominent in women's stories of menarche and discusses women's memories of relationships with sisters and other girls. Fathers and brothers tend to figure less significantly here, or, more specifically, they enter as people from whom women have learned to hide evidence of monthly bleeding. This also goes for male strangers, and, in particular, male peers. Associations with boys figure prominently in the scripted heterosexual dramas of early adolescence, and have important implications for women's sense of themselves and for their future development. We discuss how the normative constraints of a patriarchal society and its pressures for girls to be in particular kinds of relationships with others encourage girls to lose their sense of themselves and affect their abilities to connect authentically with others.

Chapter 6, "Older Women's Bodily Histories," analyzes the voices of older women who remember both menarche and the menopause. It explores how dominant sociocultural constructions of the bodily processes of these life transitions are reflected in individual women's experiences as menstruators, as well as their relationships to their bodies, over the life course. In this chapter we analyze how women's early experiences surrounding menarche have developmental implications for how they conceptualize and experience menopause, and their bodies more generally, in the second half of life.

Finally, in our conclusion, "Consciousness and Resistance," we explore the ways that women have survived and coped with the negativities surrounding menarche in their everyday lives. While women have complied with and replicated the discourses and disciplinary behaviors associated with menarche, they also have shown their consciousness and resistance to these destructive and alienating practices through insight and analysis, the telling of their stories, and the many other ways that women have learned to cope. Some women spoke of increasing solidarity with girls, of using menstruation as a way to manipulate others and get their way; many spoke of having done or having a desire to do things differently when their own daughters started or start to menstruate. This chapter discusses compliance and resistance as they affect psychological health and well-being, political insight and action.

1

Bodies and Blood

> Throughout patriarchal mythology, dream-symbolism, theology and language, two ideas flow side by side: one, that the female body is impure, corrupt, the site of discharges, bleedings, dangerous to masculinity, a source of moral and physical contamination.... On the other hand, as mother the woman is beneficent, sacred, pure, asexual, nourishing; and the physical potential for motherhood—that same body with its bleedings and mysteries—is her single destiny and justification in life.
>
> —Adrienne Rich, *Of Woman Born*

Woman and the Body

The human body is a cultural artifact. While our bodies are biophysical entities, what our bodies mean and how they are experienced has much to do with the sociocultural and historical spaces they occupy. Both men and women have bodies, but what male and female bodies signify tend to be two quite different things in most cultures. Specificity here is important: discourses about the body exhibit cultural and historical variations such that there can never be one official "bodily history," despite what scientific discourses assert. While corporeality brings with it certain universal experiences—such as birth, development, aging, pain, desire, and death—one typical human body does not exist; there are as many bodily histories as there are human beings. The corollary is that a phenomenon such as menstruation—while a nearly universal physiological process among females—is characterized by specific historical, cultural, and personal meanings and practices. Menarche, accordingly, is a maturational event that originates from inside the female body and collides with meanings and practices originating from outside the female body.

In Western societies women have been associated with the body and the earth, while men, because of their association with the spirit and the sky, have been allowed to transcend the mundane toward abstract reason and the veneration of the mind. Such deep, myth-based connections have strongly informed gender ideologies, and have reinforced the determinism implied by the biological capabilities of the female body to bleed without injury or trauma and to bring forth and sustain life. Women's monthly bleeding has been taken as evidence of and justification for their association with a debased, mundane body and their exclusion from the domain of reason. Scientific and medical models have exacerbated these gendered dichotomies, have framed the female body in denigrating and often dangerous ways, and have encouraged the idea that women's lives are directed and circumscribed by their reproductive systems (Fausto-Sterling 1985; Highwater 1991; Martin 1987). At the same time, as Adrienne Rich's statement at the start of this chapter suggests, there is a cultural place for the reverence of women's bodies as sacred vessels for men's children. To put these two meanings together is to invoke the familiar juxtaposition vis-a-vis cultural messages and sexual scripts: the reproductive mother or asexual "madonna" versus the sexual being or "whore." And, in most cultures, it is at menarche that these two expressions of the feminine first come into conflict, as menarche simultaneously symbolizes the onset of reproductive and sexual potential. As Helen Deutsch (1944) suggested over half a century ago, menarche is when young women confront the double function of the female as sexual creature and as "servant of the species."

The development of Western civilization has been predicated on the philosophical and practical opposition between "culture" and "nature" (Lloyd 1989; Wilshire 1989; Tarnas 1991). The separation between mind and body, flesh and spirit, is also rooted in this fundamental duality, which was formalized and codified during Hellenic times and has been reinforced and perpetuated for centuries since (Sheets-Johnstone 1992). According to this Western dualistic metaphysics, human beings as embodied creatures are part of nature and are stuck in space and time. This state implies that since experiences and thoughts are shaped and limited by the temporal and spacial location of the body, the mind's projects—rationality, objectivity, and self-realization—are compromised. "Objectivity" and self-realization require dis-embodiment, that is, rejection and transcendence of the "mucky, humbling limitations of the flesh" (de Beauvoir 1952; Dinnerstein 1976). Despite historical variations in the images attached to the body, what lies at the core of all such images is the construal of the body as a thing of nature, separate from and subordinate to the mind as a thing of culture.

The domination of culture and mind over nature and body underlies the hierarchical dualism that is at the foundation of Western thought, giving us our cultural and bodily heritages (Berman 1989). Such thought is organized into polarities of either/or and is based on the belief that reality can be separated into categories of binary opposites in which one member of the pair is "normal" and the other "abnormal" (Highwater 1991). Further, this dualistic metaphysics is gendered. While a generic human body is located on the nature side of the culture/nature duality, the female body is the prototypical body from which this duality is engendered. Because of the unique biological capabilities of the female body, it is seen as being closer to nature and the organic realm than is the male body. As a result, the things women's bodies do have been construed negatively and used as the justification for every variety of denigration and oppression. The natural, normal processes of the female body are symbolically marked as abnormal and taboo, distasteful, not to be trusted and potentially evil. Western civilization's progress required "giving up the female gender—the material, passive, corporeal, and sense perceptible, for the male—active, rationale, and incorporeal" (Highwater 1991: 23).

Through the denigration and domination of nature and body, and the alignment of femaleness with "passive, indeterminate matter" (Lloyd 1989), women have become essentialized as bodies, seen at best as hopelessly part of the natural world of disorderly, decaying matter, and at worst as slaves to sinister bodily impulses and excretions meant to corrupt men and prevent their transcendence. Further evidence of the ways this complex system of interrelated dualities plays out can be witnessed in the continual endeavor of Western peoples to dominate the natural world and transcend the reality of embodiment. By disavowing the primacy and necessity of the body in the reality of being a living being, the Western human subject has attempted, and still attempts, to transcend the inevitable membership in nature. As a result, Western "civilizations" have tended to become alienated from nature and "her" processes of birth, growth, decay, and death. A case in point: one of the central goals of contemporary Western cultures is to harness technology in order to defy disease, mental and physical disability, aging, and ultimately death, so that true disembodiment can be achieved (see Berman 1989; Esposito 1987; Morgan 1982). Paradoxically, at the same time that we attempt to transcend the confines of the flesh, we make dieting, fitness, and cosmetic surgery—those things that alter how the body looks—religious pursuits. We suggest that behind both cultural preoccupations is the insidious belief that culture and nature, mind and body are indeed separable, that essentially the body is an object that can be manipulated.

Susan Bordo explores the meanings connected to the female body as cultural expressions of society's ideals and anxieties in her book *Unbearable Weight: Feminism, Western Culture and the Body*. She discusses at length the cultural expressions of mind-body dualism and the association of women with the debased and passive body, emphasizing the systemic and embedded nature of these metaphysics, as well as the consequences these ideologies and behaviors have on women's lives:

> (The) mind/body dualism is no mere philosophical position, to be defended or dispensed with by clever argument. Rather, it is a *practical* metaphysics that has been deployed and socially embedded in medicine, law, literary and artistic representations, the psychological constructions of self, interpersonal relationships, popular culture, and advertisements—a metaphysics which will be deconstructed only through concrete transformation of the institutions and practices that sustain it. (1993: 11–12)

In other words, issues concerning the body are deeply embedded into social institutions and behaviors. They prescribe and proscribe so much of what we take as "normal" everyday life. Since women are associated with the body, earth and nature, and men with the abstract powers of reason, women's bodies remind humans of their vulnerability and mortality. On the one hand, woman is associated with life, while on the other, her bleeding and oozing body—reminiscent of earthly vulnerabilities—is met with disgust. Male bodies are not so symbolically marked with such connotations. Men are more easily able to imagine their bodies free of such constraints, and they project their fears and hatred of frailty and mortality onto women's flesh (Dinnerstein 1976).

Certainly, the practical metaphysics manifested in the objectification and separation of the body from the self is not endemic to the experiences of women alone, but is part of our sociocultural heritage, and thus is shared at some level by us all. However, we feel justified in asserting that women are differentially and more seriously affected by this cultural ideology because women are both defined as and yet separated from their bodies. While women and men alike experience the mind-body split, women, unlike men, are told in countless subtle and not-so-subtle ways that they are essentially *only* bodies—reproducers and (hetero)sex-objects. These ideas are elaborated upon in two important texts: Frigga Haug's *Female Sexualization* and Jane Ussher's *The Psychology of the Female Body*.

As already noted, the female body functions as a "text" of culture; it is one of the symbolic forms upon which the norms and practices of society are inscribed. Women's bodies can be approached as cultural artifacts; culture is embodied and literally inscribed on the body, where it reproduces itself and maintains social categories. The female body is a site where different cultural discourses compete for attention. Women are affected by this cultural preoccupation with the body-as-object. The vulnerabilities of women's status encourages us to be obsessed with body issues, and, as a result, suffer in the daily ordering of our lives. Women suffer because they are encouraged to internalize these discourses, and thus their bodily experiences become circumscribed and defined by dominant systems of thought and practice. This means that the separation of mind from body is not only an extremely durable philosophical construction, but for many women an experiential reality as well. The ways we live with our bodies, and the ways we think about processes such as menstruation, are fundamental expressions of our cultural values and ideologies.

Feminists have long been concerned about the body. Indeed, it was radical feminists who first explored the control of women's bodies in both public and private spaces as essential for the maintenance of patriarchal societies. Writers and activists such as Gloria Steinem educated a generation with such witty pieces as "If Men Could Menstruate," published in *Ms.* magazine in the 1970s. Alongside these efforts, scholars such as Susan Brownmiller, Rosalind Coward and Susie Orbach have worked to educate on the politics of appearance. They have focused on the enslavement of women by the media and by the products we are encouraged to buy and use, as well as the effects of the politics of appearance on women's lives, most especially in terms of eating disorders. In *Female Desires*, Coward asks the relevant question: "How is it that the definitions addressed to clothes and women's bodies become women's own language? How is it we come to speak the words that are written on our body?" (1985: 30) Other texts on the politics of appearance—such as Wendy Chapkis' *Beauty Secrets*, *The Obsession* by Kim Chernin, Naomi Wolf's *The Beauty Myth*, and the more recent *Many Mirrors* edited by Nicole Sault—continue to explore similar questions, stressing the social construction of beauty, its normalizing consequences on the reproduction of femininity and gender, the regulation of dominant relations in society vis-a-vis gender, race, class, age, ability and size, as well as the differing ways that the body is constructed through these systems of power.

Another perspective on the politics of appearance is offered by Patricia Hill Collins' *Black Feminist Thought* (1990). Collins writes poignantly about the effects of white "beauty" standards on the lives of Black women, suggesting that externally imposed standards of beauty demoralize Black women and create feelings of inadequacy. This size and beauty debate, in both academic and more popular literary circles, has tended to center on the everyday realities of white women. Less has been written on the intersections of "looksism" with race and ethnicity, especially as it concerns racial groups other than Black women, although women in other racial groups have shared their understandings of these issues through poetry and fiction, as well as through more traditional texts (*c.f.* Wong 1995; Hernandez-Avila 1995). A collection on women, food, and body image edited by Catrina Brown and Karin Jasper, titled *Consuming Passions*, has an article on "Creating Beauty and Blackness." In this piece, author Kim Shayo Buchanan explains the hesitancy expressed by some Black women about focusing on body issues in light of other more urgent material issues. She writes that women of color have rightly prioritized addressing the strict inequalities of racism and sexism such that "discomfort with appearance pales in comparison" (1993: 36). Other notable exceptions to the silence on issues of race and beauty are Nedhera Lander's article in *Shadow on a Tightrope*, an anthology on fat oppression edited by Lisa Schoenfielder and Barb Wieser (1983). Here Lander discusses the particular effects of a fat oppressive culture on the lives of Black women. bell hooks's *Black Looks*, and her chapter in *Sisters of the Yam* entitled "Dreaming Ourselves Dark and Deep," explore these issues as well. In these writings, hooks analyzes Black internalization of and resistance to white supremacist images of anglo "beauty," and seeks to remind Blacks of "their beauty and dignity in a world where their humanity was assaulted daily" (p. 83). She focuses on hair, feet, body size and color, and raises the important issue that for many Black women, class and ethnic notions encouraged "a utilitarian approach to the care of the self." She writes: "Now, living as we do in a racist/sexist society that has, from slavery on, perpetuated the belief that the primary role of Black women should play in this society is that of servant, it logically follows that many of us internalize the assumption that our bodies do not need care, not from ourselves or from others" (1993: 88).

Other than scholarly work on the looks and beauty debate, theoretical and philosophical writings on the body tended to be underrepresented in the United States until relatively recently. New texts on "the body" are appearing with regular consistency: bell hooks's *Black Looks*, already mentioned, Judith Butler's *Bodies That Matter,* Patricia Foster's collection *Minding the Body*, Elizabeth Grosz's *Volatile Bodies*, and *The Bodies of Women* by Rosalyn Diprose are cases in point. However, as far as we are aware, no one has theoretically problematized menstrual bleeding in the context of this new scholarship on the body, and very few scholars writing on the body ever do more than mention menstruation briefly in passing.

Elizabeth Grosz, in her introduction to a special issue of *Hypatia* on "Feminism and the Body," articulates the philosophical ambivalences concerning scholarship on the body. She writes of the body as:

> a theoretical domain that has been relatively underdeveloped in feminist writings, and not without good reason: if feminists have tended to neglect and ignore the concept of the body this has to a large extent been as a reaction to the pervasively misogynistic treatment of women's bodies, and to various patriarchal attempts to reduce women to their bodies when these bodies have been conceived in the most narrowly functionalist and reductionistic terms. (1991: 1)

Grosz alludes here, of course, to the tiresome "biology is destiny" argument. She raises the feminist dilemma of either addressing the body as essentially different and celebrating these (biological) differences as sources of strength and power, or attending to the conflation of sex with gender and emphasizing the need to move beyond such prescriptive and troublesome categories. Both issues are important for analyses of menstruation and our hope is to address and be explicit about these problematics and tendencies. However, we would ultimately like to move beyond these dualities by recognizing the potential strengths individual women who perceive their bleeding as connected to issues of power and efficacy experience in their lives, and, most importantly, by deconstructing gendered relations of domination implicit in scripts associated with menarche and menstruation.

Susan Bordo's exploration of the metaphors of control and self-containment endemic to androcentric definitions of femininity provides a conceptual anchoring for our approach. In "The Body and the Reproduction of Femininity: A Feminist Appropriation of Foucault," she emphasizes that it is "through table manners and toilet habits, through seemingly trivial routines, rules and practices, culture is '*made* body,' ...converted into automatic, habitual activities" (1989: 13). Importantly, Bordo also suggests that "through these disciplines, we continue to memorize on our bodies the feel and conviction of lack, insufficiency, of never being good enough. At the farthest extremes, the practices of femininity may lead us to utter demoralization, debilitation, death" (14). She stresses that these practices and disciplines are about power and social control, and goes on to discuss the ways in which contemporary eating disorders can be read as cultural statements about gender, statements that are imbued with political meanings, and which reflect the rules of bodily discourse that script femininity. Bordo does not deal with menstrual practices, yet her insights are crucial for understanding how the rules and practices of menarche are internalized as part of the reproduction of femininity.

Discussing the body and the reproduction of femininity, Bordo cites Michel Foucault, emphasizing how the body is more than a medium of culture, how it also functions as a "*practical*, direct locus of social control" (13). In a similar fashion, Sandra Bartky, in her book *Femininity and Domination: Studies in the Phenomenology of Oppression* and her article "Foucault, Femininity and the Modernization of Patriarchal Power," analyzes how these controls are maintained through panopticism, the internalization of discourses surrounding the body. She considers the disciplinary practices whereby the female body is transformed into a "feminine" one, emphasizing how sexuality is produced through power and hierarchical social relations are maintained. Like Bordo, while Bartky does not mention menstruation, her analysis of the disciplinary regimens of femininity is useful for us because of its explanation of the specific concrete practices that help produce feminine subjects, as well as the ways that the absence of a formal institutional structure and the decentralization of power require the internalization of sexual scripts. These tend to result in the illusion of great personal autonomy, and the idea that femininity is natural and voluntary—"The disciplinary power that inscribes femininity in the female body is everywhere and it is nowhere" (Bartky 1992: 112).

The work of Michel Foucault figures prominently in these scholars' works. His texts *The History of Sexuality* and *Discipline and Punish* tend to be widely cited by all who do scholarship on the body. Foucault wrote about the regulatory mechanisms and everyday concrete practices that circumscribe the body and form it as an historically and culturally specific entity. His work analyzes how the body is produced through power and knowledge and is constructed to legitimize societal systems of domination; as such, the body acts as both instrument and consequence of modern forms of disciplinary control. His analyses are excellent in that they focused on the body as the locus of cultural interpretation and social control without denying its materiality and corporeality. Nonetheless, as many feminists have already suggested, Foucault paid little attention to gender, assuming that the regulatory practices of embodied femininity produce genderless "docile bodies," involving little agency beyond the hold of this monolithic, deterministic force that produces such controlled and practiced subjects (Diamond and Quinby 1988; McNay 1992). What is more, Bordo reminds us that:

> neither Foucault nor any other poststructuralist thinker discovered or invented the idea...that the "definition and shaping" of the body is "the focal point for the struggles over the shape of power." *That* was discovered by feminism, and long before it entered into its marriage with poststructuralist thought. (1993: 17)

Poststructuralism, while intellectually heady and often elitist and inaccessible, is a valuable tool for tracing the breakdown in scientific "truths" and objectivity, for emphasizing epistemological fragmentations, heterogeneity and multiplicity. Nonetheless, bodies are more than the end results of continuous discursive framings and cannot be remade so easily. There is therefore a fundamental problem with the disembodied orientation of deconstructive poststructuralism or postmodernism. Bordo has the last word:

> What sort of body is it that is free to change its shape and location at will, that can become anyone and travel anywhere? If the body is a metaphor for our locatedness in space and time and thus for the finitude of human perceptions and knowledge, then the postmodern body is no body at all. (1993: 228–29)

Bleeding Bodies

Across time and cultures menstrual blood has invoked strong responses from individuals and communities. Menstrual blood has been and sometimes still is simultaneously feared and revered, considered to be magical, contaminating, and dangerous (Buckley and Gottlieb 1988; Golub 1992; Grahn 1982, 1993). Menstrual blood has great symbolic potency and cultures have constructed many elaborate rules and regulations—commonly termed "menstrual taboos"—to deal with menstrual blood and menstruating women. These menstrual taboos are found in many forms and in most cultural contexts. According to Buckley and Gottlieb, the menstrual taboo "is at once nearly universal and has meanings that are ambiguous and often multivalent" (1988: 7). Many cultures have menstrual taboos designed to protect society from the menstruating woman, either because she is perceived as dangerous and evil or, conversely and to a lesser extent, as spiritually and creatively powerful. A few cultures have taboos meant to protect the menstruating woman from the interference of others, particularly men.

Many scholars have interpreted these cultural framings of menstruation as representing the appropriation and transformation of female power and competence, and the rendering of such power as negative and contaminating. For example, an early text, *The Curse: A Cultural History of Menstruation* by Janice Delaney, Mary Jane Lupton, and Emily Toth, opens with the following statement:

> In the beginning, the menstrual process inspired fear and wonder in human beings. Both men and women saw at once that woman's blood set woman apart from man in a mysterious, magical way. This blood flowed but did not bring death or disability, it came and went with a regularity that no human act could change. Only an even greater mystery, the creation of human life, could alter its pattern. (1988: 3)

They continue by sharing some gruelling menstrual taboo stories from a wide variety of societies such as New Guinea and rural Austria.

These authors emphasize how menstrual taboos have functioned to keep the powers of menstruating women under male control, linking male power directly to menstrual practices. They overview menstrual taboos—most of which utilize notions of dirt and pollution, life and death—that enforce seclusion, warn against heterosexual intercourse, and function as metaphors for pre-industrial themes of danger and safety.

Along the same lines, in *Blood Magic: The Anthropology of Menstruation*, Thomas Buckley and Alma Gottlieb cite anthropological literature to explain the presence of menstrual taboos in seemingly consistent forms: "Ethnographers have reported that menstrual blood and menstruating women are viewed as dangerous and/or offensive among the peoples they have observed" (1988: 6). However, they go on to offer a strong caution about universalizing tendencies, emphasizing the considerable cross-cultural variety in the meanings of menstruation. They suggest that instead of seeing menstrual taboos as some inviolate reality, it is more useful to see them as "a wide range of distinct rules for conduct regarding menstruation that be-speak quite different, even opposite purposes and meanings" (7).

Anthropological interpretations of ethnographic data emphasize the necessity of understanding anthropology itself as a form of culture, and thus as infused with issues of power and knowledge as a meaning-making discipline. Such an interpretation entails an analysis of language as well: the "menstrous" women that Buckley and Gottlieb so frequently refer to sound ominously "monstrous." Perhaps this is some linguistic coincidence, perhaps not. Nonetheless, we suggest that it reflects the ease with which Western cultures accept the notions of taboo and restraint since they work so well with contemporary negative notions of menstruation, underscoring again how meanings associated with menstruation must be understood as cultural phenomena. The bottom line, of course, is the question of why menstrual blood should matter so. Irrespective of the particularities of many diverse cultures in terms of where they fall on the continuum of despising to exalting women vis-a-vis menstruation, almost all cultures studied pay attention to and interpret women's bleeding as relevant and important.

There are both obvious and subtle examples of the menstrual taboo common in the United States and Western Europe during this century: the construal of sexual intimacy with a menstruating woman as dirty and disgusting; the stereotype that women are unable to think and perform competently while menstruating; and the practical and material restrictions on the lives of women who have often been instructed to abstain from bathing, cooking, physical exertion, and socializing during their menses (Delaney, Lupton and Toth 1988; Ussher 1989). While we might reject the notion of a universal "menstrual taboo," and instead think about diverse and culturally specific forms of "menstrual etiquette," nonetheless, as Sophie Laws points out, "a very great majority of known cultures do emphasize menstruation in some way...because it is an obvious physical function for men in a patriarchal society to use as a marker of femaleness, to convey their view of a woman's place" (1990: 19).

Historically and currently in Western societies, menstruation and the "menstrual career" (Kaufert, 1986), that is, women's experiences of menstruation throughout the life course, have been viewed through and distorted by a patriarchal lens. Since the nineteenth century, the ability of the female body to bleed has been taken as evidence of the fundamental difference not only between male and female bodies, but between men and women as gendered beings. Further, because in patriarchal societies the biophysical and social function of women is to reproduce the human species, menstruation and the menopause can only signify failure of the female as "servant of the species." The cultural appropriation of women's biological processes and the role of these processes in maintaining gendered power is discussed in the work of Sharon Golub, who has edited three books about menstruation: *Menarche: The Transition from Girl to Woman*; *Lifting the Curse of Menstruation: A Feminist Appraisal of the Influence of Menstruation in Women's Lives*, and her more recent *Periods: From Menarche to Menopause*. In *Periods*, she writes: "My hope is that this book will lead to a greater understanding of women and the meaning of menstruation in women's lives" (1992: xiii). She includes a chapter "Living with periods—and without them: Using current knowledge to help ourselves and counsel others," with suggestions on talking with girls about menarche and rethinking the menopause as a rite of passage.

A fascinating book by writer and poet Judy Grahn entitled *Blood, Bread and Roses: How Menstruation Created the World* weaves together ethnography, archaeology, myth and folklore. Grahn suggests that women's wisdoms surrounding menstruation shaped cultural histories and made us human, and writes of the incredible power of women's bleeding that was at the root of social organization:

> One word recurs again and again in stories of menstrual ritual: taboo. The word comes from the Polynesian *tapua*, meaning both "sacred" and "menstruation." ...Besides sacred, taboo also means forbidden, valuable, wonderful, magic, terrible, frightening, and immutable law. Taboo is the emphatic use of imperatives, yes or no, you must or you must not. Taboo draws attention, strong attention, and is in and of itself a language for ideas and customs.... The word "regulation" is linked to menstruation in European languages in the same way.... These terms thus connect menstruation to orderliness, ceremony, law, leadership, royalty, and measurement. (1993: 5)

She maintains that women's menstrual consciousness, "the menstrual mind," became externalized and is at the root of principles of separation, synchronic relationships, and cyclical time. Further, she introduces the notion of "metaforms" to describe the ways that cultural practices and institutions embody metaphors of the body. As Charlene Spretnak notes in the Foreword to this book, Grahn's approach flies in the face of current deconstructionist, postmodern/poststructuralist scholarship on the body: "Contrary to the claims of this belief system, culture *responds to* the elemental power of the female body, not the other way around " (xiv). Nevertheless, we stress that bodies are never untouched by history and culture, and women's bleeding can never be decontextualized. Grahn goes on to talk about the way women's wisdom and power was appropriated and transformed by men:

> The accumulation of forms and ideas spill out of women's seclusion rites and pass over to the male domain, where they become public, extended completions of the cosmology of the whole people. This happens through several vehicles, among them, parallel menstrual rites that lead to hunting, blood sacrifice, ritual games and warrior battles. (1993: 249)

Grahn's work follows the tradition of feminist scholarship which attempts to reclaim the powers associated with women's bleeding and to integrate these knowledges into empowering practices and rituals. Beginning in the late 1970s and early 1980s, emerging feminist spiritualities acknowledged and critiqued the association in myth and religion of the female principle with negative will, sneaky manipulation and disordered chaos. They explored how different cultural contexts produce mythologies and images of disgust for women's bleeding that are deeply internalized into the psyche. These mythologies encourage women to hate their bodies and men to hate things they recognize as feminine in themselves. In a collection called *The Politics of Women's Spirituality*, edited by Charlene Spretnak, Kay Turner encourages readers to "see the body, not the mind, as the locus of transformation" (1982: 229). She urges us to claim sacred space for ourselves through ritual in order to "name the powers which men have found 'anomalous' (i.e., nameless)." These feminist spiritualities see menstruation as a source of female power and encourage its "reclaiming" as a way to personal and spiritual wholeness. Despite their essentialist foundations, numerous journals and magazines, such as *SageWoman* and *Woman of Power*, as well as books like Dena Taylor's *Red Flower: Rethinking Menstruation* and Penelope Shuttle and Peter Redgrove's *The Wise Wound*, do give women reason to be proud of their bodies and their monthly cycles, and therefore play an important part in destabilizing masculinist discourses. These works tend to fall into the "addressing the body as essentially different and celebrating these (biological) differences as sources of strength and power" camp, as we discussed earlier in this chapter.

Many of the texts which focus on reclaiming and transforming the negativity surrounding women's bleeding have been spurred on by historical and contemporary accounts that critique medical "progress" vis-a-vis the body generally, and women's reproductive lives in particular (see Fausto-Sterling 1985; Martin 1987, 1990). For example, Delaney, Lupton and Toth write of the ways a developing science rests on the prevailing politics of gender in any historical era:

> But nearly all menstrual theorists also imposed their own order upon their material observations, and their ordering was shaped by patriarchal preconceptions. They reasoned that menstruation was a sign of woman's otherness, hence a sign of her inferiority; their next step was to rationalize this inferiority through whatever science was at their disposal. And that kind of rationalization is hardly dead in our own era. (1988: 48–9)

A brief, topical survey of history reveals Aristotle's notion that the female role in reproduction is passive and nutritive, the female only making enough "heat" to provide the menses that creates and nourishes the developing fetal body, compared to the male who alone can transform matter with heat, make semen and provide the soul of the child. Several centuries later, Pythagoras theorized that menstruation came from an overflow of blood. Other theorists of this early period, such as Galen and de Graaf, believed that menstruation removed surplus matter, that blood escaped from such weak and defective spaces as the womb. Despite the negativities associated with women's bleeding, the act itself was not considered pathological until the nineteenth century when new metaphors were constructed about fundamental differences between men and women (Laquer 1986; Martin 1987). Menstruation came to be seen as debilitating and pathological, and women's lives and behaviors were inextricably linked to their reproductive organs (Bullough 1975; Cayleff 1992; Smith-Rosenberg 1974). The following is an account of the temporary cessation of menses or "blocked monthly sickness," known as Green Sickness or Chlorosis, in *Gunn's Household Physician* by John C. Gunn M.D., revised and expanded in its 230th edition of 1901:

> When this is the case, the girl becomes pale, or of a greenish pallor, and her face more or less bloated; she feels feeble, dull and drowsy; her stomach is out of order, accompanied by acidity, or sour belchings, flatulence or wind, occasional nausea or vomiting; palpitation of the heart; and finally the nervous system becomes deranged, often resulting in fits of melancholy....The mind often becomes depressed, and other hysterical symptoms occur, fol-

lowed, perhaps, by a gradual wasting away of the flesh, terminating in Consumption, Dropsy, and Death. (454)

Much research on the menstrual career has been conducted from a bio-medical standpoint. In accordance with the assumptions of this paradigm, women tend to be seen as controlled by their bodies, particularly by hormonal fluctuations. During the twentieth century the "biomedical paradigm"—a modern progeny of the Western dualistic metaphysics—has become the dominant cultural discourse about the "menstrual career" and women have continued to be reduced to their bodies. This is especially true if these bodies are/were "malfunctioning" (Dickson 1993; Martin 1987; Sheets-Johnstone 1992). When normal biophysical processes such as menstruation and the menopause are pathologized and medicalized, a woman's body is not her own but a specimen which is probed, cut, and medicated. Alongside this conflation of normal female processes with pathology is the insistence that these "female problems" be treated by medical experts, again reducing women to their bodies and the things their bodies do, as well as maintaining corporate power for the medical profession. By extension, a woman's experience of and knowledge about her own body is often distrusted or misappropriated. Evidence of this medicalization of the menstrual career is seen in the "modern disease" of Premenstrual Syndrome, from which three-quarters of all women supposedly suffer (Martin 1987), and in the construction of the menopause as a "hormone deficiency disease," caused by "senile ovaries," and cured by hormone replacement therapy (Voda 1993). So long as hormonal cyclicity is non-problematic and ensures fertility and fecundity, a woman-as-body is "normal." When female cyclicity is experienced as problematic, pregnancy is thwarted, or reproduction is no longer possible, woman-as-body becomes suspect of medical and cultural treason. In resistance we offer a slogan about PMS that we recently read on a woman's t-shirt. The hassles associated with premenstrual stress (PMS) were transformed into "**P**utting up with **M**en's **S**hit!" Cartoonist Stephanie Piro (1993: 61) gives a similar re-telling of menstrual ideologies in figure 1.1 below.

In spite of the reductionistic and sexist nature of the biomedical paradigm, there are some important biomedical projects being conducted on the menstrual cycle which are predicated on feminist principles. Some exemplars are *The Menstrual Cycle: Volume I*, edited by Alice Dan, Effie Graham and Carol Beecher, and *Volume II* edited by Pauline Komnenich, Maryellen McSweeney and Janice Novack; Alice Dan and Linda Lewis's collection *Menstrual Health in Women's Lives*; and the corpus of work by Ann Voda, in particular her work in the edited volume *Menopause: A Midlife Passage*. These works achieve a delicate bal-

STRIP T's by Stephanie ©88
"And every month he asks me if I've got 'the Curse'... So, finally I told him, "I must, I'm Living with you, aren't I...?"

figure 1.1

ance: they challenge the reductionistic and sexist assumptions of the biomedical paradigm while working within and contributing to biomedicine. Menstruation and the menopause are viewed as normative biophysical processes, not as diseases which must be cured. And, most importantly, women are treated as experts about their own bodily experiences, not *as* bodies which are out-of-control.

Medical myths are the topics of two influential texts on menstruation by authors that we have already mentioned: Louise Lander's *Images of Bleeding: Menstruation as Ideology* and Emily Martin's *The Woman in the Body: A Cultural Analysis of Reproduction.* Lander explores the development of medicine as culture and ideology and the meanings of menstruation for contemporary Western women:

> Modern women's constant menstrual cyclicity is a result of, is symbolic of, our escape from compulsory motherhood. When that escape becomes threatening—when the alternative to compulsory motherhood is female encroachment on formerly male domains—it becomes useful to call menstrual cyclicity a disability. Then women are disabled from full participation in social and political life either because they are having babies or because they are not having babies. (1988: 186–7)

The power of the medical model is also analyzed by Martin in *The Woman in the Body.* She explores the cultural framings of women's reproductive processes and traces the development of a masculinist medical model and its economic underpinnings that represent menses as "failed reproduction." Her goal was to discover how cultural discourses about the female body, and in particular the biomedical paradigm, translate into individual women's beliefs and experiences. To that end, she interviewed 165 North American women of various life course stages and socio-economic levels regarding their experiences surrounding menstruation, child birth, and the menopause. In the course of talking with her informants, Martin detected a striking and disturbing consistency between dominant discourses about female bodies and women's attitudes and perceptions. She found that "working-class women, perhaps because they have less to gain from productive labor in society, have rejected the applications of models of production to their bodies" (1987: 110). In comparison, she found that middle-class women "appear much more 'mystified' by the general cultural models than working-class women. They have bought the teleological aspect of medical accounts, which sees menstrual flow as waste products of a failed pregnancy and casts it in very negative terms" (111). In addition, Martin studied the power of metaphor in medical texts and practices, emphasizing how medicine reflects gendered power arrangements in society and is loaded with cultural assumptions:

> Menstruation not only carries with it the connotation of a production system that has failed to produce, it also carries the idea of a production gone awry, making products of no use, not to specification, unsalable, wasted, scrap. However disgusting it may be, menstrual blood will come out... Perhaps one reason the negative image of failed production is attached to menstruation is precisely that women are in some sinister sense out of control when they menstruate. (46–7)

Martin's work is also important because, unlike many other scholars, she approaches menstruation empirically. Very few studies have asked diverse women about their understandings and experiences of menstruation—ironic given the near-universality of the phenomenon for women, yet understandable given the politics of academic scholarship.

Another exception is Paula Weideger's book *Menstruation and Menopause*, in which she analyzes the results of a questionnaire given to 558 women in the United States in the early 1970s. She asked a variety of open-ended questions and compiled the first "real evidence" on a large scale of the shame and embarrassment, lack of information and fear associated with menstruation generally. Last but not least, a fascinating empirical account of menstruation has been compiled by Sophie Laws in her study *Issues of Blood: The Politics of Menstruation,* written in 1990. Laws interviewed British men about their understandings of, and attitudes toward, menstruation. Her book is very revealing in that it explains how men continue to maintain and benefit from the myths and cultural practices associated with menstruation.

In addition, she emphasizes how women, despite societal trends that allow menstruation to be spoken about in the popular media and the workplace, continue to maintain the "etiquette" of menstruation, and men continue to exercise their privilege vis-a-vis these so-called "liberating" trends. In other words, men enjoy their access into women's formerly "private" menstrual spaces; some enjoy participating in this liberalized dialogue, some enjoy the embarrassed reactions of women as they symbolically move into these spaces, and some get turned on by the supposed increased sexual availability of women who are menstruating. She quotes one of her respondents talking about buying menstrual products for his girlfriend:

> A bit like buying contraceptives, but in a way it's even weirder... I'm very conscious of making a big play of buying them. I do, I do. You know what you were saying about breaking the taboo about sex, there's something a bit sort of (clicking sound), "made it", sort of, you know. Well, whenever I go buy tampax, it's the same sort of thing, I do the same. I do make a big thing about it, I suppose, I suppose I put them on the side, slam them down (laughter) here, say, how much are they? (48)

Laws goes on to say that she found it disturbing that "men in the men's group find buying sanitary wear exciting, when there are a great number of women who have to do it and who are embarrassed. The flouting of convention in this way seems somehow to reinforce the convention" (48). It is important to emphasize the persistence and malleability of the discourses and practices of gender domination as illustrated in Laws' account.

First Blood

Menarche, the onset of menstruation, while an important, magical or embarrassing time, is a life transition rarely talked about and little studied. We recount with amusement an article on our project in a local newspaper that included the misspelling "menarchy"—a sort of cross between "monarchy" and "anarchy." However, several months later our presentation at a professional conference in Women's Studies carried the same misspelling, illustrating how little-spoken is this term in everyday and academic circles. The menopause is a topic much more widely discussed. A profusion of books on the subject has come on the scene over the last couple of years, and many popular magazines routinely carry articles on issues related to this life transition. Menarche still tends to remain a relatively obscure topic even though it is such a crucial juncture between childhood and adult womanhood.

Puberty is a developmental phase in the female life course marked by rapid and dramatic emotional, somatic, and cognitive transformation (Brooks-Gunn and Petersen 1983; Faust 1983; Rierdan and Koff

1991). According to mainstream biomedical and social scientific discourses, the term "puberty" refers to the biological changes that lead to reproductive maturity, and "adolescence" connotes the contextualized social/interpersonal period of the life-course surrounding puberty and bridging childhood and adulthood (Nathanson 1991). Whereas puberty is about specific maturational processes, adolescence is about the sociocultural meanings assigned and psychosocial processes related to these bodily changes (Jenkins 1983; Thorne 1993). For the most part, social and psychological development tends to be seen as being *caused by* the biophysical changes which unfold during puberty. From a life-span developmental perspective, however, the concepts of puberty and adolescence are integrated. The life-span approach "...focuses on events that occur in the same temporal space, rather than perceiving social and psychological events as necessarily being a response to biological events" (Brooks-Gunn and Petersen 1983: xxi). As such, development across the life-span is seen as an interactive and integrative process in which biological, social, and psychological events co-occur—that is, take place simultaneously—within a matrix of sociocultural values and expectations (Petersen 1980). To focus on only one factor, or to presuppose that these factors only relate unidirectionally, is to construct an incomplete and simplistic picture of development over the life-span (see Jenkins 1983).

While menarche is one change among the multitude of changes girls experience during puberty, the first menses is a unique developmental event in that it occurs suddenly and involves blood. In addition, menarche is the primary social marker of the beginning of adolescence and instigates a shift from a relatively asexual gender system of childhood to a highly sexualized gender system of adulthood (Lees 1993; Thorne 1993), and often precipitates a reorganization of self- and body-image (Tobin-Richards, Boxer and Petersen 1983). One important component of this reorganization of self is the intense preoccupation with the self and body experienced by adolescents. They tend to assume that everyone is as preoccupied with them as they are with themselves. This misperception often leads to an extreme self-consciousness whereby teenagers crave privacy as well as experience the feeling that they are unique, special and different from others. David Elkind (1978) calls this shift in perspective the "imaginary audience."

Importantly, these developmental changes occur simultaneously with and through menarche, and affect the responses of young women to their bodily changes. While we do not deny that this intense bodily preoccupation is in part developmental, we feel it is also important to ask the question of why girls' and boys' experiences are so different, and, especially, why adults respond to boys' bodily maturation differently than they do to girls' bodily maturation. The American Association of University Women's Reports (1992, 1993) document the difficulties with which girls negotiate gender in school settings as a result of structural and interpersonal inequities, and discuss the sexual harassment they encounter in the "hostile hallways" of the typical public school. Shere Hite's *Growing Up Under Patriarchy* (1994) further explores girls' experiences being raised in a misogynous society. In terms of the differential experiences of puberty vis-a-vis gender, we are emphasizing that cultural discourses frame developmental "stages" in such a way as to imbue them with meaning and power. It is these processes about which we are especially concerned.

While menarche is typically seen as the most obvious sign of the beginning of puberty, its onset is relatively late in the pubertal process. Maturational processes associated with female puberty occur between the ages of nine and sixteen, with breast development usually occurring as the first noticeable bodily change. Other changes include an increase in body hair, skin oiliness and body odor due to adrenal gland activity, growth spurts, increase in the size of the vagina and uterus, weight gain, and changes in the contours of the body. Generally, pubertal development is gradual and continuous, and, on average, the physical transformation from child to adult takes approximately four years. However, there are individual differences in the overall speed with which girls pass through puberty, as well as normal variations in the timing and tempo of these distinct body changes (Golub 1992). The age at first bleeding has steadily declined over the past century in North America and Western Europe to an average of 12.8 years due to dietary changes, improvements in overall health and environmental factors (Bullough 1983; Lott 1994). This onset seems to be triggered by critical weight ranges and fat ratios in the body.

While menarche is a normal maturational event which represents the first visible sign of the hormonal cyclicity responsible for female reproductive capability, the connection between menarche and fertility is somewhat erroneous since early menstrual cycles tend to be anovulatory, and a mature menstrual cycle, characterized by regular fluctuations in hormones associated with ovulation and menstruation, is not immediately in place at menarche, but may take several months to become established (Lott 1994). Consequently, new menstruators often will experience irregular and unpredictable bleeding during the first year after menarche. Further, even though the onset of menstruation is just one of many biophysical changes unfolding during female puberty, as we have found in our research, it is often experienced as a most dramatic and seemingly discontinuous event. In contrast to the more gradual emergence of secondary sex characteristics such as pubic hair or breast development, menarche tends to be sudden and unpredictable, and, despite preparation, a girl may be quite shocked to discover blood mysteriously issuing from between her legs.

In terms of the meanings associated with this pubertal transition, we emphasize that menarche is a central aspect of body politics, loaded with the ambivalences associated with being a woman in a misogynous society. It is an event that symbolizes both reproductive and sexual potential and centers attention on the body. Historically and today, in the West and cross-culturally, the first menstrual blood symbolizes a girl's entrance into female fecundity and adult female sexuality and serves as a social marker of movement from girl to woman (Logan 1980; Brooks-Gunn and Ruble 1982). Since, in Western cultures in particular, "woman" is over-represented through the practices and values of sexuality, menarche takes on loaded meanings that have consequences for women and their everyday lives. Relations of power associated with notions of female sexuality are scripted onto the discourses and practices of femininity.

Psychoanalytic theorists were the first to formally suggest that menarche is an important developmental event in the female life-course, and to this day, much of the theoretical and empirical work on the psycho-social aspects of menarche has been informed by, or in reaction to, psychoanalytic discourses. For the most part, these theorists consider menstruation to be the curse of womanhood and associate girls' reactions to their first blood with penis envy, castration anxiety, and other complexes of the psyche. Psychoanalyst Otto Fenichel even went so far in 1945 as to call menarche the "first pollution." Helen Deutsch (1944), one of the most influential among the psychoanalytic theorists, maintained that menarche is fundamentally a disturbing event because a girl must accept that her identity and sexuality are subordinate to her function as a reproducer. As such, healthy female adolescent adjustment requires acceptance of one's inferior status as a reproducer.

Other psychoanalytically oriented theorists have maintained that menarche is a potentially positive developmental event, provided that a pubertal girl is well prepared about what to expect (Grief and Ulman 1982; Kestenberg 1964). According to this line of thinking, menarche serves to end prepubertal girls' "disorganized" identities; the sharpness of the menarcheal experience and the cyclicity of menstruation are seen as providing the pubertal girl with regularity and order. Further, it is suggested that premenarcheal gender confusion is replaced at menarche by a well-defined self- and body-image (Hart and Sarnoff 1971). These theorists do not discuss whether the shift from identity disorganization to organization is a function of the menarcheal event per se, or a function of what menarche *means and signifies*, that is, of the social shift from girl to woman. They tend to ignore that the regularity and order thought to be provided by the menarcheal event and subsequent menstrual cyclicity is related to the imposition of gender expectations on girls during puberty. It is the internalization of these sociocultural expectations about femininity in relationship to the things women's bodies do that serves to organize and regulate girls' identities.

Psychoanalytic approaches to understanding the developmental import of menarche tend to be fundamentally reductionistic and sexist. Whether they saw menarche as inherently disruptive or organizing, early theorists located the source of the trauma surrounding menarche entirely within the female anatomy and psyche. While Deutsch's approach was creative and revolutionary for her time, it lacked critical insight into the external sociocultural forces that shape the menarcheal experience and might make becoming a young woman traumatic. In addition, the proscription that female psychological adjustment requires the acceptance of a subordinate status in society is harmful and narrow. Not surprisingly, this Freudian orthodoxy was being challenged within its own ranks, particularly by Karen Horney and Clara Thompson. During the first half of this century, they were among the first psychoanalysts to challenge traditional notions surrounding female development and sexuality. They maintained that the source of a girl's anxiety and stress at menarche was not her anatomy or psyche, but the surrounding misogynistic culture. Menarche may therefore be a problematic experience for girls not because of the symbolic loss of a penis, but because of the real loss of freedom and safety incurred upon entering the gendered world of adults. Similarly, existentialist Simone de Beauvoir responded to Freudians by re-construing early adolescence as a time when girls realize that their power comes from being submissive objects and that their envy is "power envy" rather than "penis envy."

Contemporary research from a variety of different perspectives outside the psychoanalytic tradition suggests that girls' experiences of menarche are characterized by ambivalence and even trauma, in part as a result of the absence of cultural recognition and well-defined rituals surrounding this developmental event (Brooks-Gunn and Ruble 1980; Mead 1949; Ussher 1989). The closest most of us come to receiving some symbolic representation of this life event is when we receive our first bra, arguably itself a symbol of constraint. As Judy Grahn suggests:

> Menstruation is the flower of a woman, the bloom of her potential, the signal for her to take on the offices of womanhood. When these offices have been restricted, made powerless and despised by others, she herself will despise her first menstruation as representing the beginning of a lowering in status and a bitter lot in life. (1982: 272)

The Western "cultural backdrop" represents menarche as a traumatic and debilitating experience at the same time that girls are instructed and expected to act "normal" and conceal their "inherent disability." Both public and private discourses surrounding menarche often reduce it to the biological/reproductive processes involved, and treat it as a hygienic crisis or a symptom-laden illness. Such cultural messages can be seen clearly in the educational materials distributed by the sanitary-products industry, widely used by parents and teachers to talk with young girls about menarche, menstruation, and puberty. As Ussher points out: "any discussion of the reality of menstruation or the pertinent practical issues" are avoided, as is information which has "direct relevance to the pubescent girl coming to terms with her own changing body and developing sexuality" (1989: 25). As a result, many girls learn only that they are under the control of strange biological processes that are very painful and somehow connected to reproduction, and further, that these processes must be denied and concealed with the help of certain (often expensive) products (Woods, Dery and Most 1982). The strength of these sociocultural messages is evidenced by the fact that as early as fifth grade, girls report that they expect to have menstrual symptoms and distress (Brooks-Gunn and Ruble 1982). Even more surprising is Clark and Ruble's finding that fifth grade boys believe that the menstrual cycle is problematic and symptom-ridden (1978). More research is needed to detect changes over the last decade concerning these issues. Ironically, the persistent lack of societal recognition of the developmental importance of menarche, coupled with the construal of menarche as a traumatic experience or hygienic crisis which must be concealed, can be seen as a sort of pseudo-ritual.

Sharon Golub's previously mentioned book on menarche was an important ground-breaker, especially given the "silence about adolescent girls in the literature of developmental psychology" (Gilligan, Rogers and Tolman 1991: 1). Golub begins her volume by suggesting that while menarche is a landmark event in girls' lives, it is one that is veiled in secrecy. And, despite receiving financial support from Tampax Incorporated, she points out that menarche is likely "to be treated as a hygienic crisis" (1983: xvii). Her collection covers the physiological, psychological and social issues surrounding menarche, focusing on the effects of such themes on this life transition. It assumes that menarche is a significant, organizing event in a woman's psychosexual development, and pays particular attention to how girls see themselves during this time. As Anne Petersen, writing in the section on psychological implications, suggests: "menarche is important to understand not just for its inherent qualities, but also because it is an ideal focus for understanding the complex relations among biological, psychological, and social factors" (1983: 63). She presented a group of seventh graders with the beginnings of stories based on passages from Judy Blume's novel *Are You There God? It's Me Margaret.* Petersen asked the girls how they thought a character in the book who had just started her period felt. Fifty percent of the girls ranked "scared" first, and 39 percent ranked "happy" first. Her finding underscores the ambivalence associated with menarche: girls feel some joy yet also much fear. This text also includes a chapter by Nancy Fugate Woods, Gretchen Kramer Dery and Ada Most on women's retrospective accounts of menarche. While some women spoke about menarche with pride or excitement, most reported negative emotions like embarrassment and fear.

Other interesting empirical work on menarche from a developmental approach was done in the early 1980s by psychologist Jeanne Brooks-Gunn, with Anne Petersen and other colleagues, and compiled in an edited collection *Girls at Puberty: Biological and Psychosocial Perspectives.* The articles in this volume emphasize how children learn gender and how these prescriptions guide the experience of menarche, and adolescent development generally. For example, in "The Intensification of Gender-Related Role Expectations during Early Adolescence," John Hill and Mary Ellen Lynch review the theory that gender becomes intensified at puberty due to social pressures from parents and peers. They, and others, argue that biological and social changes for girls which occur during early and middle adolescence tend to create a discontinuity in development, with girls' perceptions of self intimately connected to the social meanings attached to their developing bodies and menarcheal status.

Carol Gilligan and her colleagues have done some ground-breaking work on female adolescent development with girls at the Emma Willard School (Gilligan, Lyons and Hanmer 1990; Brown and Gilligan 1992), and have also looked at issues of resistance (Gilligan, Rogers and Tolman 1991). They focus on girls' perceptions of the self in relation to others during their early teenage years, the time when most girls experience menarche. In *Making Connections,* Gilligan and colleagues write about how societal notions of femininity affect girls' social and psychological development, and encourage women to be docile and other-directed: "Teenage girls and adult women often seemed to get caught on the horns of a dilemma: was it better to respond to others and abandon themselves or respond to themselves and abandon others?...Adolescence seemed to pose a crisis of connection for girls coming of age in Western culture" (1990: 9). Much of this dilemma is about the body: "These changes in girls' bodies visually disconnect them from the worlds of childhood and identify them in the eyes of other women and standards of beauty and goodness—physical and moral perfection" (164).

Similarly, Mary Pipher, in *Reviving Ophelia: Saving the Selves of Adolescent Girls,* explores the developmental hurdles of adolescence in the context of a sexist society which she calls "girl poisoning." She writes:

> Something dramatic happens to girls in early adolescence. Just as planes and ships disappear mysteriously into the Bermuda Triangle, so do the selves of girls go down in droves. They crash and burn in a social and developmental Bermuda Triangle. In early adolescence, studies show that girls' IQ scores drop and their math and science scores plummet. They lose their resiliency and optimism and become less curious and inclined to take risks. They lose their assertive, energetic and "tomboyish" personalities and become more deferential, self-critical and depressed. They report great unhappiness with their own bodies. (1994: 19)

Yet, despite Pipher's focus on girls' early adolescence, she makes only one reference to menarche in the whole book. Gilligan's work also contains a remarkable silence about this life transition. A further indication of the stubborn and perpetual silence that has surrounded menarche is the fact that 50 percent of American girls coming of age in the 1950s began menstruation with no advanced knowledge or preparation, from either their mothers or teachers (Brooks-Gunn and Petersen 1983). In Weideger's retrospective study conducted in the mid 1970s, 39 percent of the 588 women studied reported being inadequately prepared for menarche. Likewise, there are many anecdotal accounts of innocent and unprepared girls thinking they are dying when their first blood arrives (see Owen 1993; Ussher 1989). Not surprisingly, research on the menopause suggests that women are still unprepared for, and knowledgeless about, the *end* of menstruation (Greer 1991; LaRocco and Polit 1980).

In light of the previous discussion of Western cultural discourses on the female body and menstruation, the fact that menarche is an event so heavily laden with personal and cultural meanings and yet rarely merits community ritualization or critical attention should not come as a surprise. As we will argue in the following chapters, this cultural silence and neglect is important for girls and reflects issues of gendered body politics in contemporary society. Girls and women *are* affected by sociocultural messages about the female body, menarche, and menstruation, clearly illustrating how the cultural and the personal are fundamentally and inextricably linked. Menarche is a physiological happening, framed by the bio-medical metaphors of current scientific knowledge, yet also a gendered, sexualized happening, a transition to womanhood as objectified other. What is crucial here is that this juncture, menarche, is a site where individual girls produce themselves as women and gender relations are perpetuated.

2

Women Re-membering Firstblood

> Let yourself move back and forth, then, between your own bodily history and an examination of larger cultural processes and assumptions. It is in this back-and-forth movement that real understanding takes place.
>
> —Morris Berman, *Coming to Our Senses*

We embarked on this project out of an interest in menarche as a central aspect of body politics, as well as a desire to explore the particularities of this life transition in contemporary Western societies. We are intrigued by the notion that menarche represents the beginning of sexualized embodiment, and, as such, may impact and shape a woman's subsequent menstrual career and bodily history. We wish to locate women's bodily histories surrounding menarche in the sociocultural and historical contexts in which they have unfolded, as well as in relationship to dominant sociocultural discourses concerning the menstrual career in particular and women's bodies more generally. To this end, through a guided process of "embodied reminiscence," we explore how women give meaning to their first menstrual blood, and analyze how this important life-transition has shaped and impacted their subsequent experiences as women travelling through life with female bodies.

As we have discussed already, the menstruating body is a representation of gendered societal power in its most concrete form. Here we attempt to analyze menarche through the processes whereby a female body is transformed into a feminine one. We explore the discursive spaces (material and nonmaterial) through which this transformation occurs by focusing on the memories and experiences of women as active subjects. "Embodied reminiscences" of the first blood provide potentially rich sources of data regarding the complex interplay between historical and sociocultural discourses and individual development. In addition, what women remember about their experiences surrounding and including menarche and their subsequent bodily histories provides insight into what was most salient about the event not only when it occurred, but as it is reconsidered over time (c.f. Butler 1963).

Anne Petersen suggests that a tendency in Western societies is to ignore puberty as a major developmental passage, and that this may result in a "systematic forgetting of events at this time of life" (1980: 45). However, contrary to Petersen's notion of "pubertal amnesia," there is ample evidence suggesting that menarche is a pubertal event many women remember with great clarity, even with the passage of time (Golub and Catalano 1983; Grief and Ulman 1982; Pillemer, Koff, Rhinehart and Rierdan 1987; Weideger 1976). Menarche is a particularly salient occasion in a girl's life because it happens suddenly and without warning, involves blood, and serves to physically and symbolically thrust her out of childhood and into adolescence. For these reasons, menarche is often a highly memorable experience for women of various ages.

When asked to remember their first menses, the women with whom we spoke shared stories about other physiological changes unfolding around the time of menarche, especially developing breasts, fuller hips and bodily curves. All of these changes are part of the journey and struggle of adolescence; they signify reproductive potential and connote emerging sexuality. We do not seek to prioritize menarche over these other changes in this adolescent drama; rather, we will explore their interconnections, framing menarche within the language of sexual scripts, including it within the discourse of the sexual and emphasizing its importance as a symbol of the relationship between reproduction and sexuality. This inclusive approach is made all the more important because of the relative absence of a discussion of menarche, and menstruation generally, in the literature on female sexuality and life-span development.

Philosophical/Theoretical Positions

Our philosophical approach in this project is two-fold: feminist and life-span developmental. Both these theoretical approaches challenge the dominant, long-standing metaphysical assumptions of positivism regarding what it means to be a human being and maker of meaning. When practicing social science from this dominant, positivistic world-view, one assumes that while the characteristics of the researched are germane to the phenomenon being studied, those of the researcher are immaterial. This central assumption is in keeping with the metaphysical commitments upon which the dominant theories and approaches in the social sciences are predicated: the search for universal laws, the belief that a quantifiable and certain reality exists, the emphasis placed on reason and value-neutrality, and, most fundamentally, androcentric epistemological claims about who can be a knower and constructor of discourses about "reality." As such, an "objective," anonymous expert conducts research *on* specific, well-defined subjects. By omitting the practical reality that the researcher occupies certain social as well as ideological/theoretical positions, the influence of these positions on how research is done is effectively denied. This positivist world-view and way of constructing knowledge, while the dominant one, is only one system of meaning and not the only means for knowledge acquisition and theory building (Berger and Luckman 1966; Broch-Due 1992; Harding 1991; Nielsen 1990; Reinharz 1992; Stacey 1988).

A contrasting and fundamentally different approach has been engendered from feminist principles. What is important here is the *relationship between* the researcher and the informant—both of whom are whole persons who have certain characteristics, experience life from certain standpoints of privilege and/or marginality, and are makers of meaning (Haraway 1988; Harding 1991). The artificial, and impossible, ideals of distance and objectivity that are axiomatic to the positivistic approach are rejected and replaced by the understanding that subjectivity exists in every human enterprise, including the construction of social science. The feminist paradigm foregrounds the unavoidable reality that how research is done (*i.e.*, the questions asked; how these questions are studied; how data is interpreted) is strongly shaped by *who* is doing the research and the epistemological commitments of that *who*. The point is, *who* we are is in part a function of *where* we are socioculturally located, because these locations offer us certain vantage points, opportunities, and experiences which shape the way we construct knowledge.

We believe that there is value in making the social and personal locations we occupy (as abled, white, relatively young women from working-class backgrounds, who are now relatively economically advantaged and in relationships with men) explicit, just as we must make the characteristics of the interviewees explicit. Such disclosure on our part is particularly important because of the centrality in interview methodology of the relationship between researcher and informant; the questions asked and bodily histories derived during the interview process are not only an expression of who the interviewee is as an historical and social being, but of who we are as interviewers, researchers, and women. Lastly, as social scientists with a commitment to feminism, we believe that research should be emancipatory, that is, be *for* women, rather than *on* or *about* women (c.f. Fine 1992; Reinharz 1992). To us, this means that our research must be engendered from women's needs, experiences, and interests, must challenge androcentric, ageist, racist, heterosexist, and classist assumptions, and must contribute to improving women's lives. In sum, as feminists, our goals in this project are not to prove, generalize, and predict, but to describe, analyze, and bring diverse experiences and points of view into the construction of "knowledge," and ultimately, to work toward social transformation around issues of female embodiment.

Our theoretical approach has been informed by a narrative perspective that assumes humans are interpretive beings in the phenomenological sense, active in the interpretation of their everyday lives and in the attribution of meaning through stories or self-narratives (Epston and White 1992; White 1995; White and Epston 1990). According to this perspective humans constitute, and are constituted by, the stories that they live and the stories they tell, actively constructing their worlds and creating symbolic and representational stories to make sense of their lives (Bruner 1986; 1990). As such, individuals organize their experiences in the form of stories where such "storying" is about meaning-making. *Blood Stories* represents the storying or meaning-making associated with menarche, the meanings of which have been constructed by women against, and through, the meta-narratives or dominant cultural stories about gender, the female body, blood, and desire.

Our philosophical and theoretical commitments are also informed by a life-span developmental approach to understanding women's lives. According to life-span developmental theory, development and aging happen dialectically throughout the life course, such that the human potential for adaptation, growth, and new forms of functioning are continually possible (Baltes, Reese, and Lipsitt 1980; Birren and Birren 1990; Uttal and Perlmutter 1989). This conceptualization of how humans travel through the life course contrasts sharply with the dominant, traditional "deficit" model that positions development and growth as unique to the first half of life, and decline and aging to the second half. Further, the life-span developmental approach posits that an individual's experiences throughout the life course depend on her class, gender, race, sexual orientation, cohort, and culture. Most essentially, the life-span developmental approach recognizes that development and aging are complex, interactive, *bio-psycho-social* processes which can not be divorced from the cultural, historical—and personal—contexts in which they originate and unfold (Baltes, Reese, and Lipsitt 1980; Blank 1989; Silverman 1987).

What unites our metaphysical commitments to feminism and to the life-span developmental approach is an insistence on sociocultural and historical specificity. This means, for example, that we operate from the position that there is no essential, fixed category called "woman," nor, by extension, is there an essential, fixed menarcheal or female bodily experience. We suggest that both life-span developmental theory and many contemporary feminisms might be seen as connected to the broader poststructuralist movement, given its emphasis on context and positionality, the relativity of knowledge, and the importance and value of harnessing multiple theoretical positions and research methods (Harding 1991; Weedon 1987). Working with a sensibility informed by both the feminist and life-span developmental approaches means that our theorizing and researching is historically, socially and culturally grounded, and either implicitly (as in the case of life-span developmental work) or explicitly (as in the case of feminism) challenging to dominant systems of meaning.

Methodological Approach

As feminist researchers, we have critiqued the traditional scientific method for its grounding in androcentric (male centered) forms of knowledge and its emphasis on the prediction and control of events or phenomena studied. We feel strongly that such an approach is inappropriate for addressing our questions. We counter that, instead, our discovery and understanding of "facts" in the world is conditioned by the social matrix in which knowledge is acquired, transmitted and learned. Ultimately, given the limits of empiricism generally in terms of "documenting" unstable, multiple and unfixed aspects of social life, we can only achieve "partial truths" or glimpses into the lived experiences of others (Clifford 1983). We maintain that we humans tend to know a socially constructed reality more through the forms in which "reality" is manifested in intersubjective consciousness, and less through measurements of external empirical indicators (Glasser and Strauss 1967; Jaffe and Miller 1994). Therefore, our methodological focus in this project is phenomenological, involving an exploration of the meanings women make of their experiences, what they think and feel, and how they travel through their everyday lives. As such, our research is qualitative and focuses on intersubjective aspects of human behavior.

Such a qualitative, phenomenological approach is predicated on the epistemological position that people know about and make meaning of their own lives. Meaning is emergent, that is, meaning is something created and re-created by people, not something absolute and external to be discovered by researchers. As such, our job as researchers is to interview, analyze and interpret—with self-reflexive awareness of our power as researchers—in collaboration and negotiation with women, whom we consider experts about their own lives. This collaborative process is engendered, as Broch-Due describes, from the dialectical relation between the researcher and the interviewee who are "whole persons, where gender, race, social class, and culture are important social facts in the process of shaping their subjectivity...these facts have influenced their experience and their own interpretation of themselves" (1992: 97). We feel that this interactive, interpretive approach offers the most appropriate and interesting means for exploring women's experiences and "menstrual careers," and for understanding how these experiences relate to, and are shaped by, the broader sociocultural landscapes in which they are embedded.

The practical way this phenomenological approach plays out in our project can be seen in our use of oral and written bodily histories to explore the complex meanings that women attribute to their first blood. Oral and written histories are powerful research tools for developing new frameworks and theories based on women's lives because they are predicated on listening to women's words and recording women's voices, thus facilitating the articulation and celebration of voices that have traditionally been ignored, silenced or considered illegitimate (Bell and Yalom 1990; Gluck and Patai 1991). An exploration of the words and images women use to articulate their own experiences in oral and written histories can facilitate an awareness of the conflicting social forces and institutions affecting women's consciousness of menarche and menstruation.

We collected women's oral and written narratives about their bodily histories using a form of retrospective in-depth interviewing. This research strategy falls under the broader category of biographical methods, the rationale of which is to elicit and examine life stories, conversations and other auto/biographical accounts in order to understand the phenomenology of experience (Benner 1994; Frank 1980; Luborsky 1994; Wallace 1994). Retrospective interviewing is a collaborative method akin to guided life-review or reminiscence, an empirical and (sometimes) therapeutic process through which individuals remember, reframe, and integrate past experiences (Broch-Due 1992; Butler 1963; Haight 1993; Kaminsky 1984). In particular, retrospective personal narratives provide insight into how individuals interpret and make meaning of their past experiences in the context of the present (Allen and Pickett 1987; Bertaux 1981; Rubinstein 1988). Older women's personal narratives are especially interesting and insightful because they demonstrate the interactive relationship over the life course between sociocultural discourses and subjective experiences, both of which are historically grounded.

Oral and written histories that focus on memory work and the activities associated with reminiscence involve a framing of past experiences through discursive lenses that encourage women to make sense out of their lived experience in certain ways. Many researchers avoid using retrospective data because they see such data as tainted potentially by distortion and faulty memory; that is, experiences as they are remembered may not be "true" (c.f. Brown and Kulik 1977; Damon and Bajema 1974). This concern with the "accuracy" of women's memories, rather than with *what* and *how* women remember, is in keeping with the epistemological commitments of positivistic science. We feel that women's stories of their first period, stories which are constructed through the lenses of memory, represent the interactive nature of discourse and "experience," and are especially interesting because of this very fact. Memories are not static entities, and remembering is not a unidirectional process; instead, memories are shaped and elaborated upon over time, and different facets of an event may take on varying importance or meaning at different points in the life course (Haight 1993; Kramer 1987). Of course, this may make memories less valid as "proof" of some empirical reality, but, as we suggest, such notions of "proof" are problematic in the first place.

As an alternative vision, we propose that the methodological processes associated with constructing bodily histories highlight the interactive nature of discourse and experience, and ultimately problematize the notion of "experience" itself. Seeing the latter as "uncontested evidence," divorced from the forces that discursively position subjects and help produce their experience, is problematic because, in the words of Joan Scott: "It is not individuals who have experience, but subjects who are constituted through experience" (1992: 25-26). Women's memories of their first blood are framed by many competing discourses, and evolve via their on-going efforts to sift through and make meaning out of raw experiences. We hardly see such experiences as uncontested empirical facts; we are interested precisely in the ways discourses associated with the body have framed shifting identities and women's "experiences" of themselves.

Profile of the Women

The 104 women whose voices and words we share in this book were self-selected, having volunteered to participate as word of our project spread. They represent a group of women whose feelings and experiences were such that they were interested in and felt comfortable sharing information of a personal and intimate nature. We must comment on the fact that there are large silences around the women who, for whatever reason, did not want to be a part of the study. Perhaps they had no specific memories of menarche, their first blood was uneventful, too painful to talk about, and/or they felt uncomfortable sharing personal, especially taboo issues. Nonetheless, all-in-all, we found women very willing and eager to speak about menarche and appreciative of a space in which to share such experiences. This illustrates the importance of giving voice to women's diverse and complex experiences.

We used a series of nonprobability techniques to build our sample of 104 women: "snowball" techniques whereby self-selected interviewees suggested other potential participants (Bailey 1987); a call for volunteers locally, which included placing fliers around the Oregon State University campus, the city of Corvallis, Oregon, and in local physician's offices specializing in geriatric medicine; and lastly, via outreach through Oregon State University Extension Service. While our regional sample was relatively diverse in terms of age, class, sexual orientation and race/ethnicity, white women predominated, and a little under one third of the sample were women of color. Included were 73 white women and 31 women of color. Of the latter, seven women identified as African-American, nine as Chicana or Mexican-American, four as Asian-American, and one as Native-American. Three women who identified and were included as white, and one as Mexican-American, also said they were "part American-Indian." Eight Asian women grew up outside the United States, although all spent much or most of their adult lives in the United States. Two of these women were from Iran, two from Taiwan, and one each from Korea, Malaysia, Nepal, and the People's Republic of China. Three white women also grew up outside the United States—two in England and one in Germany. Two interviewees identified as bi-racial, African-American/white and Indonesian/white. Given the general lack of racial and ethnic diversity in this region of Oregon, we did "over-sample" for women of color. Despite this, the sample is still eurocentric, and we must emphasize its limitations and the dangers associated with overgeneralization. In terms of age, the range spanned from 18 to 94 years, with 29 women (28 percent) age 60 years or older. Ten women identified as lesbians and two as bisexuals, although only one woman said she identified as a lesbian during early adolescence. Approximately 47 percent might be considered to have grown up in working-class and 53 percent in middle-class homes. The majority of interviewees lived in semi-rural or suburban Oregon at the time of the interviews and had grown up in the western regions of the United States.

As we have discussed previously, one of our key curiosities has to do with the ways women's experiences of menarche—and their bodily histories more generally—are shaped by the sociopolitical and historical contexts in which they became menstruators and sexualized women. The women represented in our study are in a sense cohorts whose passage through history has been marked by tremendous social and economic changes (Allen and Pickett 1984). We therefore feel it is important to give an overview of the salient historical changes during this century that are pertinent to women's experiences of passing from childhood to sexualized womanhood. Note that these historical dynamics are particularly integral to the bodily histories of the older women with whom we spoke.

To begin with, it is important to be aware of the fact that adolescence as a distinct period of the life course, corresponding to the maturational stage of puberty, did not even exist until the end of the nineteenth century, arising as a derivative of certain economic, technological and social changes (Demos and Demos 1969; Elder 1987). With the "invention" of adolescence came a lengthening of childhood and youth, a shift from the family to the peer group and school system as dominant influences, and the problematization of youth as a time of "storm and stress" (Allen and Pickett 1984; Hall 1904; Modell 1989). Constance Nathanson points out that while much has been written regarding the experiences of adolescent boys during the first half of the century, relatively little work has been done on the history of adolescent girls, especially in relation to the race and class dynamics of Western industrial societies. Culturally, the social passage of adolescence for boys signified a marked "coming of age," a transition from puberty to adult freedom and responsibility; for girls, it was defined as the period between puberty and marriage. While a girl in the first part of the twentieth century was socialized by her mother to be "a better wife and a better mother," she was often not directly informed in meaningful and useful ways about matters pertaining to life with a female body (Nathanson 1991).

The older cohorts of women represented in our study had parents who were born in the latter part of the nineteenth century, and, as a result, may have experienced a clash with their parents between the "old ways" of the parental generation and the expectations and opportunities of the "modern era." Although in many unprecedented ways the world outside the family was opening up to them, young women were still being socialized to be reproducers and domestic workers. Few girls from the older cohorts represented in this study had access to accurate information about puberty, menarche and sexuality, neither at school nor from their parents. Then as now, menstruation symbolized both sexuality and reproduction, topics not part of "acceptable" public discourse (Delaney, Lupton and Toth 1988; Nathanson 1991). As a result, normal developmental processes were surrounded by silence, ignorance, and often fear.

The menarcheal experiences of older women were further shaped by the fact that most began to menstruate prior to the commercial availability of the sanitary napkin in the early 1920s and the tampon in the 1930s (Bullough 1974). In addition, the economic hardships experienced by many families during the Depression made resourcefulness and thriftiness necessary. Thus, it was common practice to construct one's own menstrual pads from rags or scraps of fabric for most of the first half of this century. These "bulky" homemade pads were inconvenient, messy, and problematic to wear, and had to be soaked and rinsed as inconspicuously as possible in preparation for the next menstrual bleeding. The lack of convenience and privacy associated with menstruation, combined with a pervasive ethic of silence surrounding women's bodies, certainly impacted the bodily histories of women coming of age during these eras, as we will discuss more fully in chapter 6.

Description of Data Collection and Analyses

The oral history research method we employed combined a general, unstructured interview protocol with some specific questions targeted to address issues that respondents did not readily include in their stories of menarche. These questions included probes to elaborate on the feelings, emotions, and meanings attached to menarche as a life transition, issues of bodily history, and the personal context in which menarche took place. As background to this narration, we also encouraged women to ground themselves and their memories in a socio-political landscape vis-a-vis racial, class, ethnic, religious, generational, geographic and other differences. We added a series of questions specifically addressed to the mid-life and older women; these questions, grounded in a life-span developmental perspective, regarded how the women related to their bodies over the life course, their menstrual careers including the menopause, and ways they might have socialized younger generations about menarche and menstruation. In sum, while orienting questions helped provide some structure to their bodily histories, women were free to describe their experiences in their own ways, using their own voices.

Of the 104 bodily histories we collected, 76 were oral and 28 written. The oral history interviews were conducted either in women's homes or in offices or seminar rooms, and sometimes in public spaces, although the latter occurred rarely. Written narratives were collected when women could not be interviewed in person, but agreed to share written accounts of their first blood experiences with us. Participants were asked if they wanted to use a pseudonym to provide anonymity;

most chose to do this, although some preferred to use their real names. With participants' consent, we tape-recorded the interviews, which were then transcribed professionally. Four trained research assistants who had experience in feminist research methodologies were hired to assist us with interviewing: Alida Benthin, Sindy Mau, Monica Molina, and Tamara Shaub. Three of these women are white and one Chicana, and their ages ranged from early twenties to mid-forties. With the exception of the older participants, we all tended to interview women who were most like ourselves. Given their interest and background in mid-life issues and gerontology, Jennifer and research assistant Sindy Mau interviewed almost all the older women.

Let us say here that, given our consciousness of how we as women have learned to mute our experiences and stories—especially when they do not fit with dominant cultural explanations and socially accepted practices for women—we found it crucial throughout the interview process to be sensitive to the silences and contradictions endemic to the women's telling of their bodily histories (Heilbrun 1988). In addition, at the end of the oral history interviews we asked the women for feedback about their experience of and feelings about being a part of our project. Overwhelmingly, women expressed enthusiasm for being able to speak the unspoken, emphasizing how great it was to be asked to share their experiences of something so rarely asked or spoken about. For a few women, this experience of remembering adolescence was painful. A few wept as they remembered incidents from their adolescence related to body issues, or talked about their families generally. This was especially true for women who identified as survivors of psychological, physical and/or sexual abuse.

As researchers, we consider our primary responsibilities to involve listening to the women's narratives about menarche and their bodily histories, grasping the subjective understandings they have of their lives, and accurately representing their perspectives and experiences. We also believe we have an equally important responsibility to interpret and assign meaning to the women's narratives in relationship to the various sociocultural discourses and social-scientific literatures we have discussed. Although J. Brandon Wallace (1994) suggests that no standardized procedure exists for analyzing narrative data, Mark Luborsky recommends some general guidelines for discovering emerging themes in texts and transcripts. Reflecting a life-span developmental and phenomenological sensibility, Luborsky suggests that themes be seen as markers of the meaning-making process, and not fixed structures, and that "we need to consider themes as emergent and changeable in their meaning and desirability to individuals over their lifetime" (1994: 194).

In keeping with Luborsky's guidelines, we began our process of discovery by reading the entire corpus of narratives, without taking notes, so that we could get a general feel for the range of women's experiences. We carefully listened to the tapes and read the narratives multiple times to ensure accuracy. As Kathryn Anderson and Dana Jack instruct: "To hear women's perspectives accurately, we have to learn to listen in stereo, receiving both the dominant and muted channels clearly and tuning into them carefully to understand the relationship between them" (1991: 11). In this way the process of analysis is subordinated to the process of listening. During subsequent readings, we looked for patterns in the data, and identified and notated topic areas and illustrative statements. We worked together to check and re-check our understandings of the data and our interpretations of women's words, and gave particular attention to relating the emerging themes to the sociocultural and historical contexts in which the women's experiences unfolded. In addition, we invited comments from participants concerning our interpretation of their words, such mutual validation being a crucial part of the negotiation of meaning. This entailed giving transcripts to participants who expressed an interest, inviting their feedback, and checking the accuracy of our initial understandings and interpretations.

Because we expected to discover differences in first blood stories based upon class, race, and age, we were surprised to find so many similarities across these demographic variables, with recurring themes arising in narratives from women representing different cohorts and life situations. We are not suggesting, of course, that there were no individual differences in women's memories of menarche and bodily histories, but emphasizing the similarities of women's blood memories. A more quantitative, less phenomenological study using more quantifiable measures might have found differences vis-a-vis sociodemographic characteristics leading to correlations and statements of variability. Ultimately, we are not sure of the accuracy and use of such generalizations. Nonetheless, we analyzed women's stories in context, looking for similarities and differences. This analytic approach reflects the purposes of this study, the nature of the data, and our epistemological commitments and theoretical positions.

Throughout the following chapters, we share verbatim excerpts from the women's oral and written narratives (in italics) in order to illustrate the major themes that eventually emerged from our analytic and interpretive processes of discovery. We provide a very brief biography of the narrator in most cases, although to avoid being repetitive we have chosen not to give exhaustive descriptions in all cases, and tend to omit biographical descriptions once a woman has already been introduced (see the index for page locations of narrators). At this point, by way of providing a context and direction for our exploration of the major themes in the women's bodily histories, we would like to share one edited "case" history, mostly in its entirety.

This story belongs to Judy, a 45 year old white heterosexual woman who is currently in school working on a graduate degree. She has been married twice, grew up in privileged home in the midwest region of the United States, and has an adult son. In particular, her story highlights issues of sexuality and the ambivalences felt by young women as they develop female bodies in a highly visual (one might say voyeuristic) culture. Her memory of menarche as the birth of manipulative sexual power is especially insightful. Judy also talks much about issues of contamination and concealment as well as opportunities for solidarity and resistance. She was interviewed by Janet Lee.

Judy

JL: Let's begin by you talking a little bit about your family and your memories of this period of your life.

Judy: *Okay. I was adopted into a very wealthy family who lived in the midwest, in Michigan. I was the first; three years after me they adopted a boy child who is not my natural brother. My parents were older; on the surface the home was, you know, looked pretty middle class. We lived in an upper middle class neighborhood. My father was the one who actually came from money; my mother sort of married up, which, in my family, my father's family, was acceptable if there was beauty. My mother was a very beautiful woman, blond, blue-eyes. This was in Detroit, and my family owned a bakery that was spread over three states...so here I am with everything money can buy—literally everything that money can buy—with two parents who are not terribly equipped to be parents. My mother came from an abusive background, alcoholic father; my father had a drinking problem that really didn't show up until later in my life, and so my early childhood with him was really great. We were really tight. My father was the nurturing one in the family, the one who put Band-Aids on your knees and read us stories, and you know, did those kind of things. My mother was the one who set the ground rules, delivered all the punishment. I mean, for the time that they lived that was typically the other way around. They are both dead now. My father died when I was in high school; he had alcohol dementia. He was hallucinating; he was uncontrollably erratic; he began molesting my brother. He came into my room and I knew he was not himself. My mother even said "your father is not himself, I really can't protect you every moment...you do not have to follow your father's rules." I listened; I was able to hear that from my mother. So I said, "no, get out!" and I was pretty empowered. I was eleven years old and he never came near me again.*

JL: You must have been a strong little kid. What about your first menstrual period, can you tell me about that?

Judy: *I was thirteen in March and in the summer it was not unusual for me to go and stay with my cousin. My mother's youngest sister had a daughter eight months older than me. Her name was Marcia. My mother was very close to her sister, and because the parents were close, they tried to make the kids close. So I spent a lot of my summer vacations at Marcia's house with my aunt and Marcia. Well, I never really liked Marcia, but I had to like her, so I guess I did. I was there when I got my period. I had to tell somebody; I had gone to the bathroom and seen blood. We had been out in the garage dancing to records with the boys in the neighborhood—me and cousin Marcia* (laugh). *She was a very good dancer and I wasn't, and she always made fun of me. Anyhow, I went to the bathroom and sure enough, there it was. And I knew what it was, and I know I had some anxiety about it, like oh, I wasn't home, and now I have to tell my aunt, and I don't want to tell my cousin because she might tell those boys. And it was that fear that the boys would, you know...do I look different? Will I smell different? Do I smile different? Do I...no, I can't go back out there, and there was this thing about not wanting those people in the garage to know that this happened. So I told my aunt. She acted like this was a wonderful gift and it was a revelation and we were going to have a party. Because that was her belief, which was different from my mother's. And I was like "no!" She actually baked a cake and told my uncle! Oh!! I was mortified!* (laugh) *And I laid on the couch most of the day with cramps, and I was thinking that people knew, but my aunt assured me that they were just told that I didn't feel good and was lying down. No one was telling them that I had started my period, that that was my business. But I still had this ungodly anxiety that they knew, and that when I walked out they would know because I would look different.*

JL: Why was it so important that they didn't know?

Judy: *Boys made jokes about girls on their periods. I had heard them from the time I was eleven, twelve, thirteen, and they were always about someone else. So I hadn't paid any attention to it, but now they might be making them about me. And so suddenly they are not funny anymore* (laugh). *Bingo! Yes, that does drive it home! I used to, in fact, I did laugh at them. I laughed at them until I became one, and then it was like, they better not do that to me. I was going to beat them up. There was no way I was going to tolerate them now that I understood how bad this felt. That was my biggest fear. Or, that some boy would want to have sex with me because that was what my mother said. I mean this whole thing was drilled home so many times about pregnancy, I was suddenly afraid. What will happen? Will I lose control of myself? Suddenly? Will I lie down and spread my legs? I didn't know what I was going to do! So I had a lot of anxieties about how I was going to behave. I really thought maybe I'd smell different and people would walk by and go "she has her period!" I mean, I didn't know. So there was a lot of shame; there was a lot of anxiety.*

There was some excitement also because the part of me that wants to grow up and get boobs, might get them now. I still don't have boobs, never did get any! (laugh). *I was kind of waiting for* [my period] *because a a lot of my friends were getting it at about age thirteen. I was comparing myself with my peers, and I seemed to be doing some of the things that they were doing. I was getting pubic hair; I was getting hair under my arms a little bit. I was real thin and small, so I wasn't getting much of a breast, though at that point wished for that. But anyway I wanted them and I had this terrible fear that I would be flat-chested. I don't think that was unusual, I mean, I think that was pretty common talk among the girls. Those girls that were my age who had big breasts hated them and I never understood. I wanted blond hair and blue eyes. You see my aunt, my mother, and my cousin were blond and blue-eyed, so I wanted to be too because it was better. The whole message was it was better and I was shamed by my body then* [at menarche]. *I was clearly aware that boys looked at and looked very specifically for certain physical attributes. Breasts were always the first. Small waists, you know, shapely hips, not too big of a butt, you know, I am sure it varies from culture to culture, but in that context I knew what most boys thought was attractive. Those were the rules.... It was better to be a very sexy, hour-glass* [shaped] *woman than a short little skinny, flat-chested brown-haired girl.*

JL: Now, did you consciously think about that around the time that you started your period?

Judy: *I did. Yeah, I was obsessed at thirteen with having a boyfriend and I had so many boyfriends—I think I changed them every week. I mean, it became an obsession which correlates real strongly with hormones, but also socialization. This getting my period was a time when I was supposed to give up my horses, dogs, give up skeet shooting with my dad, don't bowl, don't climb trees anymore; all the things that I loved, I gave up.... I was just nutso about having boyfriends and trying to do and look how girls are supposed to do and look. I padded my bra with kleenex, I did all kinds of things to have a figure. I was really jealous of my mother; I was mad at her. And it wasn't hard to have that split between my mother and I because she was so rigid and the disciplinarian, and so it was easy to put that on her. And that is what happened.*

My mother told me about my period when I was eleven, and again at twelve, and it was very clinical. She gave me very clean, clinical, nonemotional descriptions that were kind of like what a doctor would give you, and that was all there was to it, and then no discussion afterwards. It wasn't her style to talk about it, like—how do you feel? There was a lot of weird stuff about periods and sex and stuff that I never understood. About this time, just prior to my period, I remember going to my mother and asking her what "fuck" meant. She told me, and then I started asking questions about intercourse and my reaction was of total interest. I said, "oh, neat!" and she back-handed me across my mouth into the wall, and said: "It's not neat, it will never be neat. It is something you will do with your husband and you won't like one bit of it. Why can't you be like your cousin Marcia? She thought it was icky." So I thought, it's icky, must be icky. So I thought my period was going to be icky too. Because it was called "the curse." My mother always called it the curse.

JL: Did you connect your first period with sex?

Judy: *Yes, period meant sex and getting pregnant. My mother very clearly made that correlation: "once you get your period Judy, you can get pregnant." It is important to stay out of those situations, blah, blah, blah, and then she told me these horrible things about sex, I think, as a deterrent...and she knew me; she knew me that way and I am sure she is thinking that if I don't make this scary and awful, this is the kid that is going to do it. So anyway, I waited* [for my period]. *I didn't know when it was going to come. Part of me didn't want it to come at all because I didn't want to grow up. Well, the part of me that wanted to be like my mom, wanted to grow up and be a woman. There was this other part of me that just wanted to be me and was in no hurry to grow up, still wanted to climb trees and hang out with my dad and mow the lawn.*

JL: Had Marcia started her period by then?

Judy: *Oh yes, Marcia was an eleven year old who had a period! Marcia was a very mature person, unlike Judy who is very immature! She was always pinching me, "you are so immature!" She was like a parrot. And it was awful to be with her, and she still...she has never changed!* (laugh).

JL: So you had your celebration.

Judy: *Yes, I had the celebration and I remember feeling a little embarrassed over all this fuss. My aunt showed me how to use these little belts. I remember I showed her in the bathroom the kleenex that had the blood on it and she said, "oh, you are a woman now," and said, "I'll go upstairs and get some Kotex and get a belt and I'll come down and show you how to use it." She just assumed I didn't know. Good thing* (laugh) *because I would have never asked, and I would have tied that thing around me or done something; I would have never wanted to admit that I didn't know such a thing. So she did show me, thank God, and she was very patient and very gentle and she made light of it, and it wasn't a bad thing, and I thought that was really weird. But it did help, it really did help. My mother would have said, "here, figure it out!"* (laugh). *And maybe a month later when I asked one of my girlfriends, I would have figured it out, you know. Remember those little plastic things? The long strings on the...well, that was some tricky business. I mean, you had to have a degree to put those things on!* (laugh). *And then to get them on, they are supposed to be on your hips. Hips? What happens when you don't have any hips? They slid down and they didn't work, oh, they were miserable, but at least I knew how to put them on.*

JL: So you're talking about the Kotex that had the little strings that came up that you attached with the little doo-dad.

Judy: *Right, that was on the little belt, the little Kotex belt. It was kind of like garter belts and you know, I felt belted!* (laugh) *Those belts, and then we wore nylons, they weren't panyhose then. There were all these belts around me, holding up something in place, and I was, remember, I was a kid who hung out with my dad and was athletic and climbed trees, and this was in my way. So this was the part I didn't like, this 'in the way' business. Why does it have to be so complicated? Why can't it be simple? So I stopped wearing them at one point, probably in my first year and started just cramming kleenex into my panties because I couldn't stand wearing all those belts and stuff. The kleenex didn't absorb and so I was always messing on my clothes and then that was embarrassing. So I finally figured it out and cut the tabs off the Kotex, the strings, didn't use the belt, and I did what they do now, I actually took adhesive tape, like, what is that white tape?*

JL: Scotch tape?

Judy: *Not Scotch tape, the white stuff.*

JL: Masking tape?

Judy: *Yeah, masking tape. Rolled it inside out, put it down the center of my pants and stuck the Kotex there.*

JL: You did?! You could have been a millionaire!

Judy: *I know, little did I know. And later I started using tampons. There's a funny story—I was a little bit older, I was fifteen and we had gone to Hawaii. My father didn't go that year, he was drinking too much. My mom took my brother and I and went with another woman, a friend of hers and her two kids, and we went and stayed in a condo. I think it was a getaway for my mom. And so we had a really good time. And I decided that because I was swimming a lot the Kotex wasn't going to make it. So I told my mom I really needed Tampax so she went and bought some for me, and I don't think they had sizes then, I don't remember. They were all cardboard, they weren't easy to insert and they weren't rounded on the edge, they were just terrible things. They were hard and difficult to insert. And my mother stood on one side of the bathroom door and she was giving me directions through the door and she couldn't stop laughing. My mother!*

JL: Your mother!?

Judy: *Right, she was away from my dad. I realized that a lot of the pressure, a lot of the stress came from the relationship she was in. And so there were these few moments, these few mother/daughter moments and later on when she would get away from my dad, that were kind of nice. Anyway, she was just hysterical on the other side and I kept saying "it won't go in, it won't go in," and she was just laughing, and she said "relax, I know you are not relaxing, you are all tense in there, I can see you."* [And I said:] *"How can you see me, you are on the other side of the door." And these were the kind of conversations we were having.*

I was trying to hide myself under little tiny bikinis; I always thought that the boys knew that it was there, it was a terrible fear about men knowing. It wasn't so much my girlfriends knowing, or my mom. It was men. They weren't supposed to know. Now my father never said word one about this, except one day my mother came in when I was fourteen and said my dad was mad because I had not thrown away a used Kotex. She said, please wrap it up like I showed you. Now I never knew if my father actually said that or how he said it. I believed her that he said he was grossed out, but he never treated me any different.

JL: What were her instructions about what you were to do with the things?

Judy: *You fold it up and then you take toilet paper and you wrap it around this way, and then you have to turn it and wrap it around the other way, otherwise it will come undone. And it is very important that you wrap it up for two reasons. One for sanitary reasons and two, because people get offended. Meaning men get offended* [especially] *if you are using a public bathroom like in the house where everyone, your brother, your father are going in. And she told me, always look for that little container in the ladies' room and you wrap it, even when you throw it in there you wrap it because it is probably a man who is going to empty that. All for men. I never felt embarrassed around my dad though. I mean, I wasn't very close to him at that point because of his drinking, but I still never felt any different.*

JL: What about other boys and men?

Judy: *The day that I got my first period and later on that afternoon, that very first day, my aunt gave me some Midol and I felt better and I went back outside eventually. I had just taken a ring that morning from a boy I was going to go steady with and I took a ring from another boy. They used to give you cheap little "going steady" rings, and my cousin was mad at me. She said, "you are fickle, you can't just break up with somebody just because...why are you doing that? You liked him this morning, now you like this one better this afternoon?" And I said: "I have my period"* (laugh), *like this boy doesn't fit the new image. He was the boy I was going to climb trees with. This boy is going to hold my hand. I made a complete turnaround...I mean, this is also totally in a twenty-four hour period...very scary. And my cousin even thought it was nuts.*

JL: And you actually articulated it, about having your period?

Judy: *Yes, I am not a child anymore. I can't go with him. He* [the other boy] *is more sophisticated, older, and I changed boyfriends* (laugh). *That's scary. Weird.*

JL: Do you have a staining memory? Most of us do!

Judy: *Oh yeah! Well, that first year and second year I was in an all girls private Catholic school, near my home, so I commuted. There were girls there who boarded. French nuns, so we all learned to speak French fluently. Anyway, in an all girls school, staining experiences were not humiliating. It wasn't until I went to public high school at 15 that I had an experience where I had white pants on. It was white, it was summer...why would I be wearing pants to school? Perhaps it was some kind of special day where they gave us permission to wear pants to school. Anyway, I was fifteen, and I was a sophomore in high school, and I had one of those experiences where I got up and I didn't see it. It was on the back and* [my friend] *said: "I've got to get you a sweater." It was somebody else's sweater that she got. I had to go home of course. If you have a sweater tied around you boys pulled on those; they pulled sweaters off of you; they did stuff like that. I had no way of knowing if this was going to happen, so I went home. I remembered being a little freaked out because I wondered if anyone saw; I wondered if any boys saw. Fortunately, girls took care of girls and they let each other know when something like that was occurring. It was common among us, and we all had experienced it. But yeah, there was this terrible thing about hiding it from men, like this horrible shame that somehow it was a turnoff to them. They would be grossed out.*

JL: Can you talk more about what you mean by 'turnoff'?

Judy: *The grossed out has to do with that hint of blood and the odor, but yeah, turnoff. Most boys that I knew, and the reason that I knew this is because I used to hang around with them and I kind of knew how they thought. They didn't have to say it to me. They didn't want to have sex with girls when they had their periods because they thought it was something very taboo, like, I couldn't consider that, even if I wanted to, it's disgusting, it is disgust. And then later on when I heard about people like the Hell's Angels who used to give awards to men who went out and specifically had sex with women, different kinds of sex with women who had their periods* (laugh)*, so it is still the same issue, it is just the other side of the coin. It is like, how gross can I be and I get a medal for it? It is still the idea that it is a sexual turnoff, that the real issue is that I don't want it touching my body, you know, there is blood from the vagina, is it going to shrivel the penis up into nothing? It is like it is acid, or you were dipping it in acid. Which is an interesting idea!* (laugh) *But that is the way they behaved. Like it was a disease. It is more than just getting dirty otherwise they could say, well I could wash. But it was like you couldn't wash it off. Like contamination. So girls that did have sex with boys usually let them know if it was a good time or not, and I knew boys who wouldn't even take out their girlfriends on dates the week they had their periods because they might get turned on and drink too much beer, and have sex anyway.*

JL: You said earlier that girls take care of girls. Can you talk more about that?

Judy: *Yes, it was always acceptable in my crowd and the girlfriends that I had. It wouldn't be unusual for someone to go and get you aspirin, bring you a cup of tea, carry your books, help you, you know, if you really had some...some women had different levels of cramps and different levels of problems and concerns during their period. I wasn't as sick as some of my friends were. The only time I went to bed was when I didn't want to go to school* (laugh). *And I did use it. Oh yeah.*

JL: Do you remember helping other girls?

Judy: *Well I certainly remember helping people if they were not feeling well; carrying what they were carrying, or going off and finding some Midol or some aspirin and a glass of water, but I don't remember giving out a sweater, but I think I would have. It just never came up.*

JL: Can you think of other times that you used your period or that it was a form of solidarity with girls?

Judy: *Well, yeah. I used my period when I got older to get boys to stop pushing me to have sex. I used to tell them I had my period. I had more periods than you could imagine!* (laugh) *It was so much easier than saying no because they didn't listen to no. And if you said no, you might not get a date again. So it was that real dilemma and I found it much more convenient to say, well, I have my period. And for girls, it was solidarity because it was the one thing we all had in common; it was the one thing we all used to keep the boys at bay, we all knew that we did.*

JL: And did you share that with each other?

Judy: *Oh yeah! We talked about that, at least in my group. I can't speak for all the girls in the school, but certainly the ones I hung around with, you bet. Some girls got caught lying because the boys figured out when they had their periods and knew that was two weeks ago, I mean regularly* (laugh). *Some boys were smart enough to figure it out, but most weren't. Most just took you at your word. But it was hard: how do you flirt, act sexual, dress sexual, how do you get dates and then not actually do anything and then get another date?* (laugh). *This was really incredible manipulation and I was very good at it. I was very skillful. I wasn't allowed to date until I was sixteen, but I would spend the night at girlfriends' houses and sneak out of the house. You know, there is this piece of me that I felt I lost, a powerful piece of me that was going to do all the things that the boys did, and do them as confidently as the boys did them, and be competitive if I wanted to be, be loud if I wanted to be. Yeah, so it is a loss of power, only the power I got by having my period was a different kind of power. It was much less straight-on honest. It was manipulative. But it was powerful. My ability to manipulate boys around these sexual issues was very powerful, but it wasn't good for the relationship. When I was competing with them I was even keel, at twelve. And we were playing a game and I was beating the pants off of them because I was better; I liked them when I beat them. But when I manipulated them later on, around sexual issues, and got what I wanted, I didn't like them for being so stupid as to not see what I was doing to them. So the respect I had for men was very different with those different kinds of powers.*

JL: That's really insightful, isn't it? It's so much about the struggle around femininity. Now I'm going to play the devil's advocate for a minute, and suggest, for example, what does this have to do with menarche, with periods? Wasn't this just the adolescent drama playing itself out for you?

Judy: *I don't think so. It is so very dramatic when it first occurs. But if it were just adolescence it would stop, but it doesn't. That whole ritualistic hiding and the shame involved that doesn't stop. It goes on to the thirties, forties, fifties, sixties; it may be more dramatic at thirteen. 'It' meaning all the behaviors and attitudes around men-*

struation. They don't really change, they are just bigger than life in the beginning because everything is bigger than life developmentally at thirteen or fourteen. They never go away, they just get less noisy at thirty than they were at fifteen.

JL: Yes, but how was that related to menarche for you?

Judy: *Well, menarche is the birth if you will, of manipulative sexual power, and that is how it felt to me. And until I got my period, that socialized piece of me wasn't there. My power was more genuine, more earthy, more real, less manipulative.* [The other] *is governed by hiding, shame, keeping it from other people. It is really power that is governed by society in a way, but I can't say it isn't powerful because women use it very powerfully. There is a real price to pay for using that sexual power. There was a time in my life when I was just driven by sex, driven by boys, driven by sexuality, driven by socialization. And I thought I was free.*

JL: How might you have told your story differently had you been seventeen years old?

Judy: *At seventeen, I felt the victimization so you would have had a very angry teenager. I was very angry; I would throw stuff across the room. I was giving up stuff for this craziness because I thought I had to, and I couldn't articulate and understand what was happening to me. But I have been able as a forty-five-year old having raised a teenager, and having sort of relived some of what I went through, to resolve this. I talked to my son about women more than I ever thought that I would. He knew about women's periods and he knew what it was about. I wanted to educate him. And so he grew up with that stuff in the bathroom. I didn't hide my box, my Kotex. I still wrapped them, still to this day I wrap them, but I didn't hide them away. I refused to. And* [I would say] *get used to them. And he would hide them from his friends when they came over* (laugh), *"mother, I wish you'd clean up your stuff before my friends come over." Isn't that interesting?!*

3

Contamination and Concealment

> Trust is Tampax: It's knowing a slim pad won't do when your clothes are even slimmer. Let's say you're wearing tight leggings. Even the slimmest pad is going to get in the way. But trust Tampax Tampons, and you're free to wear anything, go anywhere. And no one will ever know you've got your period. See, a Tampax Tampon gives you all the protection of a pad. But it's worn inside your body, so you can trust nothing will show. They're also really comfortable, and there's no odor to worry about. So go ahead. Slip into something really skinny. When you trust Tampax Tampons, all that'll show is your confidence.
>
> —Advertisement, *Seventeen*, January 1994

Talk about menstruation and menstrual blood is deemed inappropriate in most domains of current Western societies, except between women alone, and, perhaps, if men broach the subject. Here men exercise their prerogative in public statements and negative sanctions, through "jokes," and by the faceless messages of capitalism as demonstrated by the ad above. Society maintains taboos against positive discussions of menarche and menstruation, and, as a result, reinforces cultural values that see menstrual blood as dirty and smelly, polluting and contaminating. If menstruation were not so "icky," companies would not go to such great lengths to emphasize that if you use their products no one will know you are menstruating, be able to see unsightly bulges, or smell you. These are the messages in the *Seventeen* advertisement above: "When you trust Tampax Tampons, all that'll show is your confidence."

Note how this message also plays on girls' requirement to be thin, completely objectionable given the high incidence of eating disorders among adolescent girls. Such a discourse is especially aimed at teenagers, encouraging them to conceal natural bodily functions and keep their growing bodies small and thin lest they take up too much space, exercise power, or show evidence of failing in the disciplinary regimens of feminine bodily hygiene/care. That "hygiene" and "care" are so easily interchangeable illustrates the potentially polluting and contaminating nature of women's bodies and blood in their natural state; bodies that have to be attended to lest they get out of control, and, as a result, bodies that require the donation of enormous amounts of time, energy and money toward their on-going management.

A crucial point here is that young women play a significant role in their own subordination through these practices of femininity, even though they may experience the competence that goes along with the careful and thorough management of bodily processes. If the body, as Douglas and Foucault have suggested, functions as a text and direct locus of practical control, then we must pay attention to the internalization of discourses surrounding the body, and to the self-disciplining and policing that occurs through the everyday compulsive regimens of menstrual bodily care and control. Foucault (1977) suggested that certain disciplinary practices produce "docile bodies" that are regulated and habituated to the norms of cultural life. While Foucault overlooked the forms of subjectivity that engender the feminine body, and put too much emphasis on the deterministic nature of these forces, minimizing human agency (McNay 1992), his discussion of the disciplinary practices has much relevance for our understanding of menarche. Further, contemporary life involves the relative absence of formal disciplinary structures that perpetuate such bodily control: "No one is marched off to electrolysis at gunpoint" (Bartky 1992: 112). Bartky emphasizes that women's continued involvement in the public sphere in the late twentieth century has been accompanied by strict rules about normative femininity which increasingly center on the body, its sexuality and appearance, and which are available to a wide spectrum of women due to the contemporary power of the visual image. This involves a saving in the economy of surveillance as women discipline their own and other women's bodies.

In this chapter we explore the disciplinary menstrual practices of concealment that both result in, and are maintained by, knowledge of menstrual contamination. These reproduce gender and help construct "woman" in contemporary Western societies. Such practices and forms of knowledge are maintained in part through information and products associated with menarche that both inform and discipline. It is to these that we turn first, followed by analyses of the contaminating nature of menarcheal and menstruating women, and the practices of concealment such notions engender in women's everyday lives.

Information and Products

Suddenly Pecola bolted straight up, her eyes wide with terror. A whinnying sound came from her mouth...

"What?" Pecola's fingers went to her mouth.

"That's ministratin'"...

Frieda was on her knees; a white rectangle of cotton was near her on the ground. She was pulling Pecola's pant off. "Come on. Step out of them." She managed to get the soiled pants down and flung them at me. "Here."

"What am I supposed to do with these?"

"Bury them moron."

Frieda told Pecola to hold the cotton thing between her legs.

"How she gonna walk like that?" I asked.

Frieda didn't answer. Instead she took two safety pins from the hem of her skirt and began to pin the ends of the napkin to Pecola's dress.

—Toni Morrison, *The Bluest Eye*

Girls learn about the contaminating nature of "ministratin'" and the subsequent requirements for concealment through the internalization of messages from many different sources—the media, religion, schools, the medical system, from their friends and families, and from information included with menstrual products. Girls are exposed to a plethora of subtle and not-so-subtle messages, whispered secretly in school playgrounds, stated matter-of-factly in lectures and documentaries, and boldly exclaimed in television commercials. Sometimes girls receive no direct personal information about menstruation at all, and occasionally they receive affirming and positive messages. Frequently they get information that constructs menstruation in negative ways, and more often than not they receive enough mixed messages to make them feel ambivalent about the whole thing. A study by Stoltzman (1986), for example, found that adolescent girls tended to get more information about menstruation from the media and their peers than from their mothers, and, when interviewed, girls appeared more negative about menstruation than did their mothers. Along similar lines, Brooks-Gunn and Ruble (1983) found that unprepared girls reported more pain with menstruation, and those who received inadequate explanations were showing negative symptomologies even three years after menarche.

In terms of information, the school system in particular provides a structured system of rules and norms associated with menstruation. Barrie Thorne, in *Gender Play: Girls and Boys in School*, writes of the "official agenda" of sex education and gives rich observations of a fifth grade class who began their sex education with the "menstruation movie":

> As I participated in this uncomfortable event, I wondered how many girls had already started menstruating and how the official messages related to their varied experiences, anxieties, knowledge, and conversations with friends and family. In spite of the matter-of-fact, upbeat tone of the movie, several themes reverberated: menstruation is a secret, emotionally loaded, and shame-filled topic; adults and kids don't feel comfortable discussing these matters; these issues are charged with tension, awkwardness, and mistrust between girls and boys.... Finally, the fact that official sex education begins with such a central emphasis on girls reinforces their definition in terms of sexuality. (1993: 147)

Like Thornes' subjects, Kay, a white student and mother in her thirties, had similar experiences with "sex ed" in the schools. She articulates how schools discipline the female mind and body, not only by the information itself, but also through the way it is presented:

First, in fifth or sixth grade, at my elementary school, we were separated from the boys and shown a film about menstruation. Next we were given a packet which contained some kind of feminine hygene products and propaganda. We considered this whole affair hilarious, embarrassing and yet still it took the place of what could be considered a sort of puberty ritual for us girls. We never knew what the boys talked about or what they were told about us, reproductively, etc. But I always somehow felt that they had been given some important secret that day, that we, as girls, were not privy to, and that this was just some kind of weird, divisive act on the part of the administration, to distract and codify us. I suppose that sounds like paranoia at work, or perhaps hindsight talking, eh? But it's true, I did feel that way.

This clinical lecture, often complete with diagrams and proper medical terminology, seems to be a very popular way, among both schools and mothers, of imparting information about menarche. Robin and Jennifer J., both aged twenty-two and from middle-class homes, remembered being particularly confused about the role of "the egg." Robin is a bi-racial lesbian, and Jennifer J. a heterosexual Asian-American: *"I was very confused, but I thought that the egg was coming out and not the lining of the uterus!"* said Robin. Jennifer laughed as she remembered: *"She* [her mother] *drew me the ovaries on a piece of paper and she showed me what happened, and that is how you get your period, and da-di-da, and that was it. She never talked about it again, and nothing about sex or relationships or anything. I didn't understand a word she was saying: like the eggs are going to be here and there. It was terrible!"* As

Noreen Steven's humorous cartoon "The Egg" demonstrates, such information-giving often has some interpretive drawbacks (fig 3.1).

figure 3.1

Kari, a white, twenty-six year-old lesbian who was raised in a middle-class home in Iowa remembers her experience of the scientific, "matter-of-fact" approach to menstrual education—an approach that, like us, Emily Martin found to be associated more frequently with middle-class families. Such a mode of imparting information tends not to connect the mechanics of menstruation with girls' emotional lives:

I was raised with a scientific approach to sexuality and menstruation. My mother had to send away for "how to explain sex to your child," pamphlets to find out about sexuality for herself. So she swore to let us know about sex as soon as we asked. I remember her telling me about the shocked reactions of women in the bathroom at an interstate rest area when she explained to me, aged three, what was in the mysterious "Modess, because..." vending machine. As I was growing up, all my questions were explained in a very scientific and factual way. Given this, it is a strange thing that I didn't even realize I had my period the first time I menstruated.

Our study, not suprisingly, showed that the older women received less knowledge than the younger ones. Many of the older women remembered feelings of fear, despair and loneliness at menarche. Only a handful of the participants over sixty years had received any information at all, and usually only following menarche. After that, it was rarely discussed again. Most were left alone to figure things out. Attempts to get information from friends were often unsuccessful, because no one else had any idea, either. Instruction at school tended to be non-existent, although a few talked about going to the public library and trying to find some information. Several older women remembered a small book—"Margery May's 12th Birthday"—that had given them some idea of what was happening. Rose, aged sixty-eight years, who raised three sons and was employed for many years as a clerical worker; Joan, aged sixty, who has a doctorate from Stanford University; and Mary P., aged seventy and a mother of twelve children, reflected on their first menses:

Well, my first knowledge of menstruation. When I was twelve my mother gave me a tiny little pamphlet that explained things quite well and our total conversation was: she said, "you read this, you need this information," so I read it, and she said: "did you understand what you read?" And I said "yes." She said "very well," and went off to do whatever she was going to do and that is as far as she ever went. No discussion whatever....I felt very strange and sort of terribly self-conscious...I wouldn't dare let my father know what was going on (laugh) *you know, in those days...And I really felt sort of totally confused about the whole thing really. And I think my girlfriends were the same way when we talked about it. They didn't have any more information than I had. We had to ask other girls, some of them had good information, some didn't know anything. It was very hush hush in those days as though it were something terrible* (Rose).

I was eleven years old when my first period started while at school (sixth grade). When I returned home and informed my mother what had happened, she handed me a box of Kotex and belt. No discussion. I went into my bedroom closet to figure out on my own how to attach and wear them. I felt lonely and rejected (Joan).

I really didn't know what was happening. When it happened I said something to her and she says: "well, this is what is going on." She didn't say much to me. I just kind of floundered through it...You know there wasn't much in those days. Nobody said much of anything. You just kind of...you kinda took care of yourself and that was the end of it (Mary P.).

Similarly, Evelyn, whose story we share below, had received no direct information about menstruation at all, leading her to worry instead that she had somehow hurt herself and had caused herself to bleed. Keeping girls ignorant of such bodily processes is a way to prevent their taking control over their own bodies, encouraging them to feel shameful and at a loss as to how to deal with their physical and emotional changes. If girls do not understand menarche, they are more likely to believe negative messages about the whole process, and are more easily controlled through menstrual practices. Evelyn is fifty-four years old, part Indonesian and part European. She grew up on the Island of Sumatra but has lived most of her adult life in the United States. She is a mother, a lesbian and is currently enrolled in graduate school. Her narrative illustrates the way women have had to learn to use menstrual equipment and products to manage their periods, while simultaneously maintaining concealment. Evelyn writes:

Mother had to bring up her four children by wits and perseverence; we mostly lived in garages until I was ten, at which time we also took in two elderly great-aunts. [There was] *very little private space, so I learned to climb trees to be in my own space. I'm telling you this because I was still doing this at age twelve or thirteen when I had my first menstrual period. My mother never told me or my sisters about such personal/private things and it surprises me, looking back, that I never knew about such female 'things' with the crowded living conditions. Five people living in a (very small, one-car) garage, a space probably no bigger than ten-by-twelve or ten-by-fourteen feet (with only an outside faucet with portable straw matting for wall, our bathroom/laundry facilities, which included a six inch hole connected to the sewer system running in back of all the houses and which was our toilet), such 'facilities' should have made secrecy about menstrual periods almost an impossible task; however, I never knew about such things until I had my first period myself. I was sure that I had somehow done something wrong while climbing the tree in the backyard, where I spent most of the afternoon study time—I had a very comfortable branch which spread out over the house and which gave me the privacy that I sought to read and study. I think my mother probably was home for several hours while I worried, but I did not say anything until several hours later, and then only to my older sister. She explained that, NO, I did not split open while climbing the tree, and that (which seemed like a horrible prospect) I would be doing this bleeding every month. I was then shown the stack of old pieces of cloth/towels and the bands also out of fabric that had thinner string-like extensions (somewhat like a large H) that could be used like a diaper of sorts (the strings tied around the waist) that would hold the pieces of cloth, pinned to the 'diaper' with safety pins in place. All very uncomfortable. Since all of this stuff had to be re-used, and since there were now three women using the same 'equipment' it was very important that we washed out the cloths and other things IMMEDIATELY AND BE VERY PRIVATE ABOUT IT. We all did our laundry, most of the time, by hand in a bucket in the back yard, generally immediately after our daily bath, but these cloths had to be washed more often than that, because we used more than one change. I HATED EVERYTHING ABOUT IT.*

Whether girls are prepared or not for menarche, as the stories above suggest, they do learn about what menstruation entails and how to manage it through the use of products or commodities, sometimes bought, and sometimes made from left-over items. Women spoke and wrote specifically about the way they were socialized into the world of sanitary products, the secrecy that surrounds this whole issue, as well as the fact that they were the ones who had to take responsibility for maintaining the secrecy, the taboo associated with it, and endure the restrictions imposed on their activities. In terms of the various *"menstrual contraptions"* (as aptly named by one interviewee), there is much skill involved in their use, which can include making, buying, washing, pinning, hiding and disposing. These skills are necessary for young women in the school context, for they must conceal their sanitary supplies at the same time that they are often only allowed to carry a notebook to class and have short, structured times to get to the bathroom. Products and practices of their use regulate and impose culture on female bodies and lives.

Many women received little books and pamphlets that were supposed to explain menstrual mysteries. Often this literature was made by menstrual product companies such as Kotex, Modess or Tampax, and these product names were used interchangeably with menstrual supplies generally. This product-related information functions as a kind of "propaganda," and plays an important part in molding behavior and disciplining the body. It also, of course, maintains corporate capitalism. Concerning this wonderful world of "sanitary care," older women told stories about using rags and cloths and the complications associated with managing these items. Joyce, a white woman aged ninety-four years who grew up in a middle-class family and moved to Oregon's Willammette Valley from Oklahoma when she was six years old, remembered dealing with menstrual rags:

You took...we'll call them rags, I mean it was just material, you made them and folded them and we had to use those and then you put...you couldn't throw them away really because you wouldn't have enough, you know. They were just things...they weren't colored I mean, they were white and you soaked them in cold water and you washed them and that was...that was horrid. That was always a job you sure hated to do. Well the thing was that it was...well it was really kind of stinkin', it couldn't help but be. Because it wasn't...it wasn't absorbent you know and you had to change them oftener.

Tita and Gerta, white women aged seventy-three and eighty years respectively, also shared their reminiscences of menarche. Tita identified ethnically as *"Scotch-Irish/German and a tiny bit of Native-American"* and grew up in a poor family of tenent farmers in Washington State; Gerta was born in Oregon into a middle-class family, received a teaching degree from San Francisco State University, raised a family and eventually received a Masters in Education. They share the following:

There was no talk about "that sort of thing" at home and when I found blood on my pants—I went to Grandma C. and she handed me some folded rags, told me to "pin them on" and when they were soiled, bled through, I was to wash them out, hang them on the line so they would be ready for "next time in about a month"—well those miserable rags rubbed the insides of my legs raw and by the time the perod ended I was really hurting (Tita).

I considered the whole thing rather a bother. The sanitary belt, the pads, the deoderant powder, the chafing, the uncomfortable feeling of the pad between one's legs. In 1932 or 1933 the internal pads first appeared with Wix and then Tampax. This was better except the darned string would get damp and dangle. If you inserted it, then you had to fish for it to remove the tampon. Being a woman wasn't all it was cracked up to be! (Gerta).

For the most part, the younger women were more relaxed about their choices of menstrual products, yet still shared many, many stories about "mattress pads" and bulky, restricitive equipment. Virginia's story is particularly illustrative of the way information about products and the products themselves discipline young women. She is a white, middle-class woman, aged thirty-eight years.

I have very vivid memories of my first period. My mother, sensing that I would probably be starting, sent away to the Kotex company and got one of those big boxes, and it had all of the napkins and books and all that. I can remember my mother after dinner saying: "I have something for you," and of course I was 10 years old and I thought, "Oh boy! A present or something! And she took me in my bedroom and brought this box in and she said "I'd like you to read this book and if you have any questions, ask me." I was ten years old and I didn't understand any of it. In fact I misunderstood most of it.... There was a little elastic belt that had a little string that went down the back and front, and it had a piece of hardware on it like a bra strap, and you wrapped the napkin which had these ends that came out, you know, and you wrapped it a certain way around this little piece of hardware so it would stay. Oh, they were horrible! It reminded me of the old garter belts. I remember being very uncomfortable wearing it, sitting on it and feeling like everyone must know.

The Kotex kit and pamphlets, the huge pads and belt, the difficult instructions and procedure involved in inserting a tampon for the first time (especially when girls are taught to not touch themselves "down there," or not to use tampons because it would interfere with their virginity), all give specific messages about ways that menstruation should be managed. Linda Bourke illustrates this with the cartoon below (fig. 3.2).

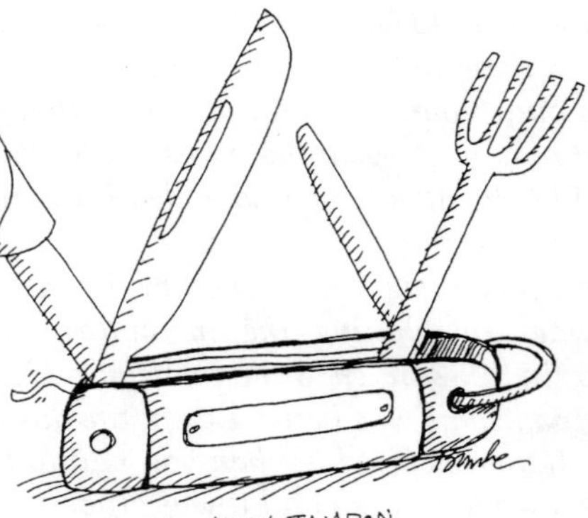

figure 3.2

Such pamphlets and menstrual paraphernalia suggest that women must collect the flow in easily disposed ways that encourage maximum cleanliness, similar to contemporary tampons with insertors that allow women to minimize touching their bodies, and the addition of perfumes and other "deodorizing" strategies to menstrual products. These deodorizing additives are bad for women's health, and the bleaching of menstrual products is very bad not only for women, but also for the physical environment. Such "sanitary" products are designed to help women de-contaminate themselves and protect others from their potential polluting influences, as well as to conceal evidence of their periods from the world. As the Tampax advertisement at the beginning of this chapter announced: "it's worn inside your body so nothing will show. They're also really comfortable, and there's no odor to worry about."

Involved here is a whole discourse of hygiene that women are expected to accept and follow to "manage" the messy and bloody aspect of menstruation, underscoring the message that women's genitals are disgusting and potentially polluting. The implication that menstrual blood is contaminating and dirty, and may lead to disease, gives added importance to menstrual "hygiene," as does the requirement for women to conceal such excretions with products that provide hygenic disposal. Companies use this rhetoric of cleanliness in their advertisements, referring to menstrual products as "sanitary products." Self- discipline and policing through the everyday acts of feminine bodily care and the use of menstrual products and other commodities perpetuates corporate capitalism at the same time that it creates disciplined bodies. Women spend considerable amounts of money on these "necessities." Fifty-five year old Marian, a white Australian woman who grew up in England, shared her thoughts on this expense. At the time of writing Marian was going through the menopause, but was still experiencing occasional periods: "If I could do one thing for the women of this world it would be to reduce the price of sanitary pads, as each period costs me approximately A$15, if it is heavy."

The requirement that corporate profits accumulate and markets expand and diversify involves encouragements to use various "different" and "new, improved" products, playing on the socially imposed fears that women have internalized. Such new products now have features that prevent leakage, for example, through panty liners with "wings," and pads with "center protection systems" that trap blood in specially designed absorbent areas. These products rely on and promote fears centered on smell and staining, maintaining the rhetoric of contamination and encouraging further self-disciplining and concealment. A humorous illustration of this new "technology" is shared in Rina Piccolo's cartoon below (fig 3.3).

figure 3.3

Contamination

I felt much more important once I had my period. I guess I did feel grown up, or more grown up. It was a little confusing though because sometimes I felt dirty. Dirty physically and perhaps ashamed.... My internal relationship to my body remained relatively unchanged for years. Sometimes I think even now, I see my body as dirty and dangerous and shameful.

—Lucie, white, aged twenty-five

In terms of menstrual pollution and contamination, as discussed in chapter 1, historically and cross-culturally, menstrual blood has been considered both magical and poisonous, and social interpretations of women's bleeding have structured and restricted women's lives. These interpretations have often tended to involve a discourse of pollution and the requirement of a separation or seclusion of individual women from the daily activities of others (especially men, and primarily husbands).

Anthropologists have argued over the meanings of menstruation, moving away from talking about universal taboos and instead emphasizing the specific nature of cultural significations that represent menarche and menstruation in particular contexts. Feminists have conducted and interpreted early work that reads menstrual taboos and seclusions as evidence of women's oppression; and they have also begun to argue that such seclusion might instead represent a genuine respect for women and for indigenous women's own self-determination. Either way, we can say that menstruation matters; it has mattered historically and cross-culturally, and it matters in contemporary Western society in the late twentieth century. Hearing women's stories today suggests that notions of pollution are still very relevant.

In 1966, Mary Douglas wrote the well-known text *Purity and Danger: An Analysis of Concepts of Pollution and Taboo*, revised in subsequent articles over the next decade. Her general thesis was that in many societies there are substances people consider to be dangerous and "out of place" that are anomalous to a general symbolic sense of order. These substances both emerge from the society and are seen as a threat to it; in the functionalist sense, their purpose is to rationalize beliefs and stabilize and maintain social order. She emphasized that bodily margins are especially dangerous: "If they are pulled this way or that the shape of fundamental experience is altered" (1966: 121). The important point here is that "Each culture has its own special risks and problems. To which particular bodily margins its beliefs attribute power depends on what situation the body is mirroring" (121).

In some societies, bodily fluids such as menstrual blood that transcend the boundaries of the body take on particular significance as lethal pollutants. As Buckley and Gottlieb suggest in *Blood Magic*: "Menstrual blood is a particularly apt candidate for analysis in terms of this theory. As blood itself, menstrual discharge is 'out of place,' breaching the natural bounds of the body that normally contain it...Menstrual blood does not issue randomly or accidently, as does the blood of wounds, but from a single source and to some extent regularly and predictably" (1988: 26). Of all societies preoccupied with and fearing menstrual blood, the Mae Enga of New Guinea are especially notorious (Meggitt 1964). Such intense responses symbolize the relations between the sexes in this society, where masculinity is reveered yet seen as vulnerable to a polluting feminine influence. Men of the Enga are involved in highly competitive social systems where wives are considered assets and signs of prestige. They choose partners from competing clans: "The Enga belief about sex pollution suggests that sexual relationships take on the characteristic of a conflict between enemies in which the man sees himself as endangered by his sexual partner, the intrusive member of the enemy clan" (Douglas 1966: 147). In this way, notions of menstrual blood as polluting function instrumentally to maintain male superiority and keep women in their place, at the same time that they work expressively to symbolize the potentially antagonistic relationship between men and women and the ambiguity or contradiction implicit in women's roles as both partners and enemies. We mention the Mae Enga because we believe that Douglas' insights about the role menstrual blood plays in maintaining male supremacy can illuminate our theoretical understandings of menstrual pollution in contemporary Western societies. However, as Buckley and Gottlieb are quick to point out, pollution theory has its limits, and the attribution of concepts of menstrual pollution to many societies where none may exist can be misleading.

Nonetheless, Douglas' work is informative for us as we try to make sense out of contemporary notions of pollution that women currently endure, help maintain, and sometimes resist. Ultimately, pollution beliefs are statements about power relations. We need only look to contemporary racist, sexist and classist ideas that people of color, the fat and the poor are less clean to provide immediate examples. Douglas emphasizes the relationship between menstrual pollution and sociostructural contradictions and ambiguities, suggesting that discourses of contamination work to offset structural gains made by some women in misogynous and patriarchal societies. Notions of pollution are components of forms of knowledge that support certain practices, practices through which the body is inscribed with the politics of culture. Women might move the world as leaders and achievers, yet still they are connected to their inescapable biological processes and bodily selves, and are sullied by this association.

As already discussed in chapter 1, psychoanalytic theory in particular has centered on issues of pollution and shame. In *The Psychoanalysis of Children*, Melanie Klein (1918, in Delaney, Lupton and Toth 1988: 75) suggested that girls unconsciously identify menstrual blood with urine and feces, and therefore with contamination. This may contribute to feelings of shame—"the deep-down-inside feeling that one is unworthy, unvalued, defective, unlovable" (Cavanaugh 1989: 2). Of course, it is more complicated than this. In terms of gender we can say that in our society language and forms of knowledge about the female body uphold practices and justify ideas, behaviors and policies that maintain patriarchal social relations and function symbolically to represent understandings of women's roles. The horror and repugnance associated with being close to another and/or her property and bodily fluids because she is seen as contaminating is a powerful indicator of the social relations of dominance and subordination: the "girl stain... the fact that girls, not boys become cast as an ultimate polluting group" (Thorne 1993: 75).

Similarly, there are few words to talk about the female sexual anatomy that are neither clinical nor derogatory. Most of these words suggest that female genitalia are smelly and unpleasant, and, in the context of a society where girls' and women's identities are so intricately linked to their bodies, this makes for internalized oppression, embarrassment and shame. These words are usually being introduced into girls' vocabularies simultaneously with their experience of puberty and menarche. It is no surprise then that Williams (1983) found that 68 percent of the elementary school girls she interviewed believed that menstrual blood had a bad odor, and 89 percent believed that increased emotionality was associated with menstruation. Sophie Laws, in *Issues of Blood* (1990), talked to British men about these very issues and found they did indeed see menstrual blood as contaminating. Other scholars have also found that men have more negative views of menstruation than women, and use the term "on the rag" more often and in more demeaning ways (Ernster 1975). In Laws' study, men spoke about how they felt menstrual blood was unclean and how they found the smell offensive. Her respondents shared the following:

> I still think of it being dirty or whatever...more like afterbirth or something like that...not something I'd like to be touching...whereas ordinary blood, I wouldn't mind that at all.

And

> I think, in all honesty, I would say it has a measure, something of a measure of impurity about it, which an ordinary cut, it doesn't seem, because it

has the connotations of discharge...I just sort of feel there is that element in it, in terms of the body functions [unclear] discharge...presumably therefore contains elements which the body is therefore rejecting, I suppose...mainly because people I know who're on what I call a pure diet, a balanced diet tend to have very little menstrual bleeding. (33–4)

In her discussion of Sheri Hite's (1981) research on men's attitudes towards women, Laws writes: "[from their] preoccupation with smell and generally with the dirtiness of women's genitals...I am inclined to see this insistence on the need for washing to be an observance of menstrual etiquette: men's manhood in some way requires that women acknowledge their possible impurity before coming into contact with a man" (61–62).

Over and again, in the interviews and in written narratives, women in our sample remembered feeling dirty and ashamed when they started their periods. Almost half specifically mentioned "the curse," "on the rag" or another negative term that they or others among their family and friends had used to describe menstruation. Eve, for example, a white, working-class student in her forties, literally spelled out her first period as a *"demeaning damn curse"*:

The day I got my period sh sh sh. It was a hot summer day, I was fourteen years old feeling very happy that maybe just maybe I had been one of the chosen few that would escape this curse that befell women, but no, lurking in my body, brewing up was the p-pain, e-eroding, r-red, i- irregular, o-odorous, d-demeaning damn curse.

Others stated that their first menstrual blood made them feel unclean, ashamed and fearful. Bertha, a Jewish woman in her forties, remembered her menarche as similar to *"a feeling I used to feel when I was young and wet my pants...It was a feeling of having soiled myself."* Similarly Julia, a twenty-two-year-old white woman, recalled the painful embarrassment of being teased by her brother about blood stains in her underwear that he called *"skid marks."* The association of blood stains with soiling her underwear from a bowel movement were especially humiliating to her. Such experiences and feelings affected women's senses of self and worth, and helped set up the idea that the female body and sexuality are bad and corrupting. So many women talked about worrying that they might smell bad and/or had learned to associate menstrual blood with a bad odor. Further, some women said that the feelings of being unclean that they experienced at menarche were still present. Jo, a white student also in her twenties, reported the following: *"Umm...I felt kind of I mean...I wanted to keep taking showers. Yeah, and it still does make me feel dirty sometimes."* Such memories of shame and embarrassment were shared by Northstar, who was about the same age as Julia and Jo, but who grew up in Taiwan:

I feel I have a big diaper. I feel everyone can see me...very embarrassed.... I know sometimes when I went to my uncle's house that sometimes my aunt would forbid my uncle to take garbage out because she said that we have "women's mess" inside so men cannot carry the garbage out because there are women's pads inside.

The following narrative, representative of the ways that women internalize notions of pollution, was written by Sarah K, a white, working-class divorced woman in her forties who lives with her two sons in Central Oregon. Sarah's account illustrates how the social rules and practices of concealment inscribed upon the body are maintained by forms of knowledge which support these same behaviors. In this case, notions about contamination are internalized as shame through the practices of concealment:

My first menstrual period came unexpectedly at age twelve. My mother explained that this happens to every girl and I should get used to it. She told me I would have to wash "down there" more frequently because of the smell. I decided I didn't want any part of this. I felt dirty, smelly and felt as though everyone around me could smell me too. I was also told by my mother that I was a lady now, so I had to act like one, and not play with the boys anymore. I guessed the reason I couldn't play with them anymore was that they would smell me too, and know my horrible secret. I felt dirty, humiliated, angry. I was also embarrassed when I had to go to the store for sanitary napkins. Once a boy who went to the same school as I was in there. When I paid for them he said, "Oh, you use 'Super.'" I was so ashamed, I ran home crying. Also, the school nurse didn't believe me. She made me go into the bathroom and wipe myself and put the bloody tissue out the door for her to see. I felt I was being punished for something that should be a natural, positive part of becoming a woman. I also remember "we women" in our family had to hide our sanitary napkins, so my dad or brothers wouldn't see them. Again, I felt this was a dirty, smelly experience (secret if you will) that only women shared.

Sarah's story is about menstrual contamination. She feels "*dirty*" and has anxieties about the smell "*down there*," worrying that others might learn of her "*secret*" by being able to smell her too. She represents someone who has been explicity taught, and has internalized, the negative ideologies about menstruation as contaminating: someone who has learnt to feel shame because she is female. In terms of her developing sexuality, her mother's reference to her being a "*lady now*," carries with it all the connotations and restrictions of femininity. Her mother also tells her to stay away from boys, implicitly communicating that it is her responsibility to control heterosexual relationships. Sarah misses the point on this and assumes that she must stay away so that the boys won't be contaminated by her.

About one-quarter of the women in our sample spoke or wrote about experiences of incest or child sexual and/or physical abuse. Almost all of these women said that they felt that their bodies were dirty and shameful, and connected the violation of their bodies to menarche as a contaminating experience. Hannah, a working-class, white, twenty-five year-old lesbian spoke poignantly of the way her feelings about her contaminated body as a survivor coincided with her feelings about her menstrual flow. She felt very dirty and ashamed:

> *The abuse made me feel awful. It colored everything, so much of what I did, how I felt about my body and my self esteem.... I felt really dirty and you know because I was on my period, and I would cramp more and I just felt dirty, I felt icky, I felt horrible, like people could smell me and I just felt subhuman.... I felt kind of shameful to be around men and I don't want to be around people and I don't want people to know at all.... I hated the feeling of flowing, I hated just that warm feeling whenever...I felt as if it was something dirty, something horrible coming out and I wanted to not flow as much as possible and if I got really active I would flow more and I didn't want to flow. I just wanted it to stop.*

Child sexual-abuse surviviors' words illustrate the way the vulnerabilities associated with women's emerging sexuality (and in these cases, the exploitation of what little girls' bodies signified in the context of a society that denigrates female sexuality), become integrated so that the body is seen as something that is acted upon, used and soiled. As Iris and Opal suggest here, menarche symbolized their biological femaleness, and they perceived femaleness as one origin of their abuse:

> *I was scared because my brother sexually molested me and he had been doing that for a long time and I knew that meant I could get pregnant and I was scared to death.... I had this sense of being dirty and contaminated or shameful because of the abuse.... I associated it with being female, with the whole business of being a woman* (Iris, white, aged thirty-three).

> *My older male cousin sexually abused me several times when I was about eight years old. As I found myself developing as a woman and I started my period I thought often about this and I remember the guilt and deep shame associated with it. It was all mixed up in my mind* (Opal, white, aged forty-five).

Concealment

You don't know what you want. You've got one hand in a bowl of sugary sweets and the other in a bowl of salty snacks. Your hormones make you feel like screaming one minute and yodeling the next. You're having dinner with your parents and your father notices you're getting taller. You realize your double plus super maxi adds two inches to your height whenever you sit down.

It sure is swell being a gal, isn't it?

Oh joy. It's that time of the month again. You don't know what you want. Yes you do. You want a super maxi that doesn't feel like one. Introducing New Freedom Maximums. Extra Long Pads tapered at the ends so they're designed to feel thinner and fit better. Yet they're 20 percent longer and wider than other super maxis, and up to 70 percent more absorbent. That's because our unique Center Protection System—it helps direct fluid to the center then traps it there in a highly absorbent inner core.

New Freedom

As good as it gets until it's gone

—*Self,* March 1994

The College of Liberal Arts at Oregon State University organizes a yearly all-College meeting where faculty and staff gather to begin the new academic year; new colleagues are introduced and department chairs and program directors are expected to give information and news. As the new Director of Women Studies, I (Janet) was asked to introduce myself and speak briefly about my research. So I said the word "menstruation" in this public setting several times, as well as such phrases as "women's bleeding" and "menstrual blood." Now, several years later, I still occasionally run into women who say, yes, they remember me, didn't I talk about menstruation at the college address? They often add how great it was that I should have talked so openly about such a little-mentioned topic in such a setting. Some also seemed to relish how uncomfortable many of their male colleagues looked during this brief interlude, suggesting how "out-of-place" such discourse is in an academic domain. I had, in effect, violated the etiquette of concealment. The disciplinary practices associated with the menstrual etiquette of concealment, whereby feminine bodies are constructed out of female ones, is the focus of this section.

Menstrual etiquette entails the concrete, everyday language and practices of menstrual concealment that women internalize, and which are at the root of their shame and embarrassment. This intense preoccupation can not be explained away merely as a developmental phenomenon. As we have already noted, while adolescence is a time of great self-preoccupation and embarrassment generally, if we start to answer the questions "why girls?" and "why menarche?" we begin to uncover the politics of gender, and the complex discourse on menstruation that gets acted out during this developmental period. Concealment anxieties sap women's energy, time and money; they "contain" the body therefore controlling women's lives:

It's just, it's just uncomfortable, and I remember whenever I had it I just thought everyone was looking at me, and they all knew somehow that it was happening to me. And it was kind of inconvenient. I couldn't go swimming and my family swims a lot and so I couldn't swim when it happened. I had to to plan what I wore, and it was such a big stress thing for me. I had to plan out all dark clothes for me to wear (laugh), *and I couldn't wear any light clothes and I just...I don't know...I had to make sure that there were times in the day where I could go to the bathroom like every couple of hours, so I would plan that out and make sure I didn't go anywhere where I was kind of stuck out somewhere with no bathroom facilities anywhere. And I just had to plan my day around it. I had to plan my week around it and just hope that nothing did fall on that week because I wouldn't want to have my period when I wanted to do something exciting* (Sally L., Korean-American, aged nineteen).

One study found that it was only after several menstrual periods that girls would share their experiences with any one other than their mothers, and many hid menarche from their mothers, too (Brooks-Gunn and Ruble 1983). Several women talked to us about using toilet paper and tissue for months, or hiding soiled underwear at the back of drawers and closets rather than let even their mothers or female care-givers know about their "condition." Concealment was especially important around boys and men, brothers and fathers. "*When I didn't have my period I didn't mind playing with the guys, but when I did, I was afraid someone would see me, like something might leak through or things like that,*" said Crystal P., a white woman in her early nineties. With similar affect, Jennie, white and in her early twenties, shared the following: "*I was paranoid that any of the boys might see; it was most important that this should be concealed from them.*"

The disdain associated with menstrual blood encourages women to go to great lengths to hide evidence of their contamination from the potentially disapproving gaze of others. Also, since a girl's world at adolescence is one where her repuation is constantly under threat, concealment becomes doubly important, censuring and constraining her life. Most women relied on their mothers to buy menstrual supplies late into their teenage years, even when they were buying other toiletry items for themselves. As Inez' story below illustrates, many had figured out ways to avoid the perceived embarrassments associated with buying menstrual products. Inez is twenty-two years old, grew up in a working-class home, and identified as a Chicana:

I was thirteen in January, when my first period happened, I just wore a pad. But then I was...the second time I had my period which was in June, I started...I was working at the hospital and I'd spend quarters on buying tampons because I didn't want my mom to buy them for me (laugh). *I was, how would you say, I was really embarrassed to go to the store and buy tampons or pads. I was really shy about that, about having to go to cash registers and buy that stuff. I worked as a volunteer at the hospital and they had tampons in the machines, so I'd take a whole bunch of quarters in and stock me up for a week or so, put them all in my bag and use them this way. So I spent a lot of money!* (laugh).

The many euphemisms for menstruation that girls start to use at menarche are further evidence of their sense that it must be kept secret; at the same time, the useage of made-up "code" words can create, as we will discuss later, solidarity and resistance among and between girls. Ernster (1975: 3–13) discusses menstrual euphemisms used by United States women, organizing the euphemisms into the following categories (we have inserted examples from our sample of women): references to a female, friend or visitor: *Having company, a guest, the visitor, Aunt Maggie*; references to a male: *George, Uncle Harry*; to time: *That time of the month, monthlies, moon time*; references to illness and distress: *unwell, the curse, the plague*; references to blood, red or materials used during menstruation: *red day, on the rag, Bloody Mary, and the river floweth from the red river valley*. Such euphemisms encourage and help maintain the practices of concealment.

Sophie Laws frames practices of concealment in the context of a menstrual etiquette that is taught to young women and reinforced in social practices. She suggests that concealment occurs because of "half-hearted threatening talk from men, which enforces the rule of silence, which is the essence of the etiquette of menstruation for women" (1990: 208). The accompanying menstrual etiquette requires women to uphold taboos against themselves through their own behaviors of silence and concealment. Laws discusses how men specifically use knowledge of menstruation to embarrass, intimidate and show dominance over women, as well as giving the go-ahead in (usually) intimate relationships for individual women to lighten up on issues of concealment. Remember Sarah K., whose story we shared earlier, being very concerned that her father or brothers might know she was menstruating, and taking great pains to conceal it from them. Her experience with the store clerk and the school nurse are examples of the prerogatives of entitled others, male or female, to break rules of concealment. But when the taboo is broken, the disgrace is showered on the women, the victim, and not on those doing the breaking. This is about the power to shape discourse and public sentiment, focusing knowledge and power on the body, and maintaining social relations of dominance. As Laws suggests: "Women are discredited by any behaviour which draws attention to menstruation, while men may more freely refer to it if they choose to. Thus the etiquette expresses and reinforces status distinctions" (1990: 211).

The etiquette of concealment is illustrated in the following narrative by Edith, aged sixty-eight years, who spent her childhood in England, growing up in a working-class family. She raised two children and was employed for most of her working life as a secretary. She wrote the following about her first period:

My first thoughts were "well, it's about time," I know that much! But it's so long ago, I guess it was mid-winter, living at _______, and waking after dozing to sleep, briefly, having had a 'funny' tummy ache—to a sticky nasty uncomfortable feeling between my legs, slightly smelly if I really think deeply. Ugghh. I called for mother. The girls in my class were already with swollen breasts and had had a period, so it seemed to me, and I was without either, plus a flat chest, no pubic hair, nothing. Felt a complete failure. So when this occurred—this thing—as I call it, I got my mother running upstairs, and we are sitting there on the edge of the bed, so terribly cold in that dark bedroom. I remember the cold linoleum would you believe, and feeling embarrassed giving my description and symptoms. I am fearful I may quote mother wrongfully after all this time, but it partly comes back to me. She opened a drawer and folded some cloth, I remember it being cold also and looked like 'interlock' fabric used in underclothing. I bet it had been someone's vest I thought!! And mother saying "that's nothing"—i.e., my predicament—"you'll get used to it and get it every month!" And I think she got me a hot water bottle. In retrospect, I was glad knowing, simply, that I had caught up with the rest of the class, in fact it's a good description to say it felt, perhaps, like a Christmas present, sort of a surprise that though you know you'll receive something, except it was like getting a present wrapped in newspaper instead of gift-wrapped! There was this dark, clammy, gloominess and sort of 'dread' accompanying it. I feel mother, bless her good and kind heart, tackled the situation with a little distaste, or even perhaps she was embarrassed.

I know the next day (must have been Sunday) and [my sister's] *boyfriend or fiancé was having tea with the family (so maybe I was eleven, could be?).*

Well, anyhow, I know I was conscious of this horrible sanitary thing, huge and uncomfortable pinned to my vest. Yes, mother said I needed a 'sanitary belt' and I guess was not prepared and I had to wait till monday perhaps. Well, why else would I have this thing 'pinned to my vest'? It seems it was wet and uncomfortable and I unpinned it until I could get mother's attention to help and have it renewed, bless my soul! I have a terrible vision of walking past everyone sitting at the table and this thing fell on to the floor (coconut floor matting in those days). What a sight to behold. Everybody looked aghast. Mother like—quick as lightening—was up in a flash, pushing me headlong through the nearest doorway which happened to be THE PANTRY with this thing flying after me and words from behind the door, which was closed on me, and saying "get yourself seen to!" In all conscience I'm sure I did not deliberately do that for attention—I couldn't possibly. Because of the embarrassment, I don't recall how I had the nerve to leave the pantry and return to the family gathering!

We were told as kids not to sit on damp things or get wet when we had our periods, and never to wash your hair during this time. Can you believe it?! The 'facts of life' were hidden in a little book, completely inappropriate, written in Victorian style, all about what I should know. And this book was under the Prudential Insurance book, (which mother paid to someone who called for it every week, life or death policy or something), and this facts of life book lay in a little old chocolate box, underneath. [My sister] *knew about it too. Big deal. It's a wonder we're right in our heads! It makes me laugh now!*

Edith directly experienced the etiquette of concealment as she was pushed into the pantry. Her behavior symbolized a lapse in maintaining the taboo, and as a result she was quickly reminded of her responsibility not to draw attention to menstruation under any circumstances, but especially when there was a guest in the house (and a male one at that). Note that Edith had already internalized messages about menstrual blood as negative. She remembers with *"ugghh"* a *"dark, clammy gloominess"* and being told abruptly that she'll *"get used to it and get it every month."* In terms of menstrual information and knowledge, she remembers with a laugh the *"facts of life"* book that gave her outdated information, hidden in a chocolate box under the Prudential Insurance book. Her clear memory of the material used for the menstrual pads and how she had to manage them pinned to her vest demonstrates how these menstrual products and practices of menarche impart meaning for women in their understandings of embodied femininity.

A study by Patterson and Hale in 1985 revealed that concealment and "making sure" was one of the central elements of young women's first menstrual experiences. We emphasize the toll this "making sure" has on young women's developing sense of self, as well as the resulting costs in energy, attention, time and money. We heard and read again and again of women's fears of showing evidence of wearing pads or staining garments or sheets. Over three-quarters of all women who shared their stories with us told of an incident associated with staining or expressed a fear that it might happen to them. This illustrates how the bulge or stain becomes an emblem of their "condition" for all to see. The stain also symbolizes a lapse in women's task of maintaining the taboo, of concealing the evidence in order not to embarrass others. Many women in the study reported having to make numerous trips to the bathroom to make sure that there was no staining, and no odor. This preoccupation, as Rina Piccolo illustrates in the cartoon below (fig. 3.4), can be intense. We heard many, many similar stories:

I was a gymnast at that time and so I had to wear a tampon for the first time. My coaches, I don't know, they just knew, they just have these ways of knowing, like they can tell...because I was in the bathroom like every fifteen minutes because I was so, you know, scared about showing. And I didn't know how to use tampons and, you know, it was very awkward and untimely, uncomfortable (Jacqueline, white, aged 24).

AT 40 SECOND INTERVALS, BECKY CHECKS FOR THE LITTLE STRING

figure 3.4

Women tended to see themselves as becoming more visible and noticeable at the same time that they felt pressure to conceal and hide evidence of menstruation. Several women, such as Monica, a Mexican-American woman in her early twenties, reported wearing a pad "*a week before just to make sure it wouldn't suddenly appear."* Many women talked about wearing baggy, dark-colored clothes just in case, some wearing coats during the school day to hide their bodies and any evidence of menstruation. Monica continued with her memories of concealment, and Laverne, white and aged seventy-five years, reported the great lengths she went to in order to avoid similar embarrassments:

I was afraid I was going to leak. That was my biggest fear that someone was going to know or something horrible was going to happen, so I would stay home...the night was like, awful because I was like, I am going to leak and I had the fear of that, and then I would use like a Stay Free, a bigger pad, and then I would put like a, it's funny, a Maxi Shield like further back so it wouldn't like drip. And I remember like for the first, gosh, for a long time when I had my period I would just lay in one position the whole night so it wouldn't leak or anything and I would just lay there and I was really stiff, and I remember that I'd wake up and kind of wonder if I'd leaked or not. And I did a few times, and not like that was a big deal, but it was just this whole association with it being, it is sticky and it is messy, and I totally had this obssession of it like...ohhh, it is this dirty thing and ohhh, let's dispose of these now and everything like that...I was pretty careful about watching where they were and who saw them, and even the...we had them in this little like cupboard under the sink..and even opening that and pulling them out of the package, I was always really quiet because I didn't want anyone to hear that I was out walking around, that I was like rustling paper or anything, so I was really discrete about it, and it was funny! (laugh) (Monica).

A problem with menstruating at that time was the napkin pads. They were made out of absorbent cotton with a cotton mesh cover (no shields). They soaked through easily and you often stained your underwear. I always worried that that my skirt might be stained and would sometimes wear my coat in school all day long. At Girls High, it was the custom for the Seniors to wear all white every Friday. When I was a Junior, I happened to notice that one of the Seniors was wearing a thin white skirt which showed the outline of her sanitary pad so when I had my Senior skirt made I bought rather heavy material and had a double panel put in the back (Laverne).

Our focus in this chapter has been on the "regimes of truth" whereby notions about women's polluting and contaminating monthly bleeding, received in various discursive contexts and bolstered by the use of menstrual products and equipment, maintain practices that "manage" menarche and discipline young bodies, minds and lives. We emphasize that it is in part through the disciplinary practices of concealment associated with menarche that embodied femininities are engendered and subordination maintained. Such practices are crucial for understanding women's relationships to their bodies, and the ways in which women come to relate to their sexual and reproductive lives generally. These sexual and reproductive lives are the focus of our next chapter.

4

(Hetero)Sexualization

> 'If you don't like them they'll call you a tight bitch. If you do go with them then they'll call you a slag afterwards.' ...Girls have to develop a feminine identity in line with their cultural ascription, but to become a person in their own right they need to develop an identity in contradiction to this. From the onset of menstruation, girls have to deal with the contradictory messages about their feminine identity. Girls' identities are fractured by the widespread description of themselves as sex objects, yet indications of sexual desire on their part can render them as 'whores', 'good time girls', and 'slags'. Adolescent socialization for girls is fraught with discontinuity and conflict.
>
> —Sue Lees, *Sugar and Spice: Sexuality and Adolescent Girls*

Menstruation is a biological act fraught with cultural implications, helping to produce the female body and woman as sexualized cultural entities. In this chapter we will focus on alienation and objectification, the anxieties associated with developing female bodies in the context of the male gaze, and lastly on the ways in which processes of sexualization at menarche often involve the loss and/or transformation of female power. As Sue Lees says above, the confusions and contradictions associated with the social construction of feminine identities in a misogynous society are thoroughly "fraught with discontinuity and conflict." It is in this context that girls make meaning of menarche as a life event that symbolizes adult womanhood. We suggest that the unavoidable association of menarche with the cultural constraints and impositions of adult femininity makes its experience ambivalent and difficult. Negotiating gender and becoming a "woman" in contemporary North American society means dealing with discursive practices that frame and discipline through the constructs of the body and sexuality. In this chapter we explore themes of female sexualization, emphasizing that it is through the body that women are integrated into the social and sexual order, and it is in part through the discourses and practices of menarche that heterosexuality and "hetero-reality" (Raymond 1986: 7) are constructed in everyday life. At the onset of menstruation, girls' subjective sense of themselves as growing women develops simultaneously with a process of female sexualization whereby women's bodies are produced as sexual objects. Emily Hancock, in *The Girl Within*, explains:

> contained, adapted and sexualized long before adolescence, a girl is cowed and tamed as her natural spontaneity gives way to patriarchal constructions of female. In donning the masks provided by the culture, a girl easily loses sight of who and what she is beneath the feminine facade she adopts in her youth...her self confidence yields to self consciousness as a girl judges herself against an impossible feminine ideal. (1989: 22)

Anne, a forty-eight year-old white academic who grew up in a working-class family, articulates this sexualization clearly:

All of a sudden I couldn't wear shorts as short. I started getting lessons in keeping your legs together, you know,...what happened was basically by the time my parents tried to make me into a "lady" or feminine it was way too late because I was twelve years old. I think I had long associated this with the, you know, marks of oppression of women, because the way I remember it, I was a free spirit up until that point and all of a sudden everything clamped down. You know, I couldn't walk places by myself. In other words, the transition from asexual girl, although that sounds like an oxymoron, into a sexualized being was marked specifically and it was a dramatic difference.... So I marked [menarche] *as the transformation in the social view of me from being just a person to a gender marked person, and you know, and that one which was very constricted.*

We suggest that anxieties associated with menarche illustrate the inclusion of women as female subjects into the ordering of the sexual. Twenty-one-year-old Amy S., a white lesbian, shared an interesting first period memory:

Okay, I am in this Mormon culture where sex is like completely bad. I am not supposed to think about it or not do it and I wasn't doing it and I wasn't.... I am a lesbian and at that time I was repressing it really hard, like, you know, in a big way. I had no clue. But I would have erotic dreams about women every now and then and I would feel totally guilty about them and you know, it was more like I just repressed them.... But it was interest-

ing because I thought that because I thought about sex, that is sort of what brought on my period. Like they were somehow connected in my head! And I was like, I started! I was like, oh no! And then I was like, oh it must have been because I was thinking about sex you know (laugh), *it was kind of funny!*

Illustrative of the derogatory framing of the pubescent female body with notions of sexuality is the fact that girls who start their period early are often labelled "promiscuous," as seen in the use of the term "precocious puberty" to descibe such early menstruators in some medical literature (Delaney, Lupton and Toth 1988). While this has much to do with the assumptions in our culture that childhood is an asexual time and that chidren should be protected from sexual knowledge and action, the strong disapproval shown by many adults toward the developing *female* body, tells us that this is not the only explanation. Several women in our study commented that friends of theirs who had developed early were somehow seen as promiscuous, even though they were just young girls with no active sexual relationships. Robin, for example, shared the following with us: "*Oh, there was one person I knew who had it before any of us you know...we just, I don't...this is really terrible but I think that I thought that she was just a little more ahead of us sexually...I am positive the girl wasn't sexual, but I knew that was a part of getting older and I knew that getting older meant having sex...and I think seeing someone else with their period made me feel that they were a lot further ahead than I was and that they...I am sure they probably weren't having sex, I don't know, but I saw them as more promiscuous.*" Liz too, a forty-three-year-old Mexican-American woman, remembered those girls she knew who had started menstruating earlier than most: "*If she started early we would say, oh, somebody fooled with her or she fooled with herself or something, something is not right if she started too early.*"

Virginia remembered seeing a used sanitary napkin on the sidewalk at about the same time that she started her period. She recalled being told that this was incredibly disgusting and that it belonged to someone who lived nearby, a woman who was made out to be "*a slutty type of woman.*" Virginia reported that she made the connection then about pollution and contamination, but also that "*this is something that, you know, nice girls don't do.*" These stories stress how menarche is interpreted in the context of emerging sexuality, as well as uncontrolled desire and all its negative implications.

Importantly, patriarchal and heterosexist societies construct menarche as simultaneously signifying emerging sexual availability and reproductive potential. While we do not suggest that sexuality and reproduction must be, or have always been, conflated (c.f., see D'Emilio and Freedman 1988), to focus on menarche is unavoidably to deal with both. Menarche involves bodily changes that are coded as both procreative and sexual, aspects to be revered and/or feared/controlled. Menarche functions as a crucial signifier of female adulthood, reproducing knowledge of young women as both potentially reproductive and sexually available, and placing women in the contradictory positions of both "madonna" (the reproductive potential at menarche) and "whore" (budding sexuality). As Rosalind Petchesky suggests, young women are "infantilized by the cult of virginity" and objectified by the "cult of Lolita" (1984: 224). These representations invoke ambivalence toward menarche and women's developing bodies and provide justification for the restrictions and controls placed upon female sexuality and reproduction. The situation is also complicated by medical discourses about female bodies and reproduction, whereby women's sexuality becomes "the object of hygienization, of the splitting of cleanliness and pleasure" (McNay 1992: 31). We emphasize that menarche represents a crucial sexual/reproductive transition and plays an important role in mediating the relationship between reproduction and sexuality generally. As Mary P. wryly observed, menstruation was *"a young woman's curse and a married women's joy."*

In *Gender Play,* Barrie Thorne suggests that it is "during the transition from 'child' to 'teen' that girls start negotiating the forces of adult femininity, a set of structures and meanings that more fully inscribe their subordination on the basis of gender" (1993: 170). Similarly, in *Reviving Ophelia,* Mary Pipher writes of the ways girls in the United States are encouraged to lose their "true selves" in order to cope with the demands of a culture that is a "girl-destroying place" (1994: 44). In early adolescence "girls are expected to sacrifice the parts of themselves that the culture considers masculine on the altar of social acceptability and shrink our souls down to a petite size.... The rules remain the same: be attractive, be a lady, be unselfish and of service, make relationships work and be competent without complaint. This is when girls learn to be nice rather than honest" (39). She suggests that this splitting of the self, which has become a trademark for feminine adolescent development, has been intensified in the 1990s. Pipher, as a therapist, is concerned about girls' psychological health and safety as they attempt to weather the storms of contemporary society:

> Increasingly women have been sexualized and objectified, their bodies marketed to sell tractors and toothpaste. Soft and hard-core pornography are everywhere. Sexual and physical assaults on girls are at an all-time high. Now girls are more vulnerable and fearful, more likely to have been traumatized and less free to roam about alone. This combination of old stresss-es and new is poison for our young women. (27–28)

This process of sexualization, whereby women come to experience themselves as sexualized in current Western societies, is a thoroughly heterosexual one; the use of sexuality as a generic term implying heterosexuality illustrates the normalizing powers of language. That is to say, "sexualization" implies "heterosexualization," meaning that women are taught to live and discipline their bodies in accordance with the prescriptions of heterosexuality, experiencing themselves as sexual objects for heterosexual male viewing and pleasure, and also as mothers of men's children. The transition from childhood to adolescence is so thoroughly saturated with heterosexual discourse that young people who have lesbian or gay orientations suffer enormously. There are no public adolescent rituals to affirm and validate their needs and desires. Almost none of the lesbians in our sample identified as lesbians during early adolescence, and, as a result, they felt that they received the same dose of "hetero-reality" as their heterosexual peers. Amy S. laughed as she told us how during the time that she started her first period she ran around having crushes on all her friends. However, *"consciously there was no indication that I was attracted to women or girls. Physically it was obvious. I mean, if I had seen myself now I'd be, yeah, you are a baby dyke!"* One exception in terms of conscious awareness was Hannah, who spoke about being confused about her sexual identity. Even before she started her period at ten years old she found herself attracted to girls and wondered if perhaps she was really a boy. She felt that her period added to her confusion because it obviously marked her as female. *"it was like, no, I am a girl,"* she said. Menarche became an obvious and undesirable sign of her femaleness.

As a "text" of culture, masculine desire and its associated social policies are sketched on female bodies, framing them in the context of public discourses—popular culture and much contemporary art, academic disciplines, and various discursive contexts that involve women's everyday lives (work, the legal system, education, etc.). As such, women's subjectivities and sexualities are linked through practices and discursive strategies that include both language and representation. As Biddy Martin suggests in a discussion of feminism and Foucault: "Sexuality and identity can only be understood, then, in terms of the complicated and often paradoxical ways in which pleasures, knowledges, and power are produced and disciplined in language, and institutionalized across multiple fields. For Foucault, representation and discourses are themselves acts of power, acts of division and exclusion, which give themselves as knowledge" (1988: 9). In other words, the language of the body that becomes integrated into women's senses of themselves in the world is not neutral; it is language imbued with power that maintains the discourses that make the body an object of knowledge. Further, since it is primarily through the body that women are inserted and insert themselves into the hierarchical ordering of the sexual, the bodily changes that happen at puberty, marked by menarche and loaded with the ambivalences associated with womanhood, signify the simultaneous entry into adult womanhood and adult female (hetero)sexualization. As a result, the meanings associated with menarche in our culture, like sexuality itself, are produced through the effects of power relations in order to regulate women's lives. We are encouraged to believe, for a variety of reasons, that menarche, again like sexuality, is a "natural" phenomenon, rather than a cultural construct, and this has implications for how we make sense out of this life transition. Below is an excerpt from Lois McNay, who also writes about Foucault's understandings of sexuality and, in particular, his text *The History of Sexuality*. We share this here because McNay articulates so well the idea that the regulatory aspects of discursive strategies and representational practices require us to think of sexuality (and, we add, menarche) as essentialized, "natural" phenomena:

> The construct of 'natural sex' performs a certain number of regulatory functions; firstly, it makes it possible to group together in an 'artificial unity' a number of disparate and unrelated biological functions and bodily pleasures; secondly by unifying these disparate pleasures, it bolsters a regulatory notion of 'natural' heterosexuality; finally, the notion of sex inverts the representation of the relationship of power to sexuality, so that, rather than seeing sexuality as a phenomenon produced and constructed through the exercise of power relations, it is seen as an unruly force which power can only attempt to repress and control. (1992: 29)

It is important to contemplate menarche in the context of social constructivist theories of sexuality specifically, and to identify how changes at menarche that are coded as both sexual and reproductive have become anchored in women's interior lives. Yet there is a paucity of attention to adolescent female development, little theoretical scholarship generally on girls' sexuality, and even less on their sexual desire (Rubin 1984; Tolman 1994). In *Female Sexualization*, German scholar Frigga Haug and her colleagues in a marxist-feminist women's collective use strategies of "collective memory work" to understand the processes by which girls' bodies become objectified and transformed into objects for male desire, arousal and capitalist commodification. They write that "it is around our bodies that we construct our identities; in so doing we simultaneously reproduce femininity within a particular social relation—the relation between the sexes—which, in its present form, is marked by contradiction. Our appropriation of particular standards thus entails a simultaneous submission to dominant notions of what it is to be a woman" (1987: 119). They focus on legs, breasts, thighs and buttocks to examine the processes by which body parts become sexualized and certain notions of sexuality and gender are produced and reproduced.

In the following sections we discuss first, how women experience sexual alienation and objectification at menarche as they negotiate the social meanings applied to their developing and changing bodies and second, how issues associated with the body are enacted for adolescent women. Finally, we analyze notions of power concerning adult womanhood and the physical and social constraints on bodies and behavior, as well as power as it relates to the ontological state of being a women in contemporary Western societies.

Alienation

Alienation is a much-used and little-explained term. Put simply it refers to the progressive state of separation between our selves or personalities and everything around us that occurs when we are powerless.... Women, then, are alienated from their sexuality along several dimensions. From an early age, we are alienated from ourselves as sexual beings by a male society's ambivalent definition of our sexuality: we are sexy, but we are pure; we are insatiable, but we are frigid; we have beautiful bodies, but we must paint, shave and deodorize them. We are also alienated because we are separated from our own experience by the prevailing male cultural definition of sex—the male fantasy of active man and passive woman. From an early age, our sexual impulses are turned back upon ourselves in the narcissistic counterpart of the male fantasy world. In social relations with men, we are alienated from ourselves as initiating, self-directed persons. Only a few women are able to hold all these contradictory parts together. Far more are now beginning to question whether they shold have to try.

—Linda Phelps, "Female Sexual Alienation" in *Women: A Feminist Perspective*, edited by Jo Freeman

This excerpt is from a piece originally published in the early 1970s in response to the so- called "sexual revolution" that had mostly extended masculine sexual culture and given men more opportunities for sexual conquest. Phelps emphasizes in this article that as alienated people, women "begin to deny our own reality; to lose important parts of ourselves" (1979: 21), in part due to society's ambivalent view of female sexuality. Such alienation entails estrangement or separation from the self.

Existentialist feminist philosopher Simone de Beauvoir spoke about women and alienation in terms of seeing man epitomized as Self, and woman as Other. She sought an ontological explanation of this state of affairs based on a notion of "Being," whereby woman is urged to deny or negate herself, accept herself and her body as shameful and inferior, and succumb to such constraining roles as wife and mother which continue to turn her into an object. This object status separates her from "Selfhood" (de Beauvoir 1952: 89–90). Though de Beauvoir demonstrates the existential disdain and distrust of the body, sees its corporeality limiting opportunities for attaining freedom, and celebrates the male ideal of transcendence of the Subject (Elshtain 1981), her focus on the alienating aspects of "Otherness" which tie woman to her oppression is useful. Interestingly, in her later interviews she responded to critiques about her negative and constraining view of the body in ways that were less disdainful of human corporeality: "it's good to demand that a woman should not be made to feel degraded by, let's say, her monthly periods" (Simons and Benjamin 1979: 342).

Bertell Ollman described Marx's theory of alienation as the "intellectual construct in which Marx displays the devastating effect of capitalist production on human beings, on their physical and mental states and on the social proceses of which they are a part" (1971: 131). Under capitalism Marx believed alienation to be fundamental for human's relationships with, each other and to labor and its products. He saw the separation of people from one another to be a consequence of social and economic conditions, specific to capitalistic societies, that encourage people to speculate on "creating a new need in another, so as to drive him [sic] to a fresh sacrifice, to place him in a new dependence" (Marx 1964: 147). In other words, people become alienated from each other because they are encouraged to establish relationships that will allow them to profit from others, thereby establishing patterns of dependence and domination. This certainly rings true for the experience of women in patriarchal societies. While Marx had little to no understanding of gender as a social construct separate from the determining influences of capitalist class relations, if we consider labor in its reproductive as well as its productive aspects, and broaden it to include women's experiences of menarche and their bodies as components of the relations of both reproductive and productive activities, we find alienation to be a useful and interesting term in the Marxist sense. As menstruating humans, women are alienated from their reproductive activities and from the product of those activities (blood, potential fetus) by virtue of the fact that their bodies are objectified and "owned" by a collective patriarchal culture and male gaze, as well as by individual men in dominant relationships with women and their bodies. Menstrual bleeding, as an indication of sexual and reproductive potential, becomes tied to what this means culturally in misogynous societies: madonna or whore. Women tend to be able to neither create their own sexual realities nor control the conditions under which they birth or raise children. The following quote by Marx, while referring to inanimate objects rather than living human "products," does have significance for its conditions of women's reproductive labor:

> The alienation of the worker in his [sic] product means not only that his labor becomes an object, an external existence, but that it exists outside of him, independently, as something alien to him, and that it becomes a power on its own confronting him. It means that the life which he has conferred on the object confronts him as hostile and alien. (1970: 195)

Alongside the alienation of people from each other and from the processes and products of labor, Marx wrote of workers' alienation from their "species life." By this he meant the extent to which our experiences fall short of being sources of creativity, affirmation and our uniquely human potential. Marx was talking about the alienation of people from themselves as a result of living under relations of domination and subordination: "estranged labor tears from him [sic] his species life, his real objectivity as a member of the species and transforms his advantage over animals into the disadvantage that his organic body, nature is taken away from him. Similarly, in degrading spontaneous, free, activity, to a means, estranaged labor makes man's species life a means to his physical existence" (1964: 114). We suggest that the experience of first menstruation for girls in our culture is another example of the way that the organic body, nature, is taken away from women. The feeling of estrangement that women experience with menarche illustrates the alienation from species life that Marx wrote about so poignantly. Of course in all his treatises Marx would probably never have applied this to menstruation, it being a "degrading" act that reminds people of their similarities to animals rather than their advantages over them. A rebuttal from Marx would certainly prove interesting!

Nonetheless, at puberty, girls enter the world of women, the world of women as sex objects in the context of a male-dominated compulsory heterosexuality. In a patriarchal society, women learn quickly that their developing bodies are objects of the male gaze. It is almost impossible to avoid this fact, surrounded as we are by hundreds of images of women, set up for male viewing. The media literally hacks women's bodies apart and gives us images of disconnected breasts, bottoms and legs. Adolescent boys learn to do similar things when they refer to girls as body parts, and assess girls based upon their (boys') opinions of certain female anatomy, in part because sexism is a critical feature of male-bonding (Stoltenberg 1989). The developing breasts and hips that are the visual cues of puberty and menarche are also highly constituted in our culture as objects of male desire (to be gazed at), and contribute to the experience of menarche as feeling synonymous with objectification. Young girls are well-attuned to society's ambivalence towards female sexuality, to the normative prescriptions and contradictions of attracting boys sexually, and to pressures to manage boys' as well as their own desires and behaviors. They are surrounded by messages of women as sex objects, yet told to put a lid on their own desires. The craziness of this situation is captured by Deborah Tolman in her article "Doing Desire: Adolescent Girls' Struggles for/with Sexuality":

> These girls are beginning to voice the internalized oppression of their women's bodies; they knew and spoke about, in explicit or more indirect ways, the pressure they felt to silence their desire, to dissociate from those bodies in which they inescapably live. (1994: 325)

Alienation is implied in this dissociation. The "missing discourse of desire" (Fine 1988) that surrounds adolescent female sexuality reinforces and is an integral part of the sexual alienation women feel as a result of their sexual objectification and insertion into the scripts of male-dominated heterosexuality. This alienation is often experienced as a separation of self from body; it frequently functions as a survival mechanism, although it is just as frequently likely to be self-destructive and manifest itself in the form of eating disorders, addictions, and mental health "disorders."

For most of the women who shared their menarche stories with us, their experience was described as something that was happening "to" them, as something outside of themselves, rather than something that was a part "of" them. They talk about their periods as something they "*have*," "*get*," or are "*on*." Lisa, a twenty-six-year-old Chicana, refers to her menarche as if it were completely outside of herself: "*I just wanted to stop it or I wanted to ignore it so it would go away. I kind of wanted to strike out against it. I didn't want it to happen, it just came along out without me even knowing. I mean, it just seemed out of the blue.*" Lisa continues as if her menarche were some stray animal she has to take responsibility for: "*having to worry about it and take care of it.*" Women in our study frequently referred to menarche as "*it*," giving an illusion of a self that was split and fragmented. Examples include: "*I couldn't believe it was happening to me*"; "*we called it the visitor*"; "*I got it when I was fourteen*"; "*I remember exactly when it started*"; and (our favorite) "*when it came I was at home.*" As Sally L. exclaimed: "*At first I didn't really want it and then later I was happy that I got it because I was worried about it, because I was worried, well, what if it happens...I always thought, well what if it happens and I don't know it."*

Karin, a white, middle-class woman aged twenty-two, shared the following: *"I mean she* [her sister] *had no problem with it. I don't know if she was happy about it but she was on good terms with it.... I guess I'm not really in control of it because I just felt like it happened to me, I didn't ask for it, it just suddenly happened."* Julia echoes these sentiments, seeing her period as an *"alien"* that comes to bother her: *"I dreaded that, I dreaded my period. I didn't want it to come back. I hate it when it comes and I hate it when it is here and bothers me. At the time I thought, in the beginning, I thought of it as kind of like an alien, yeah, like it comes and goes when it wants and I hate it."*

Stories with passive imagery are especially numerous among, although certainly not exclusively to, younger white women, suggesting a response to the postmodern, fractured world in which they live, as well as to the excess sexualization of female bodies in the contemporary media consumed by these young women. Their descriptions of menarche exude a sense of fragmentation between self and body, a sense of menarche as something a woman has to cope with, adjust to, and manage. Menarche is something that seems to appear from the outside, invading the self. Such findings were also reported by Emily Martin (1987), who wrote that the women she interviewed saw menstruation as something that happened to them, rather than seeing the processes as being a part of them, emphasizing that in matters of reproduction, women tend to see theselves as separate from their bodies. Many of the mothers in her study, and especially those who had experienced cesarian sections rather than vaginal births, reported "feelings of fragmentation and objectification" (84). Martin carefully explained this phenomenon in terms of the medicalization of the female body and the way a scientifically-based society produces images of human bodies as machines. We suggest that there is more at work here since women tended to frame menarche as happening "to them" in the context of their emerging understandings of sexuality. Like Martin, we heard several women share ways to "control" menstrual bleeding with machine and medical imagery. For example, a seventy-three year-old white, middle-class woman named Louie told us the following: *"Someday, maybe they are going to be able to catch it so you can take a pill and it will stop it, and then all of a sudden, it will all pour out in five minutes and then you are done with it."*

However, alongside these reminders of medical discourses, the passive, indirect and fragmented language of menarche and menstruation is also about sexual objectification and alienation. Since femininity in this context means moving from assertive actor to developing woman, learning to respond to the world indirectly through the filter of relationships, women are encouraged to accomodate male needs, to understand themselves as others see them, and to feel pleasure through their own bodily objectification, especially by being looked at and identifying as objects of male desire (Tolman and Debold, 1994). In this way, adolescence and the journey from girlhood to womanhood involve forms of self-silencing whereby girls become preoccupied with how they are perceived by others (Brown and Gilligan 1992; Gilligan, Lyons and Hanmer 1990; Orenstein 1994).

Iris Young writes about such issues of subjectivity, alienation and the production and reproduction of femininity in *Throwing Like a Girl.* Young comments on an advertisement that asks women to "see yourself in wool": "I am seeing myself in wool seeing him see me. Is it that I cannot see myself without seeing myself being seen? So I need him there to unite me and my image of myself?" (1990: 177)

In a chapter of *Throwing Like a Girl* entitled "Pregnant Embodiment: Subjectivity and Alienation," Young explores how Western discourses on pregnancy omit subjectivity. She writes "the pregnant subject, I suggest, is decentered, split, or doubled in several ways. She experiences her body as herself and not herself" (160). Despite the fact that women who are confronted by modern Western obstetrical medicine are often alienated from their pregnant and birthing experiences, many women may experience some respite from this other alienating gaze at this time because pregnancy is desexualized in our culture. Further, "the dominant culture projects pregnancy as a time of quiet waiting. We refer to the woman as "expecting," as though this new life were flying in from another planet and she sat in her rocking chair by the window, occasionally moving the curtain aside to see whether the ship is coming. The image of the uneventful waiting associated with pregnancy reveals clearly how much the discourse of pregnancy leaves out the subjectivity of the woman" (167). Note how much the notion of waiting during pregnancy is similar to the images of menarche as suddenly happening. Both omit subjectivity in important ways.

Women and their bodies serve to enhance male subjectivity by providing the mirror (femininity) against which men can construct themselves as "not feminine" (Irigaray 1985). This mirror is tightly monitored, meaning that subjectivity is difficult for women since they are encouraged to understand themselves as others see them. Women are encouraged to feel pleasure through their own bodily objectification, to identify as objects of male desire and to accept the sexualization of their bodies. Humans tend to construct their subjectivity through the relations of looking, and in Western patriarchal societies those controlling the gaze are usually men, or women involved in masculinist pusuits. Women are encouraged to take pleasure in being looked at, and to adopt the position of the objectified other. This is an example of the production and reproduction of femininity, intimately entwined with sexuality and defined in the politicized terms of gender. These rules of gender are learned "directly through bodily discourse: through images which tell us what clothes, body shape, facial expression, movements, and behavior is expected" (Bordo 1989: 17).

When talking about menarche, women associate it with the ambivalences and uncertainties involved in feeling "looked at" as well as with generalized feelings of alienation from their bodies. Alina, a twenty-year-old, working-class Native-American/Mexican-American woman, shared how uncomfortable she felt under the gaze of male relatives as her body began to develop:

My uncles would come over and visit us. They'd notice and look at you, you know, take a double take, and I don't know, I felt uncomfortable...I felt that they would just look at me a lot and just kind of stare at me.... I left the room a lot, I'd go to my bedroom or to the kitchen and they were in the other room watching TV or something, or go outside and I wouldn't be in the room too long. And then I wore really boyish clothes.... I didn't really want people to look at me the way they did, and so I wore jeans and a big sweatshirt over that and my hair was cut really short so I looked kind of boyish. And that was good to me because now I was like another one of the boys and I wasn't really looked at.

Robin also remembered the looks and attention she received as her developing body at menarche identified her as the *"other"*: *"Then they* [her brothers] *started becoming critical of the way I dressed, and my hair and the way I spoke...and criticizing and saying you need to go over that way and you need to start wearing skirts and you need to start doing your hair, and you need to care about what you look like and not talk like this or that. So, I think there was a definite change in how they* [her brothers] *saw me.... I think it did set inside their heads she is woman, I mean, she is not a boy. Yeah, she is different, other."*

The voices of survivors of sexual assault and abuse are especially poignant in illustrating both this objectification and the reason why a girl might desparately need to separate herself from her body at this time:

Becoming a woman kind of opened up the avenues for me. I think I unconsciously kind of knew that men would start looking at me more, and this was, I think, a bit scary in a sense. I mean I was confused, I think I wanted to be accepted by the male gender, but yet this experience [of incest], *it was a frightening thing because, it wasn't even me, it was like my body, and it was hapenning to my body...it was no longer my mind or who I was, I mean it was like I was nothing. But yet my body was something, a sex object...my body was a sex object, and the menstruation process, it just defined it that much more that I was a woman...you know what I am saying? Because I related the menstrual cycle, I connected it directly with all this.... So there is a connection there, one part of me, I wanted to be that woman for the opposite sex, because it was kind of like expected of me, you know, that I be pleasing to look at, and starting that menstrual cycle was my direct link with that, wow, I am a woman. But then there is this bad incident that I don't think had a lot of negative influence on that, yet it must have somehow, you know, been buried there* (Susan, white, working-class, thirty-four years).

Before my period came, about a month, I was on my way to church. There was a guy standing at the corner and he said "how are you doing light skinned girl, little girl?" and he touched my vagina. He just grabbed it. So I felt really bad and I never told anybody; it is like I felt responsible because that man touched me down there. And then my period came after that and I started doing a lot of things in my mind, like maybe because he touched me God is punishing me. Maybe that is why I am bleeding (Juanita, Mexican-American, working-class, migrant family, thirty-two years).

The reduction of young women to nothing but bodies is a theme that runs through these stories. It accounts in large part for the alienation these women felt as girls, and it explains why they might have felt the need to split themselves off and submerge their authentic selves. The anxieties that young women experience are overwhelmingly centered on the body, as we will explore in the next section.

Anxious Bodies

> The body is a compelling mystery, a constant focus of attention.... Girls feel an enormous pressure to be beautiful and are aware of constant evaluations of their appearance.
>
> —Mary Pipher, *Reviving Orphelia*

As we discussed in chapter 3, while the preoccupation with the body at puberty is in part a developmental phenomenon, the fact that girls specifically experience these particular feelings and behaviors in these ways points to the inappropriateness of thinking that cognitive processes occur a priori of history and culture. During the processes of (hetero)sexualization, girls learn knowledge of how the "normal" female body should look, knowledge which varies based upon cultual and historical specificities, yet knowledge rarely created by women with women's interests at the center.

In phallocentric cultures women's sexuality is framed by male desire and certain body parts enjoyed by men become objectified and fetishized. Women internalize these discourses unconsciously, so saturated is our everyday existence with its representation. At menarche when girls bodies start to change and develop and more closely resemble the simultaneously prized/despised objects of male desire, girls usually feel ambivalent and uncertain and many feel acute distress, compared to boys who tend to have many fewer issues around their bodies (Debold, 1991; Pliner, Chaiken and Flett 1990). On the one hand, girls tap into the increased sexual power given to adult women; but this "power," really, as most of us learn, is not a stable or reliable entity. A "nice ass" can very easily become a "fat ass" in a different context and under different conditions. The inevitable result of playing up to the male gaze is the fact that objectified bodies are property, commodities, and thus can never be entirely owned by women. And when the context shifts, women can find their commodities worthless. Perhaps it is the contradictions that girls experience, when they know they can entice boys' glances and attention one minute, yet have their bra straps snapped and their shirts pulled up another, that gives them understandings of these complex issues. As Jeanne, a young white student in her early twenties, remembered: *"I remember the first day I wore it* [a bra]. *I wore the tightest, lightest colored t-shirt I could find to show I was wearing a bra. But it was weird. It was like I wanted everyone to know I wore it, but I was so embarrassed that I wore it because the boys would snap it."* Whatever the processes, these "understandings," as conscious or unconscious as they might be, faciliate the ambivalences associated with menarche and their developing bodies. This section explores these anxieties.

In *Sugar and Spice,* Sue Lees examines the effects of misogynous, patriarchal discourse on emerging female sexuality. She analyzes the sheer magnitude and effects of language depicting female anatomy in derogatory ways on girls' sense of themselves, and of boys' and mens' jokes about menstruation that have "quite explicitly portrayed women as sex objects and as interchangeable" (1993: 214). These jokes and male unease are, of course, related to male discomfort with the realities of their physical and emotional dependence on women, but these realities seriously affect women's internalization of sexism around body issues. It is important to emphasize that these masculinist attitudes about menstruation are inseparable from attitudes about women's bodies and sexuality generally. Lees goes on to write more specifically of the anxious bodies of female adolescence:

> Depictions of a girl's body are the raw material of sexist abuse. At the same time her appearance is presented as her passport to success both in private and public life. One of the strongest bases of self-esteem rests on pride in

> body image. The widespread dissatisfaction that girls express about their physical attractiveness is startling. Not one girl expressed pride and confidence in good looks. Anxiety often focuses on their bodies. (1993: 207)

For many women raised in Western societies, adolescence is a difficult and vulnerable time when girls focus attention on the body in the context of a culture that demands perfect female bodies. In a study that asked pre- and post-menarcheal girls to draw pictures of women, Elissa Koff (1983) found that girls who had experienced menarche drew considerably more sexually differentiated bodies. Koff writes about how girls come to experience themselves as more sexually mature at menarche: "It appears that regardless of the actual physical changes that are taking place, the girl at menarche anticipates and experiences a reorganization of her body image in the direction of greater sexual maturity and feminine differentiation" (1983: 83). And, as we have emphasized, to experience oneself sexually as a woman in our culture is often to experience oneself as an object.

The stories of the women with whom we talked illustrate the anxiety and self-consciousness associated with developing bodies at menarche. Breasts were especially problematic. Over and again, women of all ages talked about anxieties associated with developing breasts in the context of their memories of menarche; they desparately wanted breasts, but at the same time were ashamed of them. In this sense breasts come to represent the socio-political construction of this developmental crisis; they, like menarche, symbolize femininity in both its sexual and reproductive aspects. Breasts, as Frigga Haug writes: are "never innocent"; they are highly sexualized and easily recognized as objects of male gaze and perusal (1987: 139). We remember stories from our past of women whose husbands did not "allow" them to breast feed their babies because they felt that their wives' breasts were their own sexual property, not to be confused with the suckling of young. Note how the power of the breast to feed and to so unsettle that it must be controlled and regulated is suggested in the idea of the "ultimate" radical feminist action of "bra burning." As Iris Young suggests, breasts are a "scandal" in our phallocentric, misogynous society because they "disrupt the border between motherhood and sexuality" (1990: 190). Like menarche, which also disrupts this border, such a predicament causes ambivalence for women.

It is interesting how many women remembered wearing baggy clothes to hide developing breasts; this is a theme repeated over and over again. For example, when asked about menarche, Jennifer L., a white sixty-one-year-old nurse, shares her memory of being an "early bloomer":

Oh, it was really hard for me because I am five-foot ten and I had gained my height by the time I was eleven, and I was very tall, and I developed very early and I was teased a lot by the boys...you know, that is when I started wearing, you know, I wore big shirts and I kept a coat on all the time because I didn't want to be teased. But they would say, they would call me, oh, "twin peaks" and "gee if I let you wear my shirt, will you put bumps in it like that?" And, like I said, I was really kind of puritanistic in my, you know, what I thought was right, ideas of right and wrong. And I was ashamed of my body.

In a similar fashion, Madeleine, a white, heterosexual woman in her early thirties, talked at length about the anxieties associated with her breasts; these memories were still strong and painful despite the passage of time. She started off by saying how she felt that menarche "*was just something that was happening and it wasn't really me*"—another good example of separation and alienation. She felt that her large breasts, representing her femaleness, were a betrayal of her personhood:

I also remember when I was in sixth grade and this boy called me "stuffy," in other words he was accusing me of stuffing my bra, because I wore a sweater that was, you know, more fitted than the day before and I was developing very early as a sixth grader and I didn't like my body at all, in fact I had a breast reduction when I was in tenth grade...so I had a lot of hang-ups about that and they were very painful to me. My boobs were just so big that, I mean, I am still busty and I mean, they are huge, and I was a small person, and they got in my way! (long laugh) *I really hated them. I just remember feeling that I was going to grow up and the only thing that I would be good for was something like a playboy bunny or something, you know, disgusting, or just be a housewife which was like a fate worse than death...how was I going to be a professional person if I had these big boobs? It would be like people would be just staring at me...and they used to instead of talking in my face, they would talk to my boobs, you know...it was totally degrading...I'd walk by construction sites and you know, the cat calls were just horrible. So, I guess that maybe that's why I felt so angry about my period, because I associated it with these feelings about my boobs. I don't know if that makes sense, but I felt like my large chest size was a kind of a betrayal of my personhood.*

Many others also remembered being very self-conscious and being overly concerned about bodily changes. Laurence, for example, a twenty-year-old woman from Malaysia, shared the following: "*Yes, I guess mentally I became more aware of my body and what you would you say 'the journey to womanhood,' yeah, and I became more self-conscious when I had my period.... I did become more self-conscious.*" Inez actively worked on keeping herself small; she explicitly tied these activities to the onset of her period:

I felt that my period started when it did because I used to tie a belt around my waist to keep my waist tiny. I felt that that night, I put it a little extra tight just to make sure I wouldn't gain. I don't know why I did this, I just wanted to keep my waist small, and that night I did that and then the next morning when I got up I had to go to the bathroom and had blood, and so oh no...and that is why I was scared that my period started earlier because I was doing that to my body, just trying to keep myself slim and really small. Deep dark secrets! (laugh).

At the time of menarche then, physical bodies start becoming more problematic; women report that their breasts are too small or too big, hips tend to become enemy sites and there is the overwhelming fear of fat. These reports span generations as Isabel, an eighty-year-old Jewish woman, remembered feeling *"ugly and fat."* She shared the following: *"I had been told so many times how ugly I was and how dumb I was, especially the dumbness, that I did not have a good image of myself at this time* [menarche]." Eighteen-year-old Marie, decades apart in age from Isabel, shared similarly feelings when asked how she felt about her body at menarche: *"I had a really low self esteem about my physical appearance and stuff...it was pretty heavy dislike."* Ambivalence is a good word to describe the feelings that many women report, since, while many felt okay about their developing bodies (especially in the context of competition with girl-friends and the relief from the embarrassment that goes along with being undeveloped, of not "measuring up," so to speak), these were accompanied by strong negative experiences of self-consciousness and embarrassment and the internalization of ambivalence about women's flesh and sexuality.

Loss/Transformation of Power

Trust. It's knowing you don't have to stop when your period starts. You don't have to let having your period slow you down. Not when you could use a Tampax tampon. Unlike a pad, a Tampax tampon is worn inside, so you can't see or feel it. Sounds more comfortable than a pad, right? And because it expands three ways, you know you can trust a Tampax tampon for great protection.

If you want the freedom to do what you want, when you want, (and who doesn't??), then you want the freedom of Tampax tampons.

—*Seventeen*, July 1994

The above advertisement in a popular teenage magazine was sandwiched in between the articles "When Bad Dates Happen to Good People: Preventing 12 Tales of Dating Embarrassments," and "Friends, Sex and Pressure." Another advertisement on the page before this heralded the wonders of an astringent and facial cleanser. It read: "Out of control is dialing 911 when you wake up with a zit/Under control is knowing what you can do to get rid of a zit; Out of control is believing your zits are the size of Texas/Under control is deep cleaning with a pharmaceutical ingredient." Metaphors of power, control and freedom are used intentionally in these advertisements; such notions of liberation are trivialized and reduced to women's control over their bodies and behaviors in the context of an explicit compulsory heterosexuality—cleanliness, hygiene, being able to make a pimple disappear, the freedom to wear a tampon, not a pad. These messages (which rely on adolescents' internment in the "imaginary audience" phase—i.e., "having zits the size of Texas") work on young women's real desires and needs for acceptance and autonomy; they function to maintain dominant gendered relations by equating these with bodily discipline aimed at attracting men. This would not work if it were not obvious that (hetero)sexualization in patriarchal societies involves a loss of female power, autonomy and efficacy, and an imposition of norms and restrictions that are internalized by both women and men. The cartoon (fig. 4.1) below by Nicole Hollander humorously illustrates this situation!

figure 4.1

This section explores first, the physical restrictions associated with menarche that constrains girls' activities; second, the increasing restraint and discipline at menarche associated with the double standard of sexual conduct that controls girls' lives; third, feelings of loss of authority and integrity associated with impending womanhood that girls sense at menarche; and finally, the experience that girls often have of the transformation of authentic efficacy into a sexualized manipulative form of power.

First, women involved with this project shared many stories of specific physical restrictions at menarche, although these restrictions changed somewhat with the advent of tampons. It is especially the older North American women and women raised outside the United States who shared stories of severe restrictions. However, the younger women also emphasized that menarche brings with it certain constraints on behavior, especially concerning activities with water (showering, washing hair, swimming), since most used pads rather than tampons during their early menstrual lives. Sally S. spoke of the customs that surrounded her menarche in the early 1980s in Iran, Nancy shared memories of starting her period in rural Oregon in 1941, and Maria, who grew up in Louisiana in a very poor rural family, remembers the restrictions associated with menarche when she started in 1937:

We can't pray...you can't be with your husband...for me it was no riding our bicycles or playing soccer...you shouldn't eat sour things like vinegar, lemon, or very cold things (Sally S.).

I remember feeling like one moment I am grown up now and the next thinking I don't want to grow up. And I believe probably my aunt told me that when this happened you had to curtail physical activity, you couldn't do anything strenuous, you couldn't take a bath, or wash your hair. You must not get cold, but that may have been picked up over a period of time, but that was how you were treated then. In gym class you didn't dress and when the roll was called, you answered "observing" and sat out.... I had no idea of what was going on with my body. I had not a clue why this was happening. So, I did what I was told. That meant no riding the bicycles, no hide and seek. So I would just make up excuses, little lies to cover my not participating in my usual activities (Nancy).

Back then, and bear in mind that this is the deep south of superstitions, you were not allowed to wash your hair. I never asked why. And among the Cajuns if you were menstruating you weren't allowed to help put up jams or jellies or vegetables or fruits. And if there is a newborn baby and you menstruate, you would somehow contaminate the baby. Way back in the Bayous it's still like that (Maria).

Several women shared stories of telling lies to hide their menarche and avoid a pre-planned activity of which now they felt they could not be a part. Women at first blood often curtailed their activity, internalizing and maintaining the taboos associated with menarche and menstruation, and preventing others from suffering embarrassments. Such secrecy and restrictions seem symbolic of a future that both encourages women to hide evidence of their monthly bleeding and restricts women psychologically and physically because of their gender. Crystal T., age twenty-one, shared memories of her menarche that occurred abroad on a visit to Australia. She remembered starting her first period at the same time that she met a male pen-pal. Eliza and Ann, white women aged seventy-eight and sixty-six years respectively, shared their memories too:

I don't know, it was just a real big trial thing for me. And then the next day after Christmas we went to these people I used to write to as pen pals and you know, I went there and of course they asked me if I wanted to go swimming and I said "no" because I didn't know anything about tampons...and I didn't know what to say. I told the girl, his sister, see the guy was my pen pal and I didn't want to say anything to him.... I explained it to his sister, you know, he didn't understand why and because "I don't want to." He kind of pressured me a little and I said "no I don't want to." But I think I would have went swimming if I knew more about tampons probably (Crystal T.).

I was almost twelve when my first period commenced. I don't recall what my reaction was, guess I just accepted it as part of growing up. My second time I remember very well! It was July and we were camping in Yosemite National Park with neighbors [who had a car]. *In those days it took hours to get there—the first day I met a nice young man and the following day we were going to go swimming together in the* [freezing] *Merced River. So, was I disgusted and embarrassed that I couldn't go and I don't know what kind of an excuse I made up—it must have been pretty feeble as I never saw him again after that—my first broken heart!* (Eliza).

Oh gee, you know, if I was going anywhere or if I was going to a dance, or going out on a date and I was going to have...I knew my period was going to be close, I didn't want to go. Because my flow was heavy and I was afraid I might have an accident. And we didn't have the padding that they have now, these pads. They were rather thin and I didn't want to go. I would just go home. I wouldn't go. I had a headache (laugh) (Ann).

Second, in terms of restrictions associated with the double standard of sexual conduct, Clara Thompson, as early as 1942, had described menarche as traumatic because of the real effects of loss of freedom. In 1952 Margaret Mead also asserted that the disjuncture or loss of continuity between cultural expectations for pre-menarcheal and post-menarcheal girls was related to the roles they were able to play in society. What this implies is that society views female sexuality in different ways than it does male sexuality, and, as a result, parents tend to see their daughter's emerging sexuality as more being problematic than their sons (Fine 1988). In a similar vein, as already discussed, we can talk about an "intensification of gender roles" at puberty whereby early sexual maturation is associated with greater achievement and independence from parents for boys, but to a lesser extent for girls (Hill and Lynch 1983). Many adolescent girls experience more family turmoil and parental control in the first six months after menarche than at any other time (Hill and Holmbeck 1987). This tends to be related to parental concern about girls' emerging sexuality, a process symbolized by menarche as a potentially reproductive juncture.

A strong memory of parental control was shared by Jewell, a white woman in her early forties: *"My family doctor wanted to put me on birth control pills when I was thirteen (because they greatly reduce cramps), but my mother wouldn't hear of it; she thought I would become promiscuous, so I suffeed for another five years until I put myself on birth control pills. I still experimented sexually despite my mother's feeling on the subject."* In predictable ways, the double standard of sexual conduct plays itself out as boys are encouraged to sow their wild oats and girls are chastised for similar behaviour and monitored more closely. These "oats" were literal for Louie, who was told *"not to get close to boys because they'd put a seed in me* (laugh), *and I stayed away from boys because I was afraid they were going to put a seed in me somehow!! I thought it was something like this* (gesturing)!"

The following excerpt by Inez illustrates the internalization of restraint and discipline that centers on the potentially reproductive and sexual female body at menarche. Girls' behavior starts to be more tightly controlled at menarche, a control that is directly related to the perception of adolescent girls as sexual beings, and especially as sexual beings who might get pregnant, bring shame on families, and be used by others. As a result, girls often respond by monitoring themselves and each other. Such restrictions and monitoring emphasizes how girls, as potential sexual victims are regulated, and, in turn bear the responsibility for regulating the sexual behavior of others. Inez descibes her self-monitoring as "watching":

> *What bothered me* [about menarche] *was the fact that once you get your period that means that you can get pregnant and have kids. Second of all the fact that I have to carry around a purse now really because you have to carry your pads or your tampons or whatever, and I wasn't too excited about that either, having to do that and having to wear not white when you, you know, just in case, or the fact that when you are flowing you know, once and a while you do mistakes, or sometimes a period comes up all excited, and then you have to be more careful. The fact of having to go to the bathroom every four to six hours, you know, to change and make sure things are okay,*

was just too much for me and I wasn't ready to do that. Because that meant slowing down and being more, watching, to take care more of myself which I wasn't ready to do. I wanted to be as free as a bird and be like the guys.

For many such as Vanessa, a twenty-year-old American Indian woman, not wanting to grow up is associated with a strong desire to remain a "tomboy" and access the privileges of masculinity:

I was really a tomboy. I did everything I could to be, to emulate a boy. I had my hair cut short, I played with boys, soccer, football, anything I could play. I mean I identified as female, but felt that women were too restrained in my town, they were meant to do girl things, they were meant to play with Barbies and things like that and it wasn't really acceptable for them to play in the dirt with the guys. I really didn't want to develop as a woman. I wanted to be totally flat chested and not look anything like a girl, and so when that happened it was kind of like an end of an era.

As women constructed the narratives of their adolescence, many used the word "tomboy" to describe themselves. Barrie Thorne has an interesting musing on this term: "'Tomboy' may be an identity that consolidates more in retrospect than in the present. Reflecting back in time, adults use the term to describe a pathway through the stereotyped and real gender arrangement of their childhoods, and to make claims about their present selves, for example, about their independence and flexibility" (1993: 115). As Pipher suggests, being a preadolescent tomboy is remembered fondly as a word that connotes "courage, competency and irreverence" (1994: 18).

Third, beyond the significant and immediate restrictions on behavior associated with controlling sexuality and potential reproduction, the women's stories also revealed a distinct loss of power associated with the ontological state of being a woman in contemporary Western society. We want to emphasize that this had less to do with actual restrictions on their behavior than with the perception of the state of embodied, sexualized adulthood and associated feelings of loss of competency and efficacy. Several women talked about *"grieving"* that loss. *"I felt it more like a loss and I was so involved with the grief"* said Alice, a forty-six-year-old Mexican-American/Indian woman. Similarly, Hannah remembers:

"Mom, what is this?" And she said: "well, honey, congratulations you are a little lady now." I am like, "say what?" And she said: "You started your period." I began bawling; I sat on the toilet and I just cried because I didn't want to have my period. I had this feeling that it was...that I was going to become this little woman, that I was going to have to somehow fit into this

mould or something.... I felt bad for being me, for being female. When I started my period that reinforced that femaleness which was bad already. By starting my period, it made it worse.

It was especially the teenage athletes who associated budding womanhood with loss of competency. Twenty-two-year-old Karin, whose words we shared earlier in this chapter, was actively involved in sports during her childhood and adolescence, performing as a gymnast and running track. Her words illustrate the perceived loss of efficacy and competency associated with menarche:

Gee, maybe sports are going to be more of a hassle now or they are going to be more difficult because I had always been into sports. So it kind of made me think like for some reason I couldn't be a girl, I had to be more of a woman and maybe I wouldn't be doing as many sports. I thought, gosh, you know, maybe my days are numbered as an athlete you know!...You know I had always been someone very strong and assertive and I really thought, well, gosh, does this mean I am a woman now?...I felt like a power difference there, I didn't really like it, between women and men. I thought, I had always been successful in sports and things that I thought, well, I can do anything I want, and maybe I thought being a woman meant you couldn't do everything you wanted. So it kind of scared me I think.

Finally, however, despite real feelings of loss of authentic power, there is also another message. This concerns the way that women come to understand that the relative freedoms and authorities of girlhood are replaced by a certain power involved in sexuality; again, not a sexuality that involves the ability to define one's own reality and desire, but certainly an awareness of some kind of sexual authority. As Tita remembers: "*Frankly, I felt very excited—a sexual sort of excitement (even now I remember) at this brand new thing that was going to happen.*" Remember Judy in chapter 2; she articulated the indirect "*manipulative power*" she felt she had inherited at menarche that replaced the truths of her childhood:

There is a piece of me that I felt I lost, a powerful piece of me, that was going to do all the things that the boys did and do them as confidently as the boys did them and be competitive if I wanted to be, be loud if I wanted to be. Yeah, so it is a loss of power, only the power I got by getting my period was a different kind of power. It was much less straight on honest, it was manipulative.

From a developmental perspective, as Mary Pipher suggests, in place of the authentic pre-adolescent competence and power of girls' true selves is the "false self," the self which girls learn to cultivate in order to cope with everyday life under patriarchy. Importantly though, this false self that girls become so good at portraying gives them a different sense of competency, scripted by compulsory heterosexuality and framed by contemporary notions of femininity. A component of this is a form of sexual "power"; menarche brings an ability to entice and lure, and in some sense control the behavior of, boys and adult men.

At menarche, girls become looked at, talked about, and judged against often unattainable standards of perfection and ideals of relationship. Girls learn to "look at their 'looks'" and to listen to what people say about them. As Lyn Mikel Brown and Carol Gilligan, in *Meeting at the Crossroads: Women's Psychology and Girls' Development*, suggest: "Seeing themselves seen through the gaze of others, hearing themselves talked about in ways that imply that they can be perfect, and that relationships can be free of conflict and bad feeling, they struggle between knowing what they know through experience and knowing what others want them to know and to feel and to think" (1992: 164).

While women's bodies have been the object of both derogation and admiration, women themselves often do not have the power to control how their bodies look, act and feel. For women and others in their lives, menarche is an event that centers attention on the body, symbolizing the transition from childhood to womanhood. Since "woman" is over-represented by the practices and values of sexuality, menarche takes on loaded meanings that have consequences for women and their everyday lives, scripting relations of power into the discourses and practices that surround women's bodies. The themes explored here are themes of the body and of body politics; bodies contextualized in a society that devalues and trivializes women. Adult womanhood carries with it the stigma of the inferior sex, a lower status in society and certain restrictions on body, mind and soul.

5

Intricate Relationships

Are you there God? It's me, Margaret. I just told my mother I want a bra. Please help me grow God. You know where. I want to be like everybody else. You know God, my new friends all belong to the Y or the Jewish Community Center. Which way am I supposed to go? I don't know what you want me to do about that.

—Judy Blume, *Are You There God? It's Me, Margaret*

The experience of first period is contextualized in the complicated, changing, and rich web of relationships that girls have with their families and friends. Interactions with family members are often fraught with conflict and struggle around issues of independence and autonomy, and friends help teenagers navigate these troubled waters, setting patterns for future adult relationships. Such friendships also have their own prerequisites for conformity, and thus serve to both constrain and facilitate girls' individuation (Duck 1983; Raymond 1986; Rubin 1985). Menarche, in particular, tends to be experienced through the tensions associated with the developmental activities of adolescence: separating from parents and growing closer to peers (Danza 1983; Ulman 1992). Our data suggest that the quality of girls' same-sex relationships prior to menarche is central to understanding their experiences at this crucial juncture, and that the context of these relations—how they are wound-up with the politics of gender in the family, school, and society—are important. In other words, when girls have positive communications and relationships with their mothers or primary female caretakers prior to menarche, the older women tend to be sources of support rather than sources of conflict for girls. However, given the role mothers often end up playing in the perpetuation of patriarchal social relations, positive relationships with mothers prior to menarche do not ensure that this transition will be experienced positively. Many women shared that while they felt their mothers tried to make menarche a positive experience, they also felt their mothers were responsible for imposing restrictive femininity on them and on their bodies. When it comes to relationships with fathers, brothers and other boys, we find that for most women, menarche involved negotiating gender through the societal discourses and social relations of dominance that get acted out in the family. These discourses tend to separate males and females, framing gendered practices that start to govern new behaviors, and imposing different expectations on individuals and their bodies. As a result, girls usually end up negotiating new ways to relate to males that are not necessarily tied to their prior relationships with boys and men.

These are the issues that we will discuss in this chapter. The first and longest section centers on girls' relationships with mothers at menarche and the influence mothers have on their daughters' lives at this time, followed by a discussion of friendships with sisters and other girls in the second section. The third section focuses on relationships with fathers, brothers, and boys generally, emphasizing how girls learn during this developmental time to negotiate newly configured relationships with males.

Mothers

Of all the relationships in a girl's life, her relationship with her mother is one of the most emotionally salient, complex, and lasting (Apter 1990; Debold, Wilson, and Malave 1993; de Waal 1993). Mothers and daughters are deeply connected through their bodies—bodies historically and socially situated, bodies at once the same and different (Schreurs 1993; Tolman 1991). It is in the context of this paradoxical, transgenerational connection that a girl-child learns about going through life with a female body. Adrienne Rich uses the phrase "the deepest mutuality and the most painful estrangement" to describe one of the abiding issues in mother-daughter relationships—the struggle to balance autonomy and connection, sameness and difference (1986: 226). This issue is present throughout the lifetime of a mother-daughter relationship; however it takes on central importance during a daughter's adolescence. As Elizabeth Debold says so eloquently "The transformation of the daughter's body transforms the relationship between mother and daughter" (1991: 174).

Often, mothers are intimate witnesses to and participants in their daughters' transformations from girls to women. We have discussed in previous chapters the multitude of challenges girls face concurrently with their first blood, in particular the process of sexualization which ensues, whereby girls' bodies are produced as objects of male desire. Around the same time, girls begin to experience their bodies in new ways, but often without the cognitive framework and emotional maturity necessary to make sense of and integrate what they are feeling (Flaake 1993; Tolman 1991). Mothers often recognize that while their daughters' bodies are beginning to look womanly, in terms of their social and psychological development, their daughters are still very much girls in need of guidance. As Louie so wisely stated: *"It is kind of hard making the switch from childhood to young adulthood."* Sally L., a nineteen-year-old Korean-American, shared: *"I was fighting with my mom a lot, I guess about power and control and stuff because I wanted to be more independent and she was like 'No, you are still a little kid, you still need these rules and stuff,' so we would fight over that a lot."* Truth be told, in this culture, adolescence is a problematic time for most children and their mothers, regardless of the quality of their relationship and openness of their communication (Apter 1990; Orbach 1986; Pipher 1994).

Traditional, mainstream models of adolescent development predicated on Western, androcentric principles maintain that the central developmental task of this life course stage is separation from the mother (c.f. Deutsch 1944; Erikson 1968). This is illustrated by Mary Pipher in the following passage:

> Mothers are expected to protect their daughters from the culture even as they help them fit into it. They are to encourage their daughters to grow into adults and yet to keep them from being hurt. They are to be devoted to their daughters and yet encourage them to leave. Mothers are asked to love completely and yet know exactly when to distance emotionally and physically...Girls are encouraged to separate from their mothers and to devalue their relationships to them. They are expected to respect their mothers but not be like them. In our culture, loving one's mother is linked with dependency, passivity and regression, while rejecting one's mother implies individuation, activity and independence. Distancing from one's mother is viewed as a necessary step toward adult development. (1994: 103)

While conflict is somewhat endemic to the adolescent struggle for independence and individuation, a severing of the connection between a girl and her mother need not be. Feminist theorists and researchers, most notably Carol Gilligan and her colleagues, have questioned whether models of adolescent development mandating distancing from the mother reflect the experiences and feelings of most girls and women. Instead, Gilligan talks about adolescence as a "crisis of connection" for girls, a time when they struggle to maintain their relationships with their essential selves, their families and friends, all the while feeling increasing pressure to conform to the rules and standards of patriarchal culture (Gilligan and Rogers 1993; Gilligan, Lyons and Hanmer 1990). Similarly, Terri Apter (1990) suggests that the inevitable struggle that ensues between adolescent girls and their moms is about a mutual redefining of the contours of their connection—not a severing of the connection—so that both daughter and mother can continue to develop and grow. Such reconceptualizations of women's life-span development emphasize that development is fundamentally relational, that individuality and autonomy unfold *within* a rich matrix of relationships.

For most of the women in our project, the framing of womanhood at menarche occurred within the context of the complex dynamic of their relationships with their mothers. Listening to the women's memories, we noticed that while virtually every woman mentioned her mother or primarily female caretaker in connection with her first blood, only about a third of the women spoke vividly and at length about the ways their relationships with their mothers changed around the time of menarche. Perhaps this subgroup of women felt more comfortable speaking about their relationships with their mothers, or maybe their adolescent interactions with their mothers were of greater emotional salience, and therefore more readily remembered. Interestingly, the stories shared by these women tended to be filled with ambivalence, conflict and confusion, particularly surrounding the ways their mothers introduced them to the restrictions and behaviors associated with adult feminine embodiment. Also, a small number of the women experienced menarche and travelled through adolescence without the presence of a mother, and therefore had to rely on surrogate mothers for guidance and support. Keep in mind that we did not have the opportunity to speak with the mothers of the women in our project, so we derived from the women's stories a partial, one-sided picture of their relationships with these parents. In order to avoid presenting an unbalanced portrait of the diverse roles mothers play in the lives of their adolescent daughters we feel it is important to make these potential sources of bias explicit. As is often the case, the negative and the distressing become more salient and are vividly remembered, and the good things about mothers and their relationships with daughters tend to be normalized and taken for granted.

Most mothers try to do the best they can for their daughters, often in spite of their own painful and problematic experiences be(come)ing women (Apter 1990; Debold, Wilson, and Malave 1993). This is a very important point for us to emphasize in order to avoid the "mother-blaming" that can so easily frame discussions of female adolescent development. Many of the mothers of the women with whom we spoke had difficult lives, materially and emotionally. Many were not "there" for their daughters because they were not able to understand their own victimization and pain. Faced with mothering an adolescent daughter in this culture, many women fall back on what they know best—their memories of their own adolescence and the best and/or worst of how they were mothered through this passage. Unfortunately, as we have seen, generations of mothers have perpetuated the silence and ignorance surrounding the first blood and other pubertal changes, and most mothers have not explained the meaning of these changes beyond how they relate to fertility and reproduction. As Flaake (1993: 9) clearly articulates, mothers and daughters rarely speak about "emotions, or the sensations accompanying the daughter's development; about desires or fantasies, about shame or pride concerning the body, about inner sensations during menstruation, or about the desire to explore the changing body or sexual preferences" (see 1993: 9; c.f., Apter 1990; Tolman 1991, 1994). The following anecdote, shared by Bertha, age forty-four, is a vivid example of this maternal pattern of silence concerning what it means to go through life with a female body:

My one memory of asking my mother a sexual question—I thought she was going to run the car off the road! For the first time, the night before, a boy had touched my breasts and I felt horribly guilty and I asked my mother if it was okay. That is when she almost drove the car off the road! Within a week she threw a book on my bed and said "read this," and by then it was too late, really. It was a book about dating, and I was beyond the dating game. I was getting very sexually active.

Elizabeth, aged forty-two, recalled that her mother was worried that she would become sexually active once she began menstruating, yet did not discuss her concerns with Elizabeth:

When I hit my adolescent years our relationship really split because my mother all of a sudden was very suspicious of everything I did, [she had] *a kind of bad girl image of me. I still remember her just all of a sudden* [having] *a suspicion about me, maybe I was becoming sexual. I was pretty vivacious and so I think she was sensing a whole lot of things about me that she probably just couldn't deal with, and so it was not a good time.*

Often unwittingly, at the same time that they are attempting to shelter their daughters from the realities of living in a patriarchal culture, mothers socialize their daughters into the same restrictions and silences associated with femininity that they have endured (Rich 1986). This intergenerational transmission of the rules of the patriarchy ensures that their daughters will fit into society, and by extension encourages a shared compliance in the development of a submissive femininity and gendered sexual identity. Because Bertha's and Elizabeth's mothers were uncomfortable with their own sexuality, they were suspicious and silent about what they imagined their daughters were feeling and doing.

By internalizing their own oppression, mothers often become agents of their daughter's oppression as well (Orbach 1986). We remember when one of the women with whom we spoke, Anne, who described her mother as an "agent" of the patriarchy, whose purpose was to impose inauthentic gender characteristics upon her daughter—"*She started expecting me to be a lady and it was too late.*" The result of this perpetuation of gender oppression is that girls may come to resent their mothers for simultaneously protecting them from and socializing them into the patriarchy, and may fear becoming what they perceive their mothers to have become. This pattern is seen in memories shared by Madeleine and Sally L. Madeleine's poignant story vividly captures the central role her mother played in her introduction to womanhood. She explained that her sense of her self was shaped by the conflicting messages she received in her family about what it meant to be a woman:

What I remember really clearly is seeing the blood in my underpants and that I felt very distressed because I didn't want to be having my period. What I really remember specifically is going down to the basement. It was a mid-western house. They have these basements that you don't see as much out in Oregon, just an old cement basement...and dingy...that is where my mom's washer and dryer was, and she was down there ironing. I remember going down there and telling her...and crying...and she was ironing and I remember her just trying to say positive things about it, saying, "But this means that you are becoming a woman," and I said "but I don't want to be a woman." I guess I felt like it was so symbolic that here she was in this basement ironing. The association that I had was this sort of restrictiveness.

Sally L. remembered experiencing confusion at menarche regarding whether she should identify with her younger sister, who was still a child, or her mother, whom she saw as representing all of "Womanhood":

Well, a "woman" was kind of like my mom. She stayed home, took care of the kids, cooked, cleaned, she sewed, she was my Bluebirds leader and she helped in my classroom and she gave birthday parties and she took me and my sister shopping. I guess when I was little, this is what a "woman" meant to me; I always thought a woman was like my mom, doing "mom" things. When I was little that was positive, but then as I have grown up its not so anymore, because now I have been introduced to other things, and I'd rather be a career woman than just sit at home and do the cooking, the cleaning, the sewing and what not.

Is it any wonder Madeleine and Sally felt ambivalence watching their mothers ironing in the basement or doing "mom things?" This deep ambivalence is captured in the contradictory descriptions used by Sally: while she described her mother as *"involved in a lot of stuff,"* she also spoke about wanting to do more than household tasks. Such actions and tasks symbolize restrictive femininity for daughters who, as they imagine their futures, hope not to be like their mothers. For an adolescent girl, it is nearly impossible to untangle the connection between restrictions and loss of power and "Mother"—one's mother becomes so tightly associated with the ambivalences of femininity as to become one in the same. Girls at this developmental phase have a difficult time seeing their mothers as individuals who have complex, multidimensional lives; instead, they tend to define their mothers in limited and naive ways (c.f. Debold, Wilson and Malave 1993; Pipher 1994), as seen in the following statement shared by Marie: *"I guess in a lot of ways I just kind of disdained women who just kind of sat around and did their typical women things. I had always had a sort of expectation that I would be the person in the family who would accomplish something, who would go to college and get a degree, do all that sort of stuff and just be tough about it, rather than being an air head kind of like my mother sort of is."*

Not surprisingly, these issues of ambivalence and confusion are even more salient and complex for survivors of childhood sexual abuse. For Jewell and Susan, memories of menarche were inexorably connected to their experiences of sexual victimization, and their fear of becoming women like their mothers. Jewell writes:

Before I go any further, I need to let you know that I am an incest survivor. I was raped and sodomized by my own father for the first eleven years of my life, as were my two younger sisters. I have also remembered that my mother knew all along what my father was doing to me, but she did nothing about it. Being a mother myself and knowing that I would do virtually anything within my power to help my little boy, this is a very difficult pill for me to swallow. I was eleven years old when I got my first period. I remember feeling so depressed because I was in so much pain. Because of all the physical torture I had already endured, the onset of my period was terrible for me. Of course, I was also frightened to death that getting my period and becoming a woman would mean that I was going to turn into a woman like my mother. More than any driving force, I vowed I would never become a drug-addicted, perfect victim-queen like my mother.

Susan recalls that her mother's unwillingness to believe she was being sexually abused by her stepfather was one among a series of major betrayals by her mother:

I think the way my mother handled it [her puberty], *when I look back now, just makes me more aware of her, how uncomfortable she is just in the whole issue of sex, the menstrual cycle and relationships, period. I think the way she handled it affected me in sort of a negative way. Now it is easy to go back and look at my thoughts and I know what my needs were then. I was not able to clarify* [them]*—I needed my mother to come and talk to me. And if she would have done that it would have made all the difference in the world. With what I am about to say, starting my menstrual cycle would have to play a big part. At thirteen I was molested by my step-father. I woke up one night when my mother was working at the cannery, and here my step-father was kissing me on my vagina and all I saw was his big, fat, ugly, gross penis and this gross body that smelt of booze and I was holding my legs together and he was pulling them apart. That was a real frightening, horrifying experience. I pushed him away and told him to get out of there and he left. Then he tried for three to four nights after that. I never did tell my mother, but I did tell my sister just for protection. She told my mother and my mother denied it. She confronted him with it right in front of me, and he denied it. Right in front of me, too. Oh, it was kind of like, "Wow, my mother again is not even going to protect me, teach me, nothing."*

Clinical psychologist Ann Miller suggests that "the mothers' failure to hear or acknowledge their daughters' experiences amounts to a virtual attack on the daughters' sense of reality. It is as if allowing their daughters to express their point of view, or if once expressed to acknowledge it, would amount to a major threat to the mothers' perception of themselves or of their relationships" (1990: 140). Jewell and Susan desperately needed to be heard, believed and protected by their mothers; instead, they felt as though their mothers collaborated with their male abusers. Their adolescent experiences of sexual abuse—not to mention their feelings that their mothers had betrayed them—had long-term implications for how they related to their mothers, and to themselves as women.

As we have already discussed, for many of the women in our study, their first blood experience was associated with a major education in the rules of femininity. What is important here is the central role that many mothers seemed to play in intentionally teaching daughters about restrictive feminine comportment and behavior. It is important to point out that these rules about what it means to be "a young lady" originate in, as Iris Young puts it, "neither anatomy nor physiology, and certainly not in a mysterious feminine essence. Rather, they have their source in the particular *situation* of women as conditioned by their sexist oppression in contemporary society" (1990: 153). Around the time of menarche, women remember being inundated with a confusing array of messages from their mothers: they should be feminine but *not* sexual; they should dress nicely and make up their faces but with subtlety; they should take pride in their womanly bodies but learn to regulate their appetites and discipline their bodies' sizes and shapes. Many women, particularly those who came of age after the 1960s, rejected their mothers' efforts to teach them this version of what it means to be a woman.

Carol and Barbara shared stories replete with anecdotes of how their mothers wanted to change their behaviors and interests once they felt their daughters were "growing up." Carol, a white thirty-five-year-old working-class bisexual woman, remembers that when she gained twenty pounds after menarche, her mother gave her books on dieting: *"I was fairly skinny and then all of a sudden I put on twenty pounds and then I really got to be like my mother, I got to start dieting! Of course, I shouldn't have put on twenty pounds, God forbid! So I immediately started dieting, and so I think, okay, if I was doing that, I obviously was not real happy with my body."*

Barbara is a nineteen-year-old middle-class lesbian. She developed an eating disorder during adolescence and felt overwhelmed and pressured by her mother's standards of appearance:

After I began my period my mom kind of began her "you don't need a second helping, you really don't need to be eating that," whereas my brother could eat whatever he wanted when he wanted and that made me really envious. I was upset, he'd get bigger helpings and you know, it was like, "That's not fair, I worked and played just as hard as he did, mom," and she was [saying] *"no, you need to cut down, you started your period and your body will start developing and you will put fat on." She is very into image. She is skinny, and beautiful, and people are always praising her for how she looks. She dresses very meticulously. I was so scared I was getting fat and I was very careful what I ate and very conscientious how I appeared. When I got up, I always had to have my outfits checked by my mom before I'd leave for school. She would always make sure I appeared o.k.—"Barbara, you look too fat in that outfit," or "Barbara, change your clothes."*

For a number of complex reasons, mostly having to do with socialization and survival, mothers have tended to encourage in their daughters this shared compliance in the development of a submissive femininity. Carol and Barbara felt they had to live up to her mother's standards of bodily discipline, a heavy burden to bear. Elizabeth Debold, Marie Wilson, and Idelisse Malave speak at length in their book *Mother Daughter Revolution* (1993) about the damage done to girls when mothers reinforce the cult of beauty. Each time a mother unthinkingly says something critical about her daughter's appearance, when she emphasizes the importance of dieting and depravation, of a restrictive feminine comportment, she is reinforcing the harmful sociocultural standards adolescent girls are exposed to and indoctrinated with. And, sadly, in order to fit into family and society, girls learn to give up parts of themselves, just as their mothers did before them—full and conscious embodiment, an understanding of their desire, pleasure in the way they look, a decisive and honest voice, freedom of movement and thought.

A surprisingly small number of women remembered feeling closer to their mothers, and ultimately happy to be taught how to be "ladylike." Almost all these women reported good relationships with their mothers prior to menarche, recalling that once they began bleeding, they had something in common with their mothers, and this strengthened their already close relationships. One exception was Alina, who was somewhat estranged from her mother during childhood and had chosen to live with her father after her parents divorced. She felt reunited with her mother after menarche, and remembered: "*I was just relieved that now I had my mom, because I never really wanted her, but now I did. [Menarche] was kind of like the stepping stone; it helped us get back together again.*"

Similarly, Yvette, aged twenty and African-American, recalled how during her childhood, because she was the eldest child and a tomboy, she and her father were extremely close; after menarche, "*because I was turning into a young lady, our relationship declined.*" However, once she was a "*young lady,*" Yvette and her mother "*had a nice little bonding.*" Listen to Yvette's tales of the "explosion" of femininity that ensued after menarche:

It was like immediately after that my mom started buying me little pumps to wear. I wore dresses and stuff to church before but they weren't as flowery as they were [now] *and I think my mom just went overboard. I just felt really uncomfortable around guys and I don't think I was really prepared for that, a new look, new expectations. I never recognized that I was a tomboy until I saw that my mom was trying to push these things on me. I felt I was being condemned for running around with my dad and playing with all the guys in the neighborhood. My mom is really strict on etiquette and stuff, and so all this just got blown up. "You have to cross your legs like this." I didn't dress tacky, I just put on what I felt comfortable in and she would say, "No, your socks have to match with shoes and your shoes have to match with your dress." I mean, it just got to be so detailed—"you have to keep your nails painted all the time, either you keep the paint on or you keep the paint off, don't put too much makeup on your face." It was just like an explosion of things. And she told me "men are going to start looking at you differently," and I was like, "wow, are they perverse or something? I don't understand." So I just went along with my mom's lead and kind of followed her and that's when we started bonding more. I wanted to be like her and she gave me opportunities to do things that she did. She went out and bought me pretty things and nice perfumes, all those kinds of things to make me feel like a nice little pretty girl* (laugh).

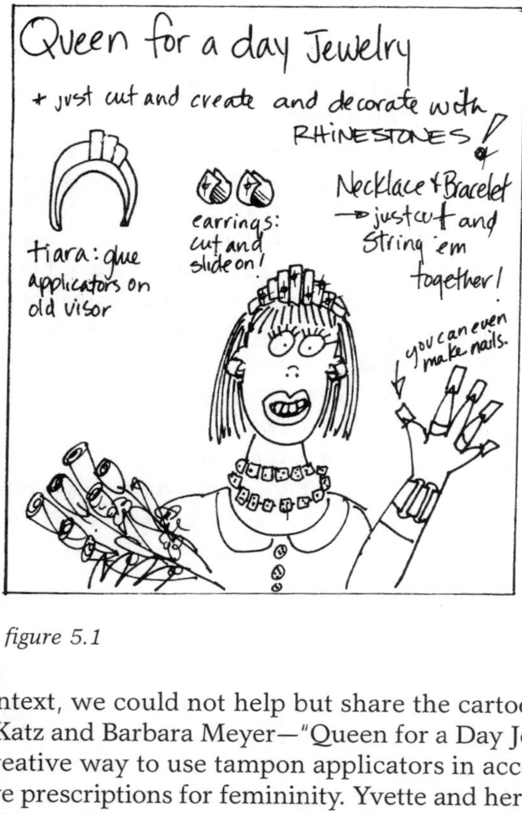

figure 5.1

In this context, we could not help but share the cartoon above (fig. 5.1) by Lori Katz and Barbara Meyer—"Queen for a Day Jewelry"—that suggests a creative way to use tampon applicators in accordance with the normative prescriptions for femininity. Yvette and her mother grew closer once Yvette accepted and internalized her mother's "etiquette" of womanhood. We sensed that Yvette came to see her transformation from "tomboy" to "nice little pretty girl" as normative and inevitable, but very difficult, and thus followed her mother's example. Acting and looking "right" were important to her mother, and ultimately became important to Yvette. While Yvette's story captures many of the issues faced by adolescent daughters and their mothers, her experience of bonding with her mother vis-a-vis her acceptance of the rules of femininity is far from typical for the women with whom we spoke.

As we have seen, the developmental issues which arise around the time of the first blood are challenging for most girls and their mothers. These issues can be even more bewildering and challenging for girls who find themselves "motherless" during adolescence, and must turn to mother-surrogates for guidance and support. When Lula, aged seventy-five, was ten, her mother died in childbirth; soon after her mother's death, her father had a nervous breakdown. At menarche, she had to rely on the kindness of neighbors and family friends for information and support. Lula shared her story with us in writing:

I was twelve when I had my first menstruation. My mother had died when I was ten, and in the schools at that time there was not a word mentioned of what was ahead in the way of growing up. When I started, I was scared to death, thought I was dying, I guess. I was crying and the lady next door asked me what was the matter, and then she tried to sooth me and tell me about what happens to all little girls sooner or later. I mentioned not one thing to my father about the situation—didn't even have the money, I knew, to buy pads, so I tore up old sheets and made some. One day a female friend of my older brother came by and wanted to take me home with her for a weekend stay. I told her I couldn't go because I didn't have any rags and had to wash and dry some and she about died! She went to town and bought me some napkins, and then told my brother to see that I had some hereafter! I remember that a girl friend who lived close to me and I got enough nerve once to question her mother about whether that was the only time to get pregnant, etc. She told us in no uncertain words "You can get pregnant anytime, so just keep the boys away from you!" I am sure, had my Mother lived, I would not have been left so in the dark.

In considering the women's stories, we learned about other sources of motherlessness besides a mother's death. Lois, one of the older women with whom we spoke, felt emotionally abandoned and betrayed by her mother. She explained that her mother focused all her energy on her older children and thus had little energy left to care for Lois, or protect her from a sexually abusive father. Fortunately, her maternal grandmother served as a surrogate-mother and positive role model while she was growing up:

When my period happened I was just kind of excited and everything, and thought how my mother would treat me. I came downstairs and I told her about it and she said "Oh, you know where the rags are, don't you?" And I said "Yeah," and she said "You know how to put them on?" I said "Well, I have some sort of idea," and so then she showed me. I felt really betrayed. I had not [had] *any sympathy or concern and it was part of my feeling of betrayal. I think my mother was very overwhelmed at that point in her life, by the time it got to my second brother and me. It was hard times. I wanted to be part of womanhood but she didn't treat me that way. My mother didn't want—she only wanted four children, I was the fifth. She was very ill when I was born. She didn't take me home with her. I stayed with my grandmother who delivered me,* [she] *was the midwife and delivered me, and when I was about three months old she brought me back to my mother. It was like I never bonded with my mother. My grandmother was a very, very stable figure in my life. Whenever I went away and came back, I always went to grandmother's house before I ever went home. Grandma's house was kind of like an anchor.*

Tita, seventy-two years old, grew up thinking her teenage mother was her older sister. When her mother abandoned her to start a new family, she was raised by her grandparents and watched over by an older half-brother. Tita wrote the following:

I was raised by my Grandparents, in fact was in my teens before I knew that my "older sister" was my mother. She had me when she was about fifteen so certainly could not have taken the responsibility for parenthood. I was always very close to the only young person in my family—he was nine years older than I. Melvin had a very different relationship with me; he filled many "roles" in my life, in many ways: mother, father, brother, and certainly my most caring friend—always from the time of my first memory, he was there for me. I'm quite sure I had my first period between eleven and twelve—no one in the family had ever told me anything...there was no talk about "that sort of thing" at home and when I found blood on my pants—I went to grandma and she handed me some folded rags, told me to "pin them on" and when they were soiled, bled through, I was to wash them out, hang them on the line so they would be ready for the "next time in about a month." Well, when Melvin came home to visit us, he told me that from then on he would see that I had Kotex and I did—what a wonderful relief! Morality, how one ought or ought not to behave with the opposite sex, babies and where they come from, intercourse, the whole "thing" of growing up just never, ever was discussed in my family—I flew by the seat of my pants, sorted things out for myself and one thing I know for sure: my period, or anything concerning my body, I would never discuss with grandma.

Hope Edelman, in her book *Motherless Daughters: The Legacy of Loss* (1994), suggests (and our data certainly support this) that a child's experience of having a mother who is physically present but emotionally unresponsive can be just as traumatic as a having a mother who is absent because of death. Similarly, being abandoned by one's mother and left in the care of others, even family members, can leave a child feeling lost and betrayed. Fortunately, the presence of at least one kind, stable adult can help a child in such a situation grow up to be healthy and well-adjusted, as seen in Lois' and Tita's experiences.

While we found evidence that menarche intensified the quality of existing relationships, especially when these relationships were contentious, we also found that women often experienced this transition with their mothers as negative, irrespective of the quality of the mother-daughter relationship itself. We think it quite provocative that when women remembered their mothers being thrilled at their daughters' impending womanhood, these same women described themselves as feeling embarrassed, humiliated, and ambivalent about the way their mothers handled their passage from child to adolescent. It seems that, regardless of the closeness and openness of the mother-daughter relationship, girls are overwhelmed and confused by the messages they receive from their mothers during adolescence. Conflicts and changes in this most essential of relationships, while necessary and inevitable, are nevertheless painful. Mothers struggle for the right balance of closeness and protectiveness, distance and release; simultaneously, their adolescent daughters struggle with their cravings for independence and individuation, mother-love and protection. We end this section voicing what we see as the central challenge for us as daughters: learning how to reject harmful cultural discourses about adult, feminine embodiment without rejecting our mothers in the process.

Friends and Sisters

At early adolescence, when girls are about eleven to fourteen years old, friendships tend to be same-sex and are becoming the most significant source of girls' feelings about themselves. As Lillian Rubin writes in *Just Friends*, adolescent attachments "take on the urgency of necessity, [and] can inflict almost unbearable pain and equally intense pleasure" (1985: 110). Such friendships are characterized by girls' needs to be understood, accepted, and validated by their peer group. Early adolescence is a time when girls are very much focused on the group and its often unspoken rules. Fear of rejection and ridicule are central, and girls of this age tend to be involved in endless talk that allows them to understand and practice the rules and behaviors of the peer group. This process is important for their understandings of acceptance and inclusion and for the exercise of group norms and the development of social skills (Lees 1993; Lempers and Clark-Lempers 1993; Parker and Gottman 1989; Thorne 1993). The cognitive changes of early adolescence that have allowed girls to assume the perspective of others contribute to their awareness of the power of group norms and their ongoing monitoring of each other in social situations. Girls see themselves reflected by their friends; they practice dealing with conflict and try out different identities (Gilligan, Lyons and Hanmer 1990). Luise Eichenbaum and Susie Orbach in *Between Women*, while not talking specifically about teenagers, capture the developmental task of adolescence as it relates to girls' friendships: "We project onto other women our fears, which are mirrored back because other women have them too.... We have a deep and passionate attachment with one another that is at once holding and binding" (1987: 70–71).

Development associated with early adolescence includes the hormonal changes of puberty as well as such cognitive changes as the transition from concrete operational thought to more formal operational thought, characterized by the ability to engage in abstract and hypothetical thinking (Piaget 1954), and to infer the views of others and coordinate those views with one's own (Selman 1980). This involves the development of the "imaginary audience," (Elkind 1978) discussed in chapter 3, and the extreme body consciousness talked about in chapter 4. Importantly, these changes occur within the nexus of power relations in society that construct meanings. In other words, developmental transitions do not occur outside of historical and social contexts; they are molded by the discourses that name, privilege and subordinate. And it is in this context that girls encounter menarche. Bodily changes work within existing socio-political contexts (which include discourses associated with the practices surrounding families, school, the media, religion, etc.) to frame the experience for individual girls.

Girl friends can be sources of intimidation and embarrassment during menarche as well as sources of support. Either way, friends matter; it is in this context that girls experience their changing bodies at menarche. Listening to women's stories we were struck by the fact that every woman with whom we spoke mentioned girl friends in some capacity as she told the story of her first period. These stories tended to center on four interrelated concepts: first, issues of timing, starting earlier or later than their girl friends and the implications of this for their relationships with others; second, concerns about acceptance, fears about rejection, and the overwhelming desire to be included in the group; third, the sharing of information with girl friends about menarche and menstrual practices and products generally; and last, the support, help and assistance that girls give each other at this time.

First, in terms of timing, girls who start their periods during their elementary school years often find the experience to be distressing and difficult. Such girls tend to be less prepared in terms of information; developmentally they may not be ready to deal with the cognitive and emotional implications of this life transition, and they are less likely to have friends who are at a similar stage or with whom they can share their feelings (Rierdan, Koff and Stubbs, 1989). So much of this has to do with the fact that adults often feel uncomfortable around such "early bloomers" and act in disapproving ways. As Barrie Thorne observed in her study of elementary school children: "Third-, fourth-, and fifth-grade girls with 'figures' (big breasts and rounded hips) are treated as deviant and even polluting because they violate the cultural ordering of age categories" (1993: 141).

Further, since the onset of menarche tends to be triggered by balances and ratios of body fat, early menstruators are often heavier than their friends. In a culture that worships thinness, having an adult female body and being in sixth, fifth or even fourth grade, can be cause for embarrassment and shame. This, of course, is because of the derogation of and ambivalence toward female bodies in our society, as evidenced by the fact that clear gender differences exist in terms of the effects of pubertal timing. Early-maturing boys receive considerable advantages in our culture while girls often suffer depression and distress (Simmons and Blyth 1987; Rierdan and Koff 1991). The advantages or disadvantages associated with early or late maturation depends upon the status that awaits adolescents at adulthood (Block 1978). For boys, maturation is symbolic of the status afforded males when they attain masculine bodies: leadership, responsibility, independence and physical prowess. For girls, maturity, as we suggest in chapter 4, is heavily associated with sexuality and girls' future roles as wives and mothers. It is early-maturing girls and late-maturing boys who seem to suffer the most, although late maturity for girls carries with it its own stigma and problems, especially within the peer group.

Almost all the women who started their period before they were in junior high spoke of embarrassments associated with their developing bodies, as compared to the child-like bodies of their peers. Not one of these women said she was happy to have started. "*Because of the fact that I developed so young, I was so much taller than everybody else, [it] was uncomfortable for me. I was treated by even grown men in a way that was wrong and I didn't feel good about this,*" said Jennifer L. Thirty-year-old Dorothy, who grew up in Korea, remembers similar feelings: "*My first experience of menstruation, my body development is much earlier than other friends, and so first time I am very ashamed.*" We might also recall the comments of Liz and Robin in chapter 4, who associated promiscuity with early maturing girls; it seems that "early developers" are automatically suspected of being sexually active. These associations are part of the logic that defines (hetero)sexuality as an essential core of individual adult identity. Yet the other side of this is that several women remembered early-maturing girls as being popular and having high status in the group. While this does not necessarily mean that those early maturing girls perceived themselves in a positive light, it does help us see the positive/negative tensions that always surround the issue of women and sexuality. In *Gender Play*, Thorne shares the recollections of several of her women students who decided that "if the most popular girls started menstruating or wearing bras (even if they didn't 'need to'), then other girls wanted those changes too. But if the popular didn't wear bras and hadn't, at least to general knowledge, gotten their periods, then these developments were seen as less desirable" (1993: 142).

Mary R., aged forty-two, a white heterosexual woman and an incest survivor, grew up in a working-class family. She shared the following about her distress:

> *I was a large girl, tall in stature, and I was developing earlier than the rest of my classmates. I kept it a secret because it is hard to be different and odd and first at things. What made it difficult is that I couldn't go to my mom. I mean, we weren't close which didn't help, but the fact that I had been sexually abused did not help either, and the fact that, you know, no one else was experiencing it. I kept it* [her menarche] *a secret from my mother because I didn't know, I didn't think it was normal. In fact I wondered if it was from the abuse. It wasn't happening to my friends.*

The women who started their periods late, usually from fifteen years on, also had negative experiences surrounding timing, but none expressed distress at their lateness, and some saw it as a reprieve from the "hassles" of dealing with menstruation. Most, though, were relieved that they had "caught up" with their friends. Kitty's story is a good example. She is a white woman, aged sixty-one years, who grew up in a farming family and worked for twenty years as a teacher: "*I was just about the only one at school among my friends that had not started and I was very slow in physical development, breast development was very slow with me. And so I remember it very well, finally, finally, finally, my period started.*"

This double standard associated with pubertal timing vis-a-vis gender is further illustrated by research focusing on pubertal adjustment and social class. Clausen (1975) found early maturation to be a more positive experience for middle-class than working-class girls, and theorized that this was because more of the former could achieve the status associated with masculinity in terms of opportunities and achievement. Perhaps another issue here is that middle-class families can afford the material "stuff" that is often so important to adolescents and tends to improve their popularity and social standings in groups, their self-esteem, and therefore their experience with menarche. We found no class differences; starting to menstruate early was difficult for most women, irrespective of class standing.

Second, women's first blood stories abound with themes about acceptance and rejection of and by female friends. Central in these stories is the importance of menarche as a marker of adult status. Even though most women experienced menarche as an ambivalent time, they also understood it as a new status that inferred the privileges associated with adulthood. As forty-seven-year-old Laurel, a white middle-class woman from California, shared: *"I remember being highly envious of girls who had begun. That girl certainly gained status in our eyes, if she had started."* What is interesting about so many of these stories are the apparent contradictions. And yet, these contradictions make sense to those of us who move through the world with female bodies. Girls are embarrassed, sometimes ashamed, and almost always ambivalent, yet they also accept their membership in this lowly club as a status in and of itself, a step up, perhaps, from girlhood, and certainly something that is important in terms of acceptance in their peer group.

Women remembered their strong need to be accepted as part of the group, and the role that menarche played in this acceptance. Forty-four-year-old Bertha laughed as she shared the following: *"In gym class when they had our names called, if we had our period we had to say 'M' and that excused us from getting completely undressed for showers. I remember feeling very self-conscious by all the girls in my class who were saying 'M' before me. I remember being very anxious to be among them. I remember feeling like I wasn't part of something."* Similarly, Amy H., a thirty-nine-year-old African-American student and mother described how she had pretended to have her period for several months before she actually experienced it in order to feel accepted by her friends. She said: *"I was happy because I didn't have to lie anymore, now I was one of the girls. It was important for me to be accepted as one of the group, it was a significant event for that reason."* Gerta, almost forty years Amy's senior, also talked about how friends who had *"joined the Club"* were closer and more significant.

Most girls felt personal ambivalence about menarche, even though for many it was a source of group bonding and acceptance. The flip side of this acceptance is rejection, of course, of not being a part of the group because you had started or because you hadn't. Gretchen, one of the "early starters" mentioned above, writes about the *"separation"* between girls that may occur at this time. She shared a story about an unpopular girl whose monthly bleeding, and perhaps first blood, was a cause for further ridicule and scorn:

I think there was a real separation then between those of us who had and those of us who hadn't. It may show how insecure we were, that we were a little bit superior than the ones who hadn't even though we were not wanting to have this period. I remember going to the girl scout camp one time and one of the girls who was pretty much an outcast. I don't remember much about her except we were really mean to her in the cabin. She had started her period and wasn't doing anything about it, wasn't using pads or anything. And we like, didn't offer any assistance, and we didn't tell our counselor or anybody that she needed help. We knew she was bleeding, [we] *let her bleed, and knew it was all over her stuff. We were like, I think, making fun of her. It was pretty funny, but I think for me it was really traumatic. I felt really horrible, like I really wanted to do something to help this person, but at the same time doing it means that you have to validate that it is also happening to you. And it was a big deal, and I was too scared.*

Third, girlfriends were also important sources of information. Susan did not get any information about menarche from her mother and instead turned to her friends: "*The only education I received as far as what menstruation was about was from my friends. I had this best friend that had started when I was twelve and she used to take me into the restroom stalls at the school and show me; she goes: 'look at this, isn't this gross!'*" Others had similar stories about getting information, sometimes inaccurate, from peers. However, friends were especially useful when it came to deciding whether to use tampons. Many women reported that their mothers did not want them to use tampons because of the sexually symbolic act of inserting something into the vagina. This was true especially for several Mexican-American women who talked about the taboo over tampons, with one woman remembering how her mother was upset that she had "*devirgined*" herself. On the issues of tampons, Inez, another Mexican-American woman, shared the following:

I used the tampons mostly because I hated the pads, until she [her mother] *asked me, are you really using them? And she was like, how do you know how to do that? And I knew because my friends told me, and my mom was kind of a little upset because I talked with my friends and I was using tampons and she wasn't really in favor of that. She said "You are not a virgin anymore." But my friends would say how tampons are the greatest things because it doesn't feel like you have anything* (laugh). *I talked more with my friends about tampons and things than with my mom.*

Similarly, Laurence laughed as she remembered the instruction she and another friend received from two older girls about inserting tampons. The older girls were giving instructions through the bathroom stall doors and Laurence and her friend were supposed to report back on their progress. Laurence, who is twenty years old, grew up in a privileged home in Malaysia and was attending a co-educational boarding school at the time of her menarche. This story is of an incident that took place a few months after her first menses: "*So they are outside going 'okay, now tell us how you are doing* (laugh)*.' One girl said, 'I am fine; I got it in, it is easy.' And I was having problems, but I kept on and I go: 'I guess it is okay.' And then she had put it up the wrong hole!* (laugh)." Laurence also spoke of the solidarity she felt with other girls when she started her period while away at boarding school:

It was during choir practice, we were just singing and I felt something weird. And then a girl said "you have a little stain on your skirt." The girls' side of the choir was really restless and the guys had no idea what was happening. A bunch of girls, about three of them my close friends, escorted me to the bathroom and everything happened, they got me the pads, told me what to do, everything.

Vicky, aged thirty-four, who grew up in a working-class family in Pennsylvania, was like many other women in remembering how she could rely on friends to check for stains. "*Everybody worried about it [staining]. You know, I remember you could walk along with your girlfriends and you know, will you check the back of my dress, it feels weird? Oh no, you are fine. And blah, blah, blah we'd go on about it.*" Alina told a story of the importance of a friend's help at school when she started her period for the first time:

It was horrible. I was in class and we were sitting there. We all had tables, we had several to each table and our table was against the wall. And so I was sitting there, and I kept feeling like I had sat in a wet puddle. And I just sat there and I was like, okay, what do I do? Luckily my friend, we had the same table, and I looked over at her and she knew something was wrong. I couldn't say anything because there were boys at the table too. But I wrote a little note, and she got my coat out and she wrapped it around me and so we stood up. We walked out to the bathroom and she ran in and we pretended that I spilled something on me, and so I got some papers and books, I covered the chair up and we left. She ran back in and told the teacher that I had to see the nurse. I started to cry, it was horrible. When we got back to the classroom, I sat on top of the book because I was still too embarrassed to wipe anything up. So the day ended, everybody left and me and my friend just kept sitting there. We are still really good friends now, actually the last time we got together and we hadn't seen each other for years and we ended up talking about that, and we were just laughing so hard!

A couple of women shared how this terrible fear of staining was used to tease each other and to negotiate their placement within peer group status hierarchies. Daniella, for example, Mexican-American and aged eighteen, reported the following: "*We used to joke about it, and one time I got really mad. They told me 'you have a stain on your skirt,' and so I went to the bathroom. I ran straight to the bathroom and then I looked in the mirror and there was nothing. They were laughing and I was so mad; I was also crying and everything.*" While girls' friendships tend to be characterized by trust and loyalty, girl friends are still often seen as untrustworthy or "bitchy." Sue Lees suggests that the double-edged nature of female friendships is a consequence of a stark reality—the result of girls having to compete with each other for male attention, as well as reflective of "the narrow tightrope a girl walks to maintain a reputation that does not open herself up to ridicule or ostracism" (1993: 77–8).

Girl friends are not the only sources of support and grief during menarche. Sisters too, provide joy and conflict for girls negotiating this crucial time (Cicirelli 1980; McGoldrick 1989). Sisters indulge in much rivalry, competing and fighting with each other, as well as supporting and covering for each other when necessary. Much of the specifics of relationships between sisters has to do with age differences and birth order, as well as such things as personality and family size, resources and dynamics. Sisters who are relatively close in age can provide friendship and support for each other at menarche. Because they are more likely to be in touch with the problems that the other might be facing, they can offer help, advise and sympathy. Girls who are embarrassed to talk with a parent might find solace in the fact that their sister feels or felt the same way and, as such, a sister is a less threatening source of support, as well as someone with whom many girls find it easier to communicate (Cicirelli 1980; Hetherington 1989). In terms of menarche, age of sisters is important. Rarely do girls share information or seek support from younger sisters, and, in fact, menarche often creates a separation between these sisters that marks one as "child" and the other as "teenager."

For girls with older sisters, about two-thirds receive information about menarche from them (Brooks-Gunn and Ruble 1983). This finding holds true for our study as well. A number of the women who grew up with older sisters reported that they became prepared for the first blood through being around their sisters and watching them deal with menarche and its disciplinary practices. Laurel, for example, remembered her older sister's first period and how that experience gave her information about menarche too: *"I walked into the bathroom and the lid to the toilet was down, and my sister shrieked all of a sudden: 'don't open it!' And it is too late, and I am screaming 'mommy, mommy, Betsy's bleeding to death!' And Betsy was just mortified, and it turned out it was my sister's first period and the toilet didn't work* (laugh). *So my mother took me aside and did a lovely job."*

For the women in our study, older sisters tended to "pave the way" at menarche; sisters' experiences affected the way girls, and sometimes their families, thought about and dealt with menarche. Marie remembered her first period being *"traumatic"* because she associated it with the shame and promiscuity associated with her unmarried sister's pregnancy:

> *I remember I started my period at school; it was very traumatic. Mostly the reason why it was such an important day in my mind, I always remember when it was, because my sister was pregnant at the time and her water broke that very same day. This made it really interesting—I mean my religion is Mormon, and I don't know if you know the sort of things that we stand for, but premarital sex is basically taboo, and so it was a really bad thing, for my mother especially. My mother was extremely upset, and I know she must have gone through some terrible times with that, seeing as how she had done the same thing with having my sister, so it is interesting how that kind of went through the generations. So basically there was a sort of negative connotation towards women's sexuality.*

Other women, especially those in mid and late life, said that menarche was so "hush, hush" that they didn't even have any indication that their sisters were menstruating, despite the problems associated with concealment in those days. As sixty-four-year-old Geri said of her sister: *"We kept this really private.* [My sister] *did not really talk about it. We just knew we had it."* However, several of the older women were sent to elder sisters for a cursory lesson about menstruation and how to act like a proper young lady. Shelly, aged sixty-one, felt that had she not had an older sister, she never would have learned about life with a female body. She is German-American, worked in special education, has three daughters and one son from her first marriage and nine stepchildren from her second marriage. She shared: *"My mother was not one...she didn't talk about anything. Nothing, nothing about sex or anything really. She just...I don't know how she assumed I was going to learn this, just assimilate it* [from] *air* (laugh)." A similar memory was shared by Tess, aged sixty-eight: *"My mother was not, you know in that generation you didn't talk about things like that, but my older sister did tell me everything I needed to know. She told me about the use of the pads and what to expect and she had terrible cramps which I didn't have until later but she told me to expect that."* And Tamako, aged sixty-eight, remembered that her mother *"dispatched"* her to her *"Second Sister"* for help with her first blood: *"I felt that Second Sister was reluctant or uncomfortable about the task to educate me about my menarche. It was a brief lesson."*

Several women found themselves competing with sisters around the issue of menarche, as illustrated by Crystal T.'s story. Crystal is twenty-one, white and bisexual, and grew up in a working-class home: *"Of course, my sister had it and she was younger than me.... I used to be jealous because I am older, and how come she started before me. She, like, developed boobs before me, I think she even had hair under her arm pits and I didn't start until later. I was jealous for a while and then I realized, man, I don't want this."* Similarly, Liz, aged forty-seven and Mexican-American, remembers some rivalry between herself and her twin sister. Her overarching memory of her sister, though, is very positive, and she appreciated their closeness. They were able to provide much support and practical help for each other as they negotiated the disciplinary practices of menarche and menstruation:

> *My twin sister started first.... She would tease me, she would go: "I am special because I am older than you; you are not a señorita." So I remember she would tease me, but I didn't even care because I didn't know what it was. I didn't know what I was missing! My twin sister and I, every time we would be on our period she would say "can you make sure that I am not spotting?" And, "okay, good," and I would do the same thing: "okay, can you watch out for me?" And so we would watch each other to make sure that we weren't spotting* (laugh).

Finally, Amy S. had fond memories of the solidarity and closeness she felt with her sisters: *"Well, I was really close to both of my elder sisters and I was also sharing a room and we actually had a real open relationship about our body stuff which is cool. And so I just said: 'Oh you guys—my period started.' And they totally helped me out and you know, gave me their supplies and everything, and they were actually really caring. It was really nice."*

Boys, Brothers, and Fathers

Women also make a clear association between menarche and changing relationships with boys through the language of the body (Haug, 1987). Many women described feeling distressed that their camaraderie with boys dissipated around this time. As we already discussed in chapter 4, women often felt that they could no longer be "one of the boys," or that their friendships had become infused with the sexual tensions of early adolescence and its budding compulsory heterosexuality (Debold, Wilson and Malave, 1993). Vanessa remembered her changing relationships with boys around the time she started her first period: "*From then on I was going to look more like a girl and then I wouldn't be able to do certain things with the guys, just because they recognized me more as a girl, and indeed that happened. The more I started appearing like a girl, developing a chest and what not, the guys actually ignored me. They didn't want to play anymore, you know, go out and play soccer or whatever. And so in a way I kind of wished it hadn't happened so young. I wanted more time to live that tomboy life style I guess.*" Barbara, a strong athlete during adolescence, also spoke about this phenomenon: "*Yeah, I think it was in the sense that it separated me from the boys, and so I felt like I was going to have to dress up and just drop sports by the wayside because now it was like some way of being notified that well, you have had your fun as a tom-boy but it is time to really do what you are 'supposed' to do.*"

In terms of potential sexual relationships with boys, the risk of pregnancy which sets in at menarche influences family dynamics (Danza 1983; Hill and Holmbeck 1987). Again, research suggests that parents tend to see their daughter's emerging sexuality as more problematic than their sons, with early sexual maturation being associated with greater independence and achievement from parents for boys, but to a lesser extent for girls. The double standard of sexual conduct is obvious here. Mary P. remembered receiving instructions from her father when she first started her period: "[He said] *now you stay away from boys, don't mess with boys. So I wouldn't get pregnant, that was the idea and that was the end of it...I can just remember my parents telling us. I know that was really drilled into your head. You don't come home pregnant, you know.*" The remarks of Gerta, widow and retired teacher, illustrate the responsibilities of potential sexual relations that girls have to assume at menarche: "*During the curse, as we termed it, I was concerned about odor and spotting. My mother made it clear that now necking and petting could have serious results if we went 'all the way'—which could happen if emotions got out of hand. She also explained that if a boy's penis were allowed to touch the vaginal area that preseminal fluid often contained sperm and a pregnancy could result.*" At menarche, as girls internalize the responsibility for controlling access to their bodies, relationships with boys necessarily begin to change.

Girls learn that they are supposed to attract boys and that power comes from receiving attention from boys: "*I wanted to be more developed in my breasts and more developed in my hips, yet I did not have the breasts or the hips. You want to fit in, and a lot comes from trying to impress the boys or something. The talk around boys was, you know, egg sized and football sized breasts. And it is almost a sense that I wasn't going to be accepted by the boys either and at that age you want to be accepted by the boys* (laugh)." (Susan).

Rowena, aged sixty-two, middle-class and white/American-Indian, illustrates the ambivalence associated with this cultural directive to attract the opposite sex—the "what if he notices me, what if he doesn't?" dilemma. Girls want the attention because society says that they should, and they receive status when they get it (so long as the conditions are right); yet they often know at some level that they pay (or have paid) a price. Rowena's story exemplifies the complexity of connections between menarche, the body and changing relationships with boys and other girls:

I felt ambivalent about my body even before my period started as my breasts began developing in fifth grade. On the one hand, it was clear that it made me "more popular" with the boys. By sixth grade I was the only girl who really needed to wear a bra. The girls were mostly envious and sometimes mean and jealous, and the boys were obviously—and I thought stupidly—affected by my "womanly" body. I think I thought less of the boys because of their reactions (and still see this reaction as superficial of men who seem to remain "boys" for life in this regard). But I know I sometimes took advantage of the effect it produced, especially with the older boys who were my brother's friends. My father was obviously proud of my appearance and used to tell me "some day you will be almost as pretty as your mother." Incidentally, I still wished my breasts were smaller so that buttons on blouses would stay buttoned. In high school I purposely bought oversized sweaters and blouses to "conceal" my breasts a little. I still do! Though at sixty-one no man is looking at me who is under seventy! I think [after my period started] *I began to regard boys as more important than before. I began to act "careful" at school, to not act "too smart" although I continued to get straight A's. That was stupid!*

Part of the dilemma associated with this acting out of compulsory heterosexuality is that young adolescent males experience the entitlements associated with male privilege at the expense of girls (Lees 1993; Thorne 1993). Women talked vividly about boys who pulled at their bra straps, and dragged sweaters off their bodies that were knotted around their waists. They also recall boys asking them if they were "on the rag" when they were assertive or voiced displeasure. Ivy, a white heterosexual woman in her late twenties, shared the memorable occasion of her first period and her ride home on the school bus where she was harassed by a particularly obnoxious boy:

I felt uncomfortable because, you know, I was afraid I might have bled through or something. The bus home was crowded that day so I had to sit next to an asshole. He always bugged people, especially me for some reason, but this day he was particularly annoying. He had some kind of sculpture, it was like a swan, and I was feeling real self-conscious anyway. As I was getting off, he just kind of stuck it [the swan's neck] *right in my butt basically; he was making some kind of obscene gesture and joke, and it was like, God! I was so embarrassed!*

Compare Ivy's experiences to those of Laurel, who went to an all-girls school. In this all-female environment she remembered menarche as a badge of honor and was able to avoid a school context where boys' presence affected girls' behavior and relationships with each other. She attended an elite high school in Southern California:

I went to a private girls' school, and it was small, and I think a girls' school is such a different social environment than a public school with a mixed population. And we had all sorts of training in the facts of life; we all were exposed to the film "You Are a Young Lady Now," all about menstruation. We all knew it was coming; we were all busy whispering and buzzing amongst ourselves starting from about sixth grade on. And we felt very adult-like. It was really a rite of passage. And I think our whole school really, all the girls, we felt the same way, that it was something we talked about a lot because there was no possibility of boys overhearing it. And it was common knowledge who had started and who hadn't, and it became quite an object of envy. I remember being highly envious of girls who had begun. And the word spread like wild-fire: "She started! She did!" And then we would all look at her differently. That girl certainly gained status in our eyes, if she had started.

An important aspect of women's experience of menarche as it relates to brothers, as we have already discussed in chapter 3, is that women must conceal evidence of menarche and menstrual bleeding from them. Girls were told over and again to hide menstrual products and any evidence of their bleeding bodies from their brothers. This is usually one of their first lessons in concealment: "*She* [her mother] *said that men can smell it. She said when you go the bathroom make sure your brothers don't see paper with blood. And she said now that you have this, you can have babies, and so you make sure no boys touch you down there*" (Juanita). These messages set up a self-consciousness for girls who, prior to menarche, were used to peer relationships with boys and their brothers.

When telling their first blood stories, several women discussed how particularly negative relationships with brothers affected how they felt about themselves during this transition. In almost all these cases, their families were especially dysfunctional and girls were usually experiencing abuse of one kind or another, especially sexual abuse from either their brothers or other male relatives. Iris was in her early thirties at the time of her interview. She grew up in an abusive, fundamentalist Christian home and was worried when she started her period because her brother was sexually molesting her. She feared she might get pregnant:

It was a combination of feeling like I can't do things now because I am a woman, a most terrifying feeling of getting pregnant and having some mutant (laugh) *or some messed up child because I started my period. I knew my brother's idea of menstruation was being 'on the rag' and that was when women were bitchy and in a bad mood and that he wanted to stay away from them because you couldn't get what you wanted out of them, especially sex.*

Similarly, Hannah, who grew up in a family where she was abused and where there was open disgust for women and their bodies, remembered seeing pornography in her brother's room. She connected it to her shame associated with starting her period, and remarked: "*It was a pisser of an experience.*" Several other women had memories of pornography in their home during their early adolescence and felt that it affected their understandings of women's sexuality and thus clouded their feelings about menarche.

Several women had especially positive relationships with brothers. Remember Lula and Tita, who found older brothers supportive during this time. Others tended to feel that while they were able to maintain their good friendships, menarche separated them from their brothers in important ways. Barbara stands out as someone who talked about the importance of this relationship for her and the distance that menarche seemed to impose:

My brother and I growing up were like best friends. We did everything together and we looked like each other. People thought we were twins. When I was twelve we started to separate and I think he was really envious of the whole experience. I think he thought it was neat the way my mom celebrated it and I think he felt like he was missing out. And also the attention, I mean, when you are eleven years old and your sister [who] *has always been treated as equal, all of a sudden gets a lot more attention, that's got to be difficult. And so I think it was more like he felt left out.... That was hard.*

In almost all cases, fathers tended to dwell on the margins of women's stories about menarche. This finding is consistent with studies that have looked at how puberty affects father-daughter relationships (Apter 1990; Block 1978; Danza 1983; Pipher 1994; Ulman 1992). Fathers generally have been found to exhibit more gender differentiating behavior with their children than have mothers, and they encourage their daughters less than they do their sons (Power 1981). Fathers' influence and presence did not seem to figure in markedly important ways for the women in our study, except in the context of embarrassments and concealments, sometimes because of abuse, and very occasionally because of particularly close positive relationships with fathers. Rose briefly recalled memories of her father during menarche: *"Nothing was ever said about it. I wouldn't dare let my father know what was going on, you know* (laugh)!" (age sixty-eight, white and working class). Similarly, Elizabeth, who grew up in a home with thirteen brothers and sisters, and who was a whiz at menstrual concealment, remarked in response to a question about her father: *"There is nothing to mention!* (laugh) *I would certainly NEVER talk to my father about anything like this!"* Women often felt embarrassed or even betrayed when their mothers told fathers about their new "condition": *"I think I remember him* [her father] *talking to me and at first I was really angry. I thought well, gosh, Mom shouldn't have told him and I felt betrayed, but then I realized for some reason I kind of thought it would change my relationship with him because we had always been so close."* Fathers often acted embarrassed and uncertain how to behave, adding to girls' uncertainties and ambivalences at this time. Many women reported that their fathers were relatively uninvolved and avoided such talk about women's private bodily issues. Inez was typical in her memories of her father being in the background during this time: *"My dad didn't care because that was women's stuff and he really didn't want to know; he just stayed out of it. He knew it was not his business and he didn't get into it."* Some women also remembered using this new status with their fathers to get out of doing chores around the house, and especially to avoid yard work.

A few women bemoaned changed relationships with fathers at menarche, and, like the discussion of brothers above, felt a separation from them that was often painful. Laurel shared the following:

I think a lot of it goes back to my relationship with my father. Up until about a year before I started my periods, I was considered Daddy's little boy. In moments of fright at night, I would crawl in bed with Daddy. My parents had twin beds. I climbed trees; I was your total tomboy and Daddy's little boy. I was everything my father would want in a son. One day when I was out vigorously practicing my tennis stroke against the garage door, my sisters came up to me and said, "Laurel, come with us, you need a bra; we are taking you to the store to buy you a bra." And I looked down and jeez, I had these breasts! I really hadn't even noticed them; I certainly wasn't aware of the need for a bra. And that is what I recall as being the time that my relationship with my father started to turn, because he began to see the physical evidence, and my sisters also. This is where my sisters did the parenting for my mom. They said: "You can't sleep with Daddy anymore." I intuitively understood why and that made sense to me, and I stopped. My life started going a different path and that is when Daddy and I started to separate. My period came in the wake of all that...and I stopped being his little boy.

Other women, especially those growing up in abusive families, found relationships with fathers growing worse at this time, and tried to avoid contact with fathers. Hannah hated to be around her father and other male relatives, and Lois remembered her father's *"hot pants"* comment and the way he made her feel ashamed of her developing body around the time of her first period. Robin talked about a very good relationship with her father, but also shared the mixed messages she received about women from her father. She felt that this greatly affected her experience of menarche:

So he says: "I am so happy you are growing up, you are a woman now." And I thought that was overly dramatic (laugh)*; I was like: "Oh Dad, shut up!" My brothers and my father were very respectful of me. However, they were very disrespectful towards women. He was into pornography and shared it with my brothers. He was always making rude comments, making jokes about sex. But I think the objectification I saw of women, I mean my father couldn't drive by a woman without turning his head—I was getting two different messages. One was that he was so happy that I was his daughter and that I am a beautiful person and that now I am a woman, but at the same time I was seeing him put down women, objectify women. And I am sure I didn't want to be a woman. I didn't want that.*

Overall, menarche seemed to intensify the content and conditions of prior negative relationships with fathers, triggering more distrust and sometimes anger on the part of women. However, unlike relationships with mothers, menarche tended not to enrich an already close relationship. Becoming a woman, as signified by menarche, in almost all cases seemed to instigate the reconfiguration of relationships between fathers and daughters, often resulting in separation. This is as we might expect, given the developmental and emotional changes associated with the negotiation of gender in the family in Western societies.

In conclusion, girls' experiences of menarche cannot be disentangled from their complicated matrix of interpersonal relationships. The social construction and gendering of nuclear families and schools means that girls negotiate menarche through the discourses that frame the experiences of adolescent girls vis-a-vis their friends and family.

In accordance with the developmental hurdles of adolescence, girl friends become intensely important in providing a sense of self through participation in the group, as well as crucial information and support. Boys become important too as the gendered discourses of compulsory heterosexuality frame feelings and behaviors. Gendered practices in families intensify also, with girls becoming more closely monitored at menarche, and expected to follow normatively constructed paths toward womanhood. In contrast, boys tend to be allowed to experience the entitlements and privileges associated with masculinity, and, as a result, brothers often, though not always, separate from, and demonstrate their power over, their sisters. Mothers have often colluded with this as they socialize their daughters into the same restrictions associated with menarche and femininity as they themselves, often painfully, had endured. We found that women tended to have many negative memories of the roles their mothers played at this time, often exacerbating an already contentious relationship. However, they often remembered such negativities even when their mothers were happy about daughters' menarche, and had been helpful in terms of information and care. Sisters, like girl friends, provide support and information and, again like girl friends, can also be sources of conflict and anxiety. Fathers usually stand apart from events associated with menarche, sometimes becoming more distant yet remaining supportive, and sometimes intensifying already negative or problematic relationships with daughters. With few exceptions, we found that these relationships within the family follow relatively predictable paths that are informed by the social construction of gender and relations of domination in Western societies.

6

Older Women's Bodily Histories

> We can catalogue her being: tissue, fiber, bloodstream cell, the shape of her experience to the last moment, skin, hair, try to see what she saw, to imagine each injury she survived. That she lived to an old age. (On all parts of her body we see the years.) By the body of this old woman we are hushed. We are awed. We know that it was in her body that we began. And now we say that it is from her body that we learn. That we see our past. We say from the body of the old woman, we call tell you something of the lives we lived.
>
> —Susan Griffin, *Women and Nature*

In this book we are weaving together many voices—those of the women with whom we spoke, those representing various discursive positions, and our own—into a story about female embodiment, that is, about what it means to go through life with a female body. Thus far, we have been exploring the problematic nature of female embodiment by focusing on women's memories of the developmental turning point of menarche. Since it is a significant point of confluence in the female life course, where the various streams of what it means to be a woman coalesce, menarche is a logical place to start in reading women's bodily histories for clues about how discourses shape and mediate women's bodily experiences over the life course. In this chapter, we are going to shift our focus to another major point of confluence in the female life course—the last blood of the menopause. Like the first blood, the last blood is a normative developmental passage that is burdened with the discursive and personal ambivalences surrounding women's bodies. In exploring the experiential and discursive connections between the first blood and the last blood we hope to broaden our understanding of women's embodiment over the life course.

As witnessed in the previous chapters, the women we interviewed had strikingly similar memories of, and feelings about, their first blood and the sexualization of their bodies, despite belonging to different age cohorts, and by extension, being positioned differently vis-a-vis historical and sociopolitical contexts. We initially approached the corpus of narratives supposing that these different contexts would contribute to widely varying kinds of experiences; thus we were surprised to find that, generally speaking, women's stories of their first blood did not vary significantly vis-a-vis age cohort. That is not to suggest, of course, that the contexts in which a girl becomes a woman are immaterial, or that the 104 women in our project had homogenous experiences. We have seen, for example, the various ways the older women were impacted by a lack of convenient and effective "sanitary products" and the extraordinary efforts they went to to conceal "evidence" of their bleeding bodies. Further, while the imperative toward silence about women's bodies and the things their bodies do exists even now, older women did not have access to the wide variety of information on the menstrual career, reproduction, and women's life-span development available today (Delaney, Lupton and Toth 1988; Nathanson 1991; Weideger 1976). Daisy, a seventy-four-year-old who worked as a marine during World War II, pointed out that her parent's generation "*was that generation that just didn't talk about 'it'.*" And, as many of the older women mentioned, any topic having to do with the female body was "*hush hush.*" The result, as discussed more thoroughly in previous chapters, is that normal developmental processes were more likely to be surrounded by silence, and, by extension, ignorance and often fear, for girls and women of previous generations.

Nonetheless, despite these and other important historical dynamics shaping women's bodily histories, we consider the absence of striking generational differences in the women's *memories of* and *feelings about* their first blood experiences to reflect the fact that dominant discourses about the female body—which, as we have shown, do affect how women live with and feel about their bodies—have not changed fundamentally over the eight decades represented in our study (c.f. Banner 1992). We stress that while the specific socio-cultural discourses surrounding women and women's bodies seem to differ from era to era, they are elaborate variations on a theme. What exists tenaciously at the core is the reality that in a patriarchal society women are simultaneously objectified as, and denigrated for being, bodies.

We are going to depart from the intergenerational approach we have thus far employed in order to focus exclusively on twenty of the older women who shared their stories with us. Of the twenty-nine older women in our sample, twenty women chose to speak with us about their bodily histories in mid- and later-life. At the time of the interviews, these women were between sixty and eighty years-of-age, representing the 1910 to 1930 birth cohorts. While this sub-sample is balanced in its inclusion of relatively the same proportions of working and middle class women, the majority of women were white; one was Jewish and one was Japanese-American. Nineteen of the women lived independently in the community and one was residing in a semi-independent retirement home. All of the women were mothers and none identified as lesbian. Every woman but one worked outside the home for pay at some point in her lifetime. At the time of the interview, fifteen women were married, three were widowed, and two were divorced.

We have chosen to place special emphasis on the life-span developmental aspects of older women's bodily histories for several reasons. In the context of both mainstream and feminist research on adult development and aging, mid-life and older women rarely have been asked to reflect on their bodily experiences (MacQuarrie & Keddy 1992; Sasser-Coen 1991). It is worth repeating that human life-span development is an embodied process; while women are obviously not just bodies, nor controlled entirely by biophysical processes, our experiences over the life course are shaped by the fact that we have female bodies (c.f. Ussher 1989). To us, the older women's bodily histories are exceedingly interesting. Because the older women have lived long and experienced much, they speak from a vantage point—later life—from which younger women cannot. Their reconsiderations of their first periods and subsequent bodily histories are as much about these particular experiences as they are about the subjective meanings and understandings they have devised over time to make sense of their lives (Broch-Due 1992; Frank 1980). What is more, their perceptions about and experiences of being menstruators and living with female bodies in a misogynist society may show both continuity and change over the life course. Because each of the twenty older women had experienced natural or surgical menopause, we were able to take an exploratory look at the thematic and personal connections between their menarcheal and menopausal experiences. In particular, we were curious as to whether the disembodiment many women experienced around the time of menarche continued into mid and late adulthood. Put another way: at some point in their life course, do women find a way to mend the damage that has been done to them in this culture? Can a woman learn to fully inhabit the body she is and consider the natural things her bodily-self does as, at the very least, normal and acceptable?

As a prelude to exploring the older women's experiences surrounding the last blood, we first discuss the experiential and discursive connections between menarche and the menstrual career present in their bodily histories. This is an important place to begin because the older women's attitudes toward and experiences of the menopause are shaped strongly by the contours of their careers as menstruators. Next, we broaden our analysis, looking at the parallels between the beginning and ending of the menstrual career, focusing particular attention on the medicalization of the menopause. Lastly, given that in this culture the end of bleeding signifies the beginning of female old age, we consider how women feel about and relate to their aging bodies after the menopause.

Life-Span Developmental Impact of the First Blood

As mentioned previously, Deutsch (1944) was among the first to hypothesize the existence of a strong, direct link between a girl's first blood experience and her subsequent menstrual experiences. More to the point, she suggested that emotional and/or physical pain associated with a traumatic first blood experience would be repeated each time a woman menstruated, although with less intensity. Along the same lines, Natalie Shainess (1961) found that among the one hundred women she interviewed, those women who had memories of negative first blood experiences were more likely to have current menstrual problems. Given that neither Deutsch nor Shainess looked empirically at the developmental association between menarche and menstrual experiences, their findings should be seen as suggestive.

Our examination of the few empirical studies that have focused on the relationship between the menarcheal experience and menstrual patterns have turned-up conflicting findings. Woods, Dery and Most (1982) systematically studied the connection between menarcheal and subsequent menstrual experiences, finding little support for Deutsch's theory. While most of the 193 women in their study recollected feeling great ambivalence toward menarche, there was little evidence of a relationship between the quality of the first blood experience and current menstrual attitudes and symptoms, suggesting that "the self-fulfilling prophesy that might have been set in motion by negative menarcheal experiences seems more a myth than reality" (292). Instead, Woods and colleagues found that their respondents' attitudes toward menstruation were related to their *current*, rather than their first, menstrual experience: women with problematic menstrual patterns were more likely to construe menstruation negatively, despite the quality of their first blood experience. Results from a similar study by Golub and Catalano (1983) support Woods, Dery and Most's overall findings. It is important to note that these studies predominately focused on the connection between menarcheal and menstrual *symptomology*, as opposed to the continuity or discontinuity in attitudes and meanings surrounding these phenomenon.

A different picture emerges from the work of Brooks-Gunn and Ruble, who report that their findings "suggest that some aspects of the first menstrual experience may affect subsequent experiences" (1983: 174). Girls who began menstruating earlier than their friends and girls who were not prepared for menarche had more negative first blood experiences and more symptomology during subsequent periods than girls who were "on-time" and well-prepared (c.f. Ruble & Brooks-Gunn 1982). This study points out two important factors which, as we have seen, shape girl's menarcheal experience and may have life-span developmental implications: timing, that is, whether a girl is "early" or "late" in her development *compared to her peers*; and information about and preparation for her first blood. Obviously, these two factors interact—an early-maturing girl is less likely to be prepared for menarche than an "on-time" or late-maturing girl (c.f. Rierdan, Koff and Stubbs 1989). We have already illustrated and discussed the negative impact inadequate preparation can have on girls, as well as the social stigma directed at girls who develop "precociously" (Thorne 1993). The point here is that girls whose bodies develop and bleed "earlier" than their friends may feel confusion and resentment about having bleeding bodies; because her girlfriends are not yet bleeding, the girl who reaches menarche "early" has no point of reference against which to normalize her experiences. Without a context for normalizing her experiences, she may also be more susceptible to the onslaught of cultural indoctrination that occurs at this time (Pipher 1994; Ussher 1989). An unfortunate outcome for such a girl may be that her subsequent bodily experiences, in particular her menstrual career, are impacted negatively.

In sum, despite similarities in the quantitative research measures and analyses these researchers employed, their findings provide a rather unclear picture of the developmental connections between the first blood experience and the menstrual career. A source of complexity in such studies is the fact that menarche and menstruation are phenomenologically different—while menarche is a major developmental event, menstruation is an ongoing, more-or-less cyclical process. Thus, the meaning a woman makes of her menstrual career may reflect more strongly her *current* menstrual experiences and attitudes, rather than her first blood per se. Also keep in mind that, to date, studies have been based on the experiences of contemporary girls, and thus the findings may not reflect the experiences of current cohorts of older women.

In our study, the older women's menstrual careers varied in terms of cyclical regularity, amount of bleeding, and presence of emotional and physical discomfort. However, this variation between women did not appear to be systematically related to variations in the physiological characteristics of their first blood (such as timing, amount of blood, or presence of pain), nor, given that most of the older women were sadly lacking in unbiased and meaningful information, to their amount of preparation for menarche. Rather, what seemed to be the most salient factor shaping how the older women experienced their bleeding bodies throughout their menstrual careers were the messages they received as girls about the *meaning* of women's bleeding bodies. That is to say, as adult women, their experiences of their bodies and the things their bodies do were mediated by the pervasive cultural message that menstruation is something disgusting, problematic, and to be concealed. The objective characteristics of their first blood and subsequent bleedings were of less importance than the subjective attributions these women learned to assign to their bodily experiences.

Throughout their menstrual careers, the older women considered their bleeding to be disruptive to their daily lives. This was true particularly for those women who felt they had problematic menstrual cycles. Not knowing when or if one's bleeding would begin, or having an extremely heavy flow, meant one had to be prepared at all times. The rules of menstrual etiquette that demanded planning gave the implicit message that others must not be confronted by one's physical and emotional "messiness." Rose, aged sixty-eight, would avoid planning trips or attending social events when she thought she might be bleeding. Unfortunately for her, her attempts throughout her menstrual career to plan her life around her bleeding were constantly thwarted: *"I just never knew when it was going to be and I couldn't plan anything because we never knew when* [my period] *was going to start and I had to be prepared at all times. It was very frustrating. I charted* [on a calendar] *and it was absolutely no good at all. I could be as far as three weeks late."* Similarly, Kitty, aged sixty-one, who had regular but very heavy bleeding, spoke about how important it was for her to consistently keep track on her calendar when her bleeding was due to begin. Like Rose, she scheduled her life around her bleeding *"so I could prepare myself. I think the main thing was always this worry about will I have stuff with me? The main thing for me was just being prepared, but that's just the way I live, I am very prepared."*

We find it very telling that a majority of the older women—despite whether they perceived their menstrual careers as having been problematic or not—described their bleeding bodies as *"something to dread," "a mess,"* and as *"a pain in the neck."* What Jennifer L., age sixty-one, hated was *"just the physicalness of it, the messiness of it."* Jennifer's words reflect vividly the misogynist discourses which denigrate women's bodies and the things women's bodies do. Her use of the term "physicalness" is very intuitive: women's bleeding bodies remind us of our essential physicalness, our untranscendable stuckness in the organic.

The fact that the older women began menstruating before the advent of convenient and sophisticated "sanitary products" may have contributed in part to the enormous amount of energy and time they spent, over many years, on regulating their bodies and behaviors. Not surprisingly, once these women had access to disposable pads and tampons, they quickly abandoned the more-burdensome homemade versions. However, while these new products were more reliable and less prone to leakage, women did not alter their excessive self-monitoring behaviors. We feel something deeper must be going on here. Such hyper-vigilance in managing one's bleeding body suggests strongly that at the first blood young women internalize the teachings of this culture which construe the female body as troublesome, embarrassing, and not to be trusted. What is more, these teachings have great persistence and longevity—the women's feelings of dirtiness, shame and constriction of freedom which defined their first blood defined the entirety of their menstrual careers. Bleeding never became a mundane or taken-for-granted aspect of life with a female body, something natural and integrated into one's life pattern. Not one of these older women spoke of being a "menstruator" (c.f. Martin 1987). Instead, menstruation continued to be seen as some-thing that happened to them and was out of their control—a feeling shared, as we have already discussed in chapter 4, by the younger women as well. A case in point: the pubescent tendency toward "making sure" (Patterson and Hale 1985) that one's bleeding was contained and one's body hygienic persisted for the older women until they were no longer bleeding. Ann's clever double entendre that she always "*went along with the flow*" is ironic given how excessively she regimented her life around her menstrual cycle. As she stated, "[If] *I knew my period was going to be close, I didn't want to go.*" In sum, we see here how a large proportion of these women's lifetimes has been circumscribed by natural bodily processes which are construed—and ultimately experienced—as frightfully disruptive.

Connections Between the Beginning and Ending of the Menstrual Career

The first blood and the last blood have much in common. Menarche and the menopause are normative developmental passages representing the beginning and ending, respectively, of the cyclical organization of women's bodily histories. Like menarche, the menopause is a bodily event which has psychosocial, cultural, and historical meanings (Dickson 1993). And, like the first blood, the last blood is viewed through and distorted by a misogynist lens, is pathologized and misconstrued, and generally goes uncelebrated and unritualized as a rite of passage (Greer 1991; Mankowitz, 1991; Weideger 1976).

Writers on the menopause, like many women, often use the term "menopause" to refer to all of the biophysical and psychosocial changes that occur during midlife that are associated with a woman's shift in status from reproductive to nonreproductive. In fact, the menopause is a distinct event—the cessation of the menses—which occurs as part of a long-term biophysical process, extending approximately from the ages of forty-five to sixty, and called the climacteric (Ussher 1989; Voda 1993). Among other biophysical changes, during the climacteric the amount of hormones produced by the ovaries fluctuates and steadily declines. As a result, the quality and timing of bleedings becomes harder to predict—some months a woman may bleed heavily and for many days, and in other months she may not bleed at all, or only a scant amount. In conjunction with the fluctuation of and decline in hormones women may experience "hot flashes," and vaginal and urinary changes; some women also report feeling depressed, irritable and nervous (Cutler and Garcia 1992; Ussher 1989; Voda 1993). When the ovaries no longer produce enough estrogen and progesterone (around the age of fifty for women living in western societies) the last bleeding occurs. When a woman has not bled for twelve consecutive months, she has officially experienced the menopause (Voda 1993). The only sign of the menopause that all women experience is the cessation of bleeding.

Medicalization of the Menopause

Historically, dominant discourses about the menopause have been predicated on psychoanalytic theory. Accordingly, the end of bleeding has been construed as a traumatic and crazy-making event, and menopausal women represented as irritable, depressed, and socially superfluous (Delaney, Lupton and Toth 1988; Kahana, Kiyak, and Liang 1981; Martin 1987; Ussher 1989). In a sociocultural context in which women are essentialized as reproducers and sex objects, the menopause signifies the end of a woman's sexual and social life (De Beauvoir 1952; Dickson 1993; Greer 1991). The combined forces of ageism and sexism render the menopausal woman redundant, useless, unattractive and old. If the first blood initiates the sexualization of girls' bodies, the menopause certainly initiates the de-sexualization of women's bodies.

As we have described previously, an extension of the "biology is destiny" rhetoric of psychoanalytic theory is the contemporary medicalization of the menstrual career, with the biomedical paradigm conceptualizing the menopause as a hormone deficiency disease. As such, the menopause is defined as "a cluster of symptoms, led by hot flashes and vaginal atrophy, including, also, many diffuse psychological problems" (Dickson 1993: 36), which are "cured" by hormone replacement therapy (see Cutler and Garcia 1992; Voda 1993). Despite considerable biomedical advances during the past few decades in knowledge about and "treatment" of the menopause, we still have little empirical data on the menopause as a nonpathological, normative, lifespan developmental transition. Only recently have feminist studies on the potentially liberating and positive dynamics of the menopause come on the scene. Popular works such as Dena Taylor and Amber Coverdale Sumrall's (1991) edited volume *Women of the Fourteenth Moon* and Marian Van Eyk McCain's (1991) *Transformation Through Menopause* celebrate the menopause as a developmental milestone in the female life course. Similarly, the brilliant interdisciplinary research articles compiled in Joan Callahan's (1993) *Menopause: A Midlife Passage* challenge dualistic, reductionistic, sexist and ageist discourses on the menopause.

The older women in our study are positioned historically such that their climacteric and menopausal experiences coincided with major advances in the medicalization of the menstrual career. In particular, during the 1960s and 70s, hormone replacement therapy and hysterectomy became the two most common "cures" for "female problems" (Cutler and Garcia 1992; MacPherson 1993; Ussher 1989; Voda 1993). Of the twenty older women we are considering in this chapter, seven had elective hysterectomies during midlife for heavy bleeding, endometriosis, and, in one case, fibroid (benign) tumors. Of these seven women, three were placed on hormone replacement therapy (HRT) because their ovaries were removed along with their uteruses. Six of the women experienced natural menopause without hormone replacement therapy, and seven natural menopause with HRT. In a way, HRT and hysterectomy have become the major commodities and disciplinary practices associated with the menopause; they are virtually inseparable from the phenomenology of the menopause, much in the same way "sanitary products" and concealment are inseparable from the phenomenology of menstruation. As we will see, biomedicine defines and closely manages the menopausal experiences of contemporary women living in the west.

Initially, we were shocked by the number of older women who had had hysterectomies for elective reasons (none of the women had life threatening conditions). However, we discovered that the incidence rate of hysterectomy was quite high in the 1960s and has increased steadily since; in 1962, approximately 31 percent of menopausal women had hysterectomies, and, by the 1980s, a woman had a 50 percent lifetime chance of having her uterus removed (Cutler and Garcia 1992). Currently, it is estimated that 1,700 hysterectomies are performed each day. What we find even more disturbing is that one-half of the hysterectomies performed during the past ten years may have been medically unnecessary (Ussher 1989; Voda 1993). As Voda maintains:

> Hysterectomies in this country are usually performed to correct a benign or misdiagnosed condition, such as dysfunctional uterine bleeding, whether this is caused by fibroids (benign tumors) or is simply a normal change in the menstrual bleeding pattern. Since physicians do not regard a woman's uterus as an important organ once reproductive life has ended, treatment for fibroids and/or dysfunctional bleeding has been to remove the organ surgically. (1993: 188)

And, almost as if completing Voda's statement, Ussher says: "The ease with which the medical profession removes the womb is more a reflection of misogynist attitudes toward the female body and reproduction than a reflection of the need for the operation" (1989: 114). Rather than normalizing the changes in menstrual patterns that accompany this developmental stage in the female life course, the medical profession normalizes the surgical and pharmaceutical treatment of these changes. This is seen in Kitty's experiences. Kitty remembered that, while she had a relatively easy menstrual career, the changes she experienced during the climacteric were difficult and disruptive, and eventually lead to an elective hysterectomy:

> *I had problems. I was about forty-six, which is early, and* [I had] *very irregular periods and this kind of thing, and then a lot of bleeding. And excessively so. We began lots of different medications, I can't even remember which kind, to try to get the periods back on cycle or level things off. Anyway, after many years of this I was, let's see...about five years of on-and-off problems with menopause, hot flashes, vaginal atrophy. I had everything that went along with it—no problems during menstruation, then menopause set in. I can't remember that I was irritable or blue because that is not my nature, and you hear sometimes that irritation sets in. But it was a lot of hot flashes and so forth. Because I bled so much—three weeks out of the month was bleeding—finally we said, well maybe we better just do a hysterectomy because it was just getting crazy, and nothing worked as far as pills and stuff went, and so I just had a total hysterectomy.*

Because she was inadequately informed about the normal changes she would experience during the climacteric, Kitty perceived herself as being too early for the menopause, and thus assumed the pattern of her bleeding was abnormal. We wonder how she might have thought about and managed her irregular and sometimes heavy bleeding, as well as her hot flashes and vaginal dryness, had she been aware that she was experiencing normal changes that are indicative of the climacteric process. Ussher (1989) points out that women use very subjective criteria when assessing whether or not they experience heavy bleeding—for some women very small amounts of bleeding are defined as heavy, and vice-versa. We do not doubt that bleeding three weeks out of the month can be terribly inconvenient and uncomfortable, and that one may feel desperate for some form of amelioration. Nor are we suggesting that a woman's subjective experiences should be distrusted or undermined, or that a woman has to accept discomfort even if it is "normal." However, we do question whether a total hysterectomy—a radical surgical procedure—was the best and only solution in Kitty's situation, and even then whether she would have made this choice had she been exposed to diverse and accurate information about what was going on with her body.

Equally shocking are the rates at which midlife women routinely are prescribed hormone replacement therapy, the goal of which, as Ussher candidly points out, always has been "the preservation of a serviceable vagina" (1989: 107). During the late 1960s and the 1970s, the decades during which most of the older women in our study were experiencing climacteric changes and the menopause, fifty-one percent of women in the United States used HRT, on average for ten years (Cutler and Garcia 1992). Currently, it is estimated that one-third of women over fifty are using HRT regularly (Voda 1993). Ann Voda suggests that while HRT is definitely necessary for women who have been "castrated," that is, had their ovaries removed, it is rarely necessary for women experiencing natural menopause, for whom the passage through the menopause is so gradual as not to cause estrogen deficiency. What is more, given the conflicting conclusions from recent studies of HRT's side-effects (c.f. MacPherson 1993), there are still many questions about HRT that need to be explored, such as: "What are its long-term effects? What is its relationship to heart disease, stroke, cancer, and osteoporosis? Is it advisable for all women or only some? Should it be taken for just a short time at onset of menopause or be prescribed for life? Is it worth risking the possibility of uterine cancer in order to reduce the risk of bone fracture?" (Ladd 1993: 195). Further, Rosalind Ladd cautions that while current research demonstrates that HRT is effective in reducing hot flashes and vaginal dryness, HRT's long-term affects are unknown, and its connection to emotional and psychological complaints is dubious. In the context of self-advocacy, these are vital issues about which women need information. Unfortunately, for women of earlier generations, these concerns were not even being articulated, let alone addressed.

In our study, half of the twenty older women were prescribed HRT to maintain ovarian functioning and "cure" menopausal "symptoms," such as hot flashes, vaginal dryness, heavy bleeding, irritability, and depression. Shelly had read enough to be aware of some of the risks associated with HRT, and thus decided initially to go through natural menopause "cold turkey," that is, without HRT. She soon changed her mind, however, because she was so bothered by hot flashes and night sweats. At the time of the interview, she had been taking hormones for ten years:

I had started going to a gynecologist for my yearly checkups so I did talk to him about it [the menopause]. *I am quite a reader and I do read all the articles in all the women's magazines and I am not afraid to ask questions of my doctor. I talked to him about those kinds of things and he said, "Well, of course your periods are going to stop." So, I wasn't afraid of this happening. In fact, I was kind of looking forward to not having to deal with that all the time anymore. We talked about the hot flashes and to watch out for osteoporosis. We talked about all the different things that happen to women's bodies after* [the menopause]. *He wanted to put me on estrogen, but I thought, well, I am going to go cold turkey. I don't want to deal with that. I was kind of afraid of breast cancer and uterine cancer. Oh, it was terrible without the estrogen. I was in a sweat all the time. Of course, they were worse at night when you were trying to sleep. I think I went about three months from the time I had my last period until I went in and I said, "I can't stand this, I got to do something, got to try something." So then he put me on estrogen—so many days on, so many days off and then I'd have a period. I am not sure I would want to go off of it. I think probably the benefits of it outweigh the worry.*

Tess, a sixty-eight-year-old, middle-class white woman, was prescribed HRT for depression after her uterus was removed: "I didn't ever have any real bad problems but I did have some problem with depression and that was one reason why I took hormones. I had never had anything but a sweaty clammy feeling, I never had hot flashes as such." Similarly, Rose, who experienced natural menopause, went to see her gynecologist when her periods became even more irregular than normal and she found herself crying uncontrollably at work "for no reason." Her doctor prescribed HRT:

I read some information, magazines and that sort of thing but I hadn't really thought about it because I thought that is in the future yet, I don't need to be concerned about it. [The doctor] *didn't tell me a great deal I didn't already know from what I had read. He just said that he would give me some hormones to help my nerves and that sort of thing, to help calm me, I guess, or do something. I am not really sure what it was supposed to do, but that did help and that is about all that they ever did.*

Rose's use of the phrases *"or something," "I think," "I guess,"* and *"I am not really sure"* stand out to us like beacons, pointing to the "textual unconsciousness" of her narrative (Steele 1989). What we really hear Rose saying is that she abdicated much control over her health to her doctor—she had little idea what she was being medicated with, and what effect the treatment was supposed to have, nor why her doctor had prescribed the drug in the first place.

We find it revealing that both Rose and Tess were prescribed HRT for depression, a treatment which has yet to be demonstrated effective or appropriate (Cutler and Garcia 1992; Ladd 1993; MacPherson 1993; Voda 1993). Moreover, neither physician inquired as to whether personal or family issues might be contributing to Rose's and Tess's feelings and complaints, and instead assumed their depression had a biological (hormonal) etiology. It is misogynistic and simplistic to reduce women's psychological and emotional functioning to their reproductive systems. Health care providers need to care about what is going on in women's lives, in addition to and besides hormonal changes and the end of fertility. There are many social, psychological, and biophysical challenges that arise during midlife that may contribute to feelings of depression, irritability, or sleep disturbances, such as the loss of a spouse or elderly parent, economic stress, changes in health status, and the combined effects of sexism and ageism. For example, Rose, whom we quoted from above, remembers that she and her husband were having many family problems around the time she was going through the menopause. She shared that there were *"things that were going on around us that we couldn't control,"* and felt this might have been why her emotions were close to the surface.

Let us make it clear at this point that our purpose in this chapter is not to enter into the complex debate about the pros and cons of HRT and hysterectomy, nor to position ourselves on one side or the other of the controversy. For us to suggest—from our vantage point as women who are still menstruating—that HRT and hysterectomy are unacceptable and damaging solutions under *all* circumstances is to treat women as incapable of making informed choices. However, we do feel it is important to emphasize the political nature of the medicalization of women's bodies, that for the past thirty years the medical establishment (in collusion with pharmaceutical conglomerates) has been defining *for* women what is acceptable, tolerable and normal. In the case of HRT, the ageist and (hetero)sexist sub-text must not be overlooked—the original intent of hormone replacement therapy was to keep women "feminine" and "young" for men's pleasure as long as possible (Ussher 1989; Zita 1993). According to Robert Wilson, the gynecologist who originated the rhetoric that menopause is an estrogen deficiency disease in his book *Feminine Forever,* "estrogen therapy doesn't change a woman...it keeps her from changing" (1966: 53). Interpretation: the normal, natural changes that happen to women's bodily-selves as they go through the life course should be denied, controlled, and medicated. Castrate a woman when she is no longer a reproducer and sex object (she doesn't need those organs anymore, anyway), but be sure she takes her hormones so she looks and acts like she's still a reproducer and sex object.

What we find almost more disturbing than the readiness with which the medical profession has sanctioned the cutting and drugging of midlife women's bodies is the overall lack of self-advocacy exercised by many women at the end of their menstrual careers (c.f. Ladd 1993; Voda 1993). We certainly found this to be true for most of the older women in our study. Self-advocacy in medical decision making is difficult for us all, but can be particularly difficult for midlife and older women because of the combined impact of the medicalization of the menopause, paternalism on the part of health care providers, and general lack of access to accurate and unbiased knowledge. Of "our" twenty older women, only two seemed to make informed choices about HRT, in both cases against the advice of their doctors. Even though she used the slogan "*estrogen is great*," Louie decided that the benefits of taking hormones did not outweigh her risk of developing breast cancer. She took estrogen for awhile after she had a single mastectomy, and really enjoyed the increased energy and weight control it gave her. But she "*studied up on it and chose not to take it myself....* [I] *still have one breast, so why ask for it? So I chose not to take it.*" After she discontinued HRT, Louie discovered that if she kept exercising and taking care of herself, she had little difficulty maintaining her energy level and weight.

The second woman demonstrating that she made an informed choice about HRT was Daisy. She had just started the menopause when, at the age of forty-nine, her doctor recommended she have a hysterectomy for heavy bleeding and benign fibroids. After the hysterectomy, she was prescribed HRT. She seemed to have a very down-to-earth attitude about the whole thing:

I had a young doctor who said, "Well, if you were my mother I'd insist you take hormones." And I said, "O.K., I'll try it." I tried it twice and both times I flushed the stuff down the toilet. I said, "I do not need to be a teenager again. I do not need sore breasts, I do not need my face breaking out. I do not need that." He finally gave up on me. I have a big heavy bone structure and I feel that my system must have produced estrogen for a long time after I had the hysterectomy.

How can it be acceptable for a young, male physician to say to a mature woman "if you were my mother [or wife] I'd insist you take HRT?" To say such a thing is to patronize a woman and treat her like a caricature of her younger self. Certainly, well-meaning health care providers want to prevent and ameliorate suffering and death, and many menopausal women want to be cured of the discomforts and uncertainties associated with the end of their menstrual careers. Some women, unfortunately, do have pathological conditions such as cancer of the reproductive organs and therefore need hysterectomies and HRT not only in order to survive, but to maintain an acceptable quality of life (Cutler and Garcia 1992; Voda 1993). And, some women find the natural hormonal changes associated with the climacteric too disruptive and uncomfortable to tolerate, and thus opt for HRT. The point we want to make is that women have a right (and must learn) to make *informed* decisions about what is done to their bodily-selves, about the risks they are willing to assume in order to maintain their desired quality of life. We think Ladd clearly lays out the changes that both physicians and women need to make:

> Physicians need to abandon the psychogenic model which is denigrating when applied to menopause-age women as a class. In doing so, they will be abandoning many of the myths they have inherited from past generations of the medical profession. To substitute for the old myths, they need to listen to women's voices about their own experience and explore with each individual patient her own values and preferences...Women must be willing to assert their right to participate in decision making, do the hard work of recognizing and voicing their own values and goals, and, perhaps most difficult of all, be willing to accept responsibility for making their own choices. (1993: 201)

Life After The "Good-Riddance"

Because it symbolizes the end of reproductive life, the menopause is assumed to be a traumatic and threatening event for mid-life women. Discourse frames this time in a woman's life as the brink of old age, and the end of fertility as just the first of many losses to come: loss of youth, beauty, sex appeal, grown children. As if a woman's only role were as servant to the species, the woman who no longer bleeds is thought to grieve for the end of reproduction and her permanently empty nest, to become asexual and un-womanly (Brooks-Gunn and Kirsch 1984; Greer 1991; Ussher 1989). Just as witnessed in earlier chapters, to focus on menarche is necessarily to consider the sexualization of young women's developing bodies. Similarly, when we look at dominant discourses about the menopause we witness a systematic de-sexualization of mature women's bodies, bodies which are still being defined by the male gaze. Ussher asks "Is this the fate of all women: to feel obsolete...to feel invisible and inadequate? Are the last forty years of a woman's life inevitably spent looking back in longing at the years of youth and fertility?" (1989: 195)

Given the way the menopause is construed in this culture, it is not surprising that when women *anticipate* the end of their menstrual careers, they often express quite ambivalent feelings about, and attitudes toward, this normative event. They are not sure whether they should celebrate their "change of life" as a developmental milestone or regard it as a debilitative condition requiring medical treatment (Greer 1991; Leiblum and Swartzman 1986). Not surprisingly, a great deal of women's ambivalence and difficulty before and during the menopause has to do with feeling unprepared and unknowledgeable. Many women say that the very worst thing about the end of the menstrual career was not knowing what to expect, and therefore expecting the worst (LaRocco and Polit 1980; Neugarten, Wood, Kraines, and Loomis 1963). When women do receive information and advice about the menopause from magazines, family members, friends, or health care providers it usually "reflects and reinforces the broader culture's underlying assumptions about women's biology, women's aging, and women's roles in contemporary American society" (Barbre 1993: 24).

It is quite surprising, then, that while women's expectations about the end of bleeding are strongly informed by dominant discourses, quite often their expectations are not borne out by their experiences. As Ussher suggests "This negative construing is not an inevitable process: the horrors of the menopause are not experienced by all women" (1989: 105). Echoing Ussher, Martha, aged sixty, recalled "*I was really expecting the worst but it didn't happen* (laugh)." Research demonstrates that when post-menopausal women are asked how they feel in retrospect about the menopause, most report having few regrets about the end of fertility, and do not remember the menopause as a traumatic event (Kahana, Kiyak, and Liang 1981; Ladd 1993). Similarly, in the classic empirical study of women's attitudes toward the menopause conducted in the early 1960s, Bernice Neugarten and her colleagues demonstrated that as women moved from pre to post-menopausal, their perceptions of and feelings about the menopause improved. Again, often reality does not match expectation. In contrast, and not surprisingly, young women and men of all ages have been found to consider the menopause as much more disruptive and traumatic than do postmenopausal women (Kahana, Kiyak, and Liang 1981); similar findings have been reported regarding the perceptions of physicians and nurses versus those of mid-life women (Ladd 1993).

Many women are surprised to discover positive psychological and physiological aspects of the menopause, most obviously freedom from the "hassles" of menstruation and reproduction (Engel 1987;

Neugarten, Wood, Kraines and Loomis 1963). Emily Martin (1987) reports that most of the working- and middle-class women in her study described the menopause as a natural stage in their life course; some women even found that they were happier and had greater energy at the end of their menstrual careers. For those women who are mothers, major child-rearing tasks are usually complete, and for perhaps the first time in their lives they can focus on their own interests and desires (Delaney, Lupton, and Toth 1988; Rubin 1979). There is some research suggesting that white women who define themselves primarily as mothers often find the end of reproduction disruptive and traumatic (Berkun 1985; Kahana, Kiyak, and Liang 1981; Rubin 1979). Research on the menopausal experiences of African-American women in the United States provide conflicting findings on this point (Kahana, Kiyak, and Liang 1981; Martin 1987; Ussher 1989).

What we see clearly in the research literature is that midlife women who have other roles and sources of meaning in addition to or besides motherhood, particularly employment for pay outside the home, report experiencing less biophysical symptomology, depression, or trauma in connection with the end of bleeding (Barnett 1984; Block, Davidson, and Grambs 1981; Martin 1987). Cross-cultural research on the menopause lends support to these findings as well—women living in cultures which treat the menopause as a normative passage and convey prestige and respect to women as they age report experiencing little, if any, menopausal depression and distress (c.f. Olesen and Woods 1986). Taken together, we feel these findings provide further support for the notion that women's bodily experiences over the life course are strongly shaped by sociocultural discourses (Buckley and Gottlieb 1988; Delaney, Lupton, and Toth 1988; Ussher 1989).

Because of their placement in history, we anticipated that many of the older women we spoke with would remember feeling ambivalent about the end of their menstrual careers—that is, a combination of sadness for the end of their young and fertile years, and relief at being free of a life organized around bleeding and reproduction. As we discussed in chapter 2, the older women in our study came of age during an historical era when, despite rapidly expanding educational and employment opportunities for women, girls were still primarily socialized and expected to be wives and mothers, before and above all else (Allen and Pickett 1984; Nathanson 1991). Contrary to what we supposed, however, these women tended to have no regrets about being unable to birth any more children; they had finished with that part of their lives long ago and were now happy to be liberated from reproduction. Many described enjoying *"sexual relations"* much more after the menopause since they no longer had to worry about unwanted pregnancy or schedule their love-making around their bleedings. Such feelings of liberation were true regardless of whether a woman had had a problematic or nonproblematic menstrual career or experienced surgical or natural menopause.

Lula, age seventy-five, wrote a humorous and entertaining bodily history entitled "The Scourge." She described being so plagued by menstrual cramps that she dreaded life whenever the time for another menses came around. Lula shared the following about *"the good-riddance"*:

I have not felt anything but relief since I no longer menstruate. I ended up with endometriosis, finally a hysterectomy, and was very happy to get rid of the entire mess! I felt just fine about the "good-riddance!" By the time I was ready for closing up shop, I had had three babies, been to gynecologists many, many times, and so was well prepared for anything, I think. I now wonder: If God had the making of Woman over again, would He follow the same pattern—make Her out of His rib (causes a lot of inequality), give her child-bearing (sure keeps the man in the dark), find another better way to insure her fertility (maybe just take some kind of a pill instead of men-struating?) No offense intended, God—just wondering!

Daisy, whom we quoted from earlier, described being sexually and physically liberated by the end of reproduction. Remember that Daisy, who had an elective hysterectomy for bleeding and fibroids, flushed her hormone pills down the toilet:

It was just one of those things. It is a part of aging and I'll say this, had I known what a relief it was not to have a uterus, I'd have found a quack twenty-nine years sooner and had a hysterectomy! I don't think that life ends at menopause, I think it begins. These people who feel they are less than a woman are feeling sorry for themselves. Sexually they are freer than they ever have been, and physically they are freer than they have ever been.

Jennifer L. told us that surgical menopause was *"the most liberating thing I think that ever happened to me. It is a very liberating thing to not have to worry about getting pregnant,"* and Alex declared *"I am so glad it is over with, lets put it that way. I imagine you will be too when your time comes."* Kitty, who shared with us that she felt *"freed up by the end of reproduction,"* had no regrets about the fact that her freedom came as a result of hysterectomy: *"That part of my body had served its purpose and it didn't change my feelings about myself. I am still a woman regardless of whether I have a uterus or not."* While Tess, who had a hysterectomy due to heavy bleeding, questions whether she would have a hysterectomy today, given what she now knows, she is adamant that the relief from pain she experienced following the end of her menstrual career far outweighed any grief she might have felt about loosing her reproductive ability. Contrary to what dominant discourses would have us believe, these women did not feel like "damaged goods," like castrated women. Instead, they spoke about the relief they felt to be through with the "mess" of having a bleeding body. As Shelly stated: *"I was kind of looking forward to not having to deal with that all the time anymore."*

In thinking on the women's unequivocally positive reconsiderations of the menopause it occurred to us that given that so many of these women felt bewildered and constrained throughout their menstrual careers, particularly by the changes leading to the last blood, it is understandable that they would feel freed-up by the menopause, whether natural or surgical. Just as the beginning and middle of their menstrual careers were strongly shaped by negative cultural messages about menstruation and women's bodies, the end of bleeding was as well. Considering the way women's bodies and bleeding are construed in this culture, is it any wonder that these women were relieved to vacate such symbolically loaded territory, even if such freedom came as the result of a major surgical procedure? For thirty to forty years they had felt constrained and limited by their bleeding bodies. Many of them birthed and raised more children than they might have, had they had access to birth control, and all of them shaped a large proportion of their lifetimes around taking care of their families. At the same time, they built for themselves interesting and active lives. During midlife, all of these women participated in paid work, educational programs, volunteerism, travel, or other activities. Thus, by the time they had finished menstruating or were *"closing up shop,"* as Lula put it, they had nothing about which to feel sentimental or regretful.

For these women, the few years immediately after the menopause were an oasis of sorts, a time of heightened freedom, energy and confidence in their bodily-selves. However, for the older women with whom we spoke this was also a time of transition—they described becoming increasingly aware of the passage of time, of their personal aging. For them, the issue of how to reconcile their new-found sense of freedom with the inevitability of aging became incredibly salient.

Aging Bodies

As we have discussed, the menopause functions as a crucial signifier of female old age. The combined forces of sexism and ageism (and in many cases racism, classism, and heterosexism) affect the lives of all women as they age, to one degree or another. Androcentric, advanced capitalistic, youth-oriented cultures have little use for women who can no longer fulfill the roles of reproducer and sex-object. A woman is as valuable as she is young, beautiful, and fertile (Gerike 1990; Greer

1991; MacDonald and Rich 1983; Sontag 1972; Wolf 1991). At the first visible sign of aging, women are named ugly, used-up, and sexually repulsive. While mid-life is often a time of heightened power and prestige for men, particularly white men, by mid-life a woman is considered past her prime, her opportunities few, her choices limited (Rosenthal 1990; Rubin 1979). And it is a sign of the normative and invasive nature of these cultural standards that individual women often internalize them, at once striving to maintain a veneer of youthful "perfection" so as not to be betrayed by their aging bodies, and wondering if their socially valued lives are finished (c.f. Block, Davidson, and Grambs 1981; Copper 1988; Moss 1970).

Since in the United States the majority of women can expect to live approximately thirty years beyond the menopause (Cutler and Garcia 1992), this means that for a time nearly equivalent to the menstrual career women culturally are defined as uninteresting, asexual, and redundant. Truth be told, during these thirty years, the impact of the passage of time on a woman's body becomes increasingly apparent. As Cleo Berkun recites: "Sometime around the age of fifty, unless surgical menopause has occurred earlier, menopause occurs. Other bodily changes occur: It is likely that women need fewer calories to maintain their body weight, it is harder to maintain muscle tone, breasts tend to sag, the inevitable facial wrinkles and gray hair appear" (1985: 13). The litany of changes that take place as human beings age is lengthy and complex, and beyond the scope of this chapter. The most important point we can make is that human biophysical aging is a natural, universal, and inevitable process that begins to unfold the day we are born; and yet, while both men and women age, the sociocultural and psychological meanings attached to aging vis-a-vis gender are wildly different (Berkun 1985; Greer 1991; Rosenthal 1990).

What we are interested in here is how the older women felt about and related to their bodily-selves after the menopause, whether their subjective experiences reflected and/or challenged discourses that associate the end of reproduction with old age and de-sexualization. An interesting linguistic shift took place in our conversations with the older women when we asked them to talk about their relationships with their bodies after the menopause. When they shared their stories about their first blood and their menstrual careers they were engaged in a process of looking back and re-membering, and consequently they spoke in the past tense. In contrast, when they spoke about their relationships to their bodies after the menopause, they shifted to the present tense, speaking not only in response to our questions but in terms of their present feelings about and experiences with their aging bodies.

David Karp (1988) suggests that the fifth decade of life—the time around which most women experience the menopause—is the "Decade of Reminders." The mid-life men and women Karp interviewed discussed how they began to receive messages from their bodies, from their friends and family members, and from society at large about the passage of time and their personal aging. They experienced a discontinuity between how they felt inside and how others saw them; their sense of self was ageless, but when they looked at their reflections in the mirror or in the eyes of others they realized they were becoming older (c.f. Kaufman 1986). We see examples of this discontinuity in Isabel's and Jennifer L's descriptions of how their feelings about their bodies have changed since the end of bleeding. Recall that Isabel, eighty years-of-age, was a survivor of physical and sexual abuse. She shared how changes taking place in her body due to illness and injury evoked the feelings of insecurity and ugliness she had experienced as a girl:

I did not have a good image of myself and had to cope with that for a long time. Now that I can't see myself, some of these old feelings have come back. I suddenly got these compression fractures in my vertebrae and I went down from 5'7". I am now 5'2". And I had spasms, very painful spasms, lost thirty pounds. I had always weighed about 145 to 150. In two weeks, I lost thirty pounds. That didn't feel like me. Even now, I can't believe that I am so short and thin, you know. I have felt some of these fears coming over me, because I haven't been able to see myself for, oh, about two years, and I don't know what I look like.

At the time of the interview, Jennifer was dealing with increasingly debilitating back pain related to an injury sustained earlier in life:

Now I'd like to give it [her body] *away. I was older when all of the sudden I learned to play. Now I can't square dance anymore, which I really liked to do. I feel, you may not believe this, but when you are sixty you don't feel any older than you do sitting there right now, as far as your spirit and mentally how you feel. Yeah, you know, it surprises me to look in the mirror, and I could sit and visit with you and feel just at one with you. Women are women and age doesn't have a whole lot to do with it. My body is reminding me of my age and it is a real insult. I am really insulted by my body, but I finally got past the denial stage and am admitting, o.k., you're, you know...* (laugh).... *I mean, I have to admit it because I can't do a lot of things. It is really hard right now.*

Simone de Beauvoir described this strange and painful paradox that captures many of us as we age as originating from "the insoluble contradiction between the inward feeling that guarantees our unchanging quality and the objective certainty of our transformation" (1952: 290). This contradiction is certainly reflected in Isabel's inability to visually or somatically recognize her rapidly changing body. Jennifer's eloquent statement that her body is reminding her of her age reflects this paradox as well. Jennifer feels insulted and disappointed because her body is getting in the way of her self, a self which had "finally learned how to play." We also see here how Jennifer is struggling toward acceptance. She is trying to come to terms with her limitations, to be realistic about what she can and cannot do.

Of all the older women, Ann demonstrated feelings about her bodily-self that were most reflective of the sexist and ageist discourses of the female body that we have been examining. We will excerpt at length from Ann's bodily history below. While her feelings are not representative of all the older women with whom we spoke, she expressed many of the issues that concern women as they grow older in this culture. Ann, a homemaker and mother of four, was sixty-six years-of-age at the time of the interview. In response to a question regarding how she felt about her body after the menopause, she had the following to say:

> *It was like something was taken away from you, that maybe men wouldn't think of you as a whole person. Your facial features are changing...getting wrinkles, and not being young again, and I still have that thought in mind, that I am getting older and I want to be young. I try to take care of my complexion, and my hair and my weight. I don't want to be big and fat* (laugh), *out of proportion. I want to look young. I do. I have that thought a lot.*

Joseph Esposito suggests that starting in midlife, changes in our body and appearance occur so fast that "As the changes increase, we must change to remain the same" in order to counteract the "depersonalization that takes place generally in the aging process" (1987: 60). When asked specifically how she felt about her bodily self, notice that Ann began her answer by referring to an impersonal, generic "you," and then shifted to referring to herself in first person, as "I." Her use of a passive, impersonal voice suggests that this topic may have been quite problematic and difficult for her to talk about, that she felt somewhat disconnected from her aging self. When asked whether she felt others treated her differently once she was no longer bleeding, she described how good it made her feel when people complemented her on looking so young. Ann also spoke about the efforts she made to "age-pass" (Berkun 1985; Gerike 1990), that is, to pass for younger than her chronological age:

I feel that a lot of people look at me. I don't know if they are looking at my complexion or what, but they look at me like, gee, she's got pretty complexion or she looks so young. I have had many people say to me that I don't look my age. They say, "Oh, you are just a kid." And I'll say, "Well, how old do you think I am?" "Oh, probably around forty-nine or fifty" (laugh), *"Gee, thanks a lot!" It makes you feel good, you know, that you don't look old. I am not gray haired. I color my hair and* [my husband] *doesn't want me to go gray. I tried it one time. I let my hair go gray a little bit. I don't like gray hair on me and so I do color my hair. If I let my hair go gray it would probably make me look much older.*

At this point in the conversation, Ann was asked how she might feel if she ever reached a time when she could no longer pass for younger than her actual age. She replied with the following: "*Probably devastated* (laugh). *I'd probably feel sad. I don't know what I am going to be like if I get up in my seventies, eighties, if I live that long. I don't know what my facial features are going to look like. We'll wait and see.*" Ann articulates clearly the connection between aging, de-sexualization, and invisibility for women. It is important to her to continue passing for younger than she is, and thus she colors her hair at her husband's urging and tries to take good care of her body and complexion. She knows that if she ever stops doing these things, particularly coloring her hair, she will look her age. Interestingly, Ann evaded the question "What is it about looking old that concerns you or bothers you? Is it the looking old or is it what people think...is it that people will think that you are old and treat you differently?" She returned to her previous musings about how nice it is when people tell her she looks young, which actually is an answer in itself. The point is that Ann would like it if for the rest of her life people saw her as young, and therefore *treated her as young*. Given what it means to be an old woman in this society, Ann's longings are understandable.

Attempting to look younger than one is, "age-passing," is a strategy many women of all ages adopt, to one degree or another (Gerike 1990). In this culture, for a woman to maintain legitimacy and respect, and often positive self-esteem, she must pass for the "right age," which is always younger than she is; eventually, however, she will begin to look her real age (Block, Davidson, and Grambs 1981; Wolf 1991). When such a time comes upon her, a woman must make new choices about how she will live her life—will she deny her age and collaborate with and reinforce the very sexist and ageist forces she is attempting to allude, or will she accept and celebrate the changes time has made in her, develop and live to her fullest capacity, and therefore help create a new discourse of power and liberation for aging women? Let us not minimize the fact that a woman may feel pressured to conceal her age in order to survive: to make it in a male dominated world, to ensure her job security and social visibility, to please her lover or spouse. Not surprisingly, feminists come down on both sides of this question. Some say women should fight aging for as long as possible, that altering one's appearance with hair dyes and plastic surgery can be a radical, powerful and liberating choice; others say that to do so is akin to an African-American living in a racist society lightening her skin and straightening her kinky hair. Ann Gerike puts forth a compelling argument for gray hair:

> The greatest advantage, however, is that a woman who allows her hair to gray naturally is accepting herself for who she is. She is also, in effect, challenging the ageism of a society that tells her she should be ashamed of her age and should make every effort to disguise it. (1990: 45)

Overwhelmingly, the older women described feeling ambivalent about the changes taking place in their bodies during the last third of their lives. Like Ann, a majority of the women did not like what was happening, but unlike Ann, they were circumspect about and more accepting of the changes they felt were largely beyond their control. Geri's and Shelly's words capture this sense of ambivalence, this feeling of wanting to bravely accept one's aging, at the same time wishing one didn't have to grow old. Geri, a white Mormon woman sixty-four years-of-age, worked as a public health nurse and raised two children: *"I have always liked my body. Sometimes I have been mad at my hips, but that is just the way women are you know. I feel as I have grown older I've known that I would probably put on weight, which I have, about a pound a year. I don't like growing old, but I don't think about growing old."* Similarly, Shelly shared the following:

> *It* [the menopause] *was kind of nice, I didn't have to worry about birth control. I didn't notice that intercourse was difficult or I had never broken a bone. I had gallbladder surgery about three years ago and I put on some weight and I can't seem to lose that and I don't know if any of that has to do with age or whether I am eating more calories than I burn, I don't know. But that is the only thing. I don't like the extra weight that I have right now. I think* [my daughters] *expect me to go on forever and they expect me to be able to do everything that I always did before. I have noticed a little slowing down. You know, things that I used to be able to do a little bit faster, a little bit easier, maybe I can't do anymore. And I don't know if it is the extra weight or if it is age. I don't like it. I don't like to get old. I don't want to. I don't like to look old. I don't think I can look young all my life.*

We find Shelly's last statement incredibly poignant, and illustrative of the split-consciousness many of us experience as we enter later life—

knowing that aging is normal and inevitable, but wishing it didn't have to happen so fast. These two excerpts also reveal one of the major concerns of the older women we spoke with: weight gain. Even in later life, these women are preoccupied with managing their bodies in order to fulfill unreasonable cultural standards of thinness and deprivation, standards predicated on the bodies of pre-pubescent girls. On a deeper level, however, the older women's preoccupation with weight gain (and wrinkles and gray hair) is less about wanting to look young and attractive, and more about fearing they will become unrecognizable to themselves, and others, as we witnessed in Isabel's story. Again, we see the discontinuity between inner sense of self and outer appearance that often becomes an issue during midlife, and even more so in later life.

We see throughout the older women's bodily histories the consistent and frequent use of the word "it" to refer to their bodies and to the things their bodies do. Like their descriptions of menarche, these women spoke about the menopause and aging as something happening *to* them, rather as something wholly part of them. While Emily Martin (1987) reported a reduction of this language of fragmentation among her older respondents, we did not find evidence of such in the older women's narratives. It seems that the discourse which defines women as reproducers and sex-objects during the menstrual career transforms at the menopause into an equally harmful discourse which reduces women to their aging bodies. One of the ways women attempt to resist this ongoing discursive regime is by subjectifying their ageless selves while objectifying their ever-problematic and temporal bodies (Esposito 1987; Gadow 1983). Given that over a woman's lifetime, most of her bodily experiences are eclipsed by such discursive regimes, is it any wonder that her alienation from her body may persist?

Daisy and Rowena seemed to be a bit more down-to-earth about the changes taking place in their bodily-selves as they aged. Notice, however, that they too referred to their bodies as "it":

> *Well, I don't know. Its there. You take good care of it, to the best of your ability. I don't believe in flaunting what you have. I think that people should dress tastefully and I don't think that because you are over seventy you should wear black or navy blue or lavender. Purple is fine, bright purple* (laugh)*! I think you mature, and as you mature, your body matures and I don't believe in facial uplifts unless its the eye tuck because your lids are drooping so you can't see, then that's not cosmetic, that is necessary. I think those character lines are well earned and they are part of the aging process. I like the line that says, "I may grow older but I will never grow up." Because you can keep a young viewpoint and you need to keep busy. Not busy-work busy. Something that is a challenge* (Daisy).

I have always been healthy and well-coordinated. My body has always been trustworthy and has served me well. It is often wiser than my "reasons" and I am pleased with it. Even though in this culture it could have been thinner than it seems to like to be, it always wins, so I fight only limited battles against its wish to be chubby (Rowena).

Daisy's and Rowena's use of the language of fragmentation is jarring, given the overall positive nature of their comments. However, despite talking about their bodies as if they are objects, they seem to have reconciled themselves to their aging bodies, each in her own way. Daisy has chosen as her motto a popular poem by Jenny Joseph entitled "When I am an Old Woman." Paraphrasing from the poem, she declares with delight that she will wear purple, and that "I may grow old but I will never grow up." Rowena has decided to let her "trustworthy" and "wise" body do what "it" seems to want to do—be chubby—despite the cultural imperative of thinness.

In this chapter, we have seen how many of the themes that emerged from the women's stories of their first blood are also present in the older women's narratives about their subsequent menstrual careers and menopausal experiences, suggesting that these themes may have some continuity throughout female adulthood, at least for this group of women. For example, there seems to be a continuation throughout the menstrual career of the restrictions on women's behaviors as a result of bleeding; the silence and confusion associated with the processes of the female body; and the sexualization of women's fertile bodies. Further, we found evidence in the narratives of a continuity well into later life of the medicalization of women's bodies and the things women's bodies do, as well as the use of fragmented language indicative of the splitting off of the body and the self. At the same time, we detected a transformation of sorts for some of the women when they were no longer menstruators—a celebration of the end of a life circumscribed by menstrual cyclicity and reproduction and a movement toward acceptance of the changes in their bodily-selves over time. And, just as we have seen in the context of misogynist discourses about menstruation, we find that the older women both comply with and resist cultural messages about what it means to be a woman who no longer bleeds.

Conclusion

Consciousness and Resistance

> Any deep examination of structured shadows and silences bumps up against the insight that within spaces of oppression lies the fermenting of resistance—renaming lack, filling silence, and infusing outrage into spoken talk.
>
> —Michelle Fine, *Disruptive Voices*

To study women's experiences of their first blood is to study one of the primary ways the female body is formed and contextualized vis-à-vis the sociopolitical constructs of androcentric society. As we have shown, the manner in which women make meaning of and experience menstruation—from the first blood of menarche to the last blood of the menopause—symbolizes the relationships we have with our bodies more generally, relationships which, in contemporary societies, tend to be fraught with ambivalence and often dis-integration. As women, we often comply with negative discourses about the body by disciplining our own and other women's lives, seeing and being seen through the lenses of a misogynist society that imposes restrictive scripts which serve to constrain our spirits. However, at the same time that we comply daily with the prerequisites of femininity in contemporary Western society, we are also involved in ongoing resistance to these scripts.

Running through the women's stories are tales of consciousness, agency and resistance. By "consciousness" we mean an awareness and understanding which is less "something 'within' us than something around and between us, a network of signifiers which constitute us through and through" (Eagleton 1991: 194). "Agency," as we are employing it, encompasses the power of individuals to help construct their existence, to "make things happen." And "resistance" is about the ways women survive and oppose systems of oppression in their everyday lives. That is to say, women are not merely acted upon, nor are they powerless pawns embedded in discursive struggles that determine existence. While discourses do frame the body, as we have demonstrated, the woman in the body does resist, as Emily Martin has suggested. As Martin writes: "Most women feel shame at the prospect of soiling themselves publicly with menstrual blood and try earnestly to conceal it. The same goes for menopause. But we have seen that alongside this shame and embarrassment are a multitude of ways women assert an alternative view of their bodies, react against their accustomed social roles, reject denigrating scientific models, and in general struggle to achieve dignity and autonomy" (1987: 200).

In *Women, Girls and Psychotherapy: Reframing Resistance*, Gilligan, Rogers and Tolman flesh out the concept of resistance:

> We elaborate the concept of resistance by joining girls' struggles to know what they know and speak about their thoughts and feelings. In doing so we acknowledge the difficulty girls face when their knowledge or feelings seem hurtful to other people or disruptive of relationships. Thus the word "resistance" takes on new resonances, picking up the notion of healthy resistance, the capacity of the psyche to resist disease processes, and also the concept of political resistance, the willingness to act on one's own knowledge when such action creates trouble. (1991: 1–2)

They emphasize that at adolescence, girls often face disconnections—from themselves and from others—as they start to negotiate and traverse a misogynous world with a female body. The retrenchment and "shutting down" that often occur at this time have been identified by some psychoanalysts as "natural" responses in the context of female passivity and masochism (Deutsch 1944; Freud 1954; Horney 1967; Thompson 1942). Gilligan and her colleagues challenge this notion, arguing that such behaviors must be understood in the context of systems of domination and discrimination, and, as such, can be reinterpreted as forms of survival and resistance. For many girls, difficulty occurs as a result of entering a "developmental crossroads," where the path to maturity involves a separation that conflicts with the expectations placed on her to connect (Stern 1990). As Tolman has suggested, "the energy needed for resistance to crushing conventions of femininity often begins to get siphoned off for the purpose of maintaining cultural standards that stand between women and their empowerment" (1994: 324–5). What this means for most girls—and women—is both daily resistance and daily compliance and accommodation.

Despite the strong pressure to internalize and comply with negative scripts about themselves and their bodies, the women with whom we worked on this project also showed that they resisted the destructive and alienating discourses associated with the menstrual career and female embodiment in ways that were subversive and disruptive. They did this through insight and analysis, through remembering and telling their stories and through the many ways they have learned to cope with going through life with a female body. Some spoke of increasing solidarity with girlfriends around the time of the first blood or of using menstruation as a way to manipulate others and get their way, and many spoke of having done or having a desire to do things differently when their own daughters start(ed) to menstruate. Likewise, many of the older women described the freedom, energy and confidence they felt once their lives were no longer bound to the rhythms of the menstrual career, and a few expressed empowerment at being able to resist what they perceived as a medicalization of their last blood. It is to these forms of consciousness and resistance that we now turn.

Telling the Story

Since this project involved participants who were volunteers, the voices we have shared throughout this book are the voices of women who wanted to have the opportunity to chronicle their bodily histories in some form. Some women told their first blood story as a form of lament, focusing on their grief and pain; some spoke in conciliatory tones that expressed acceptance of their experiences as "normal" or "natural"; and some spoke with righteous anger. Often, when the tape-recorder had been switched off and the interviewing was finished, women would comment on the benefits of speaking publicly about something that was an important experience in their lives, but had tended to be ignored by the society in which they lived, as well as by academia. A sentiment many women expressed is captured in the comment "I don't know if it's making any real sense, but it is starting to make more sense to me when I talk about it."

By telling their stories and speaking their truths about menarche and life with female bodies, women were able to voice the internalized oppression of their bodies. This telling of truths is especially crucial because, as Audre Lorde (1984) reminds us, silence does not protect; speaking "truths" is a brave and vital act of resistance in a society that devalues and silences women's voices; and at the same time, it creates a more inclusive conception of social reality. As the Personal

Narratives Group who edited *Interpreting Women's Lives* suggests: "For a woman, claiming the truth of her life despite awareness of other versions of reality that contest this truth often produces both a heightened criticism of officially condoned untruths and a heightened sense of injustice. This criticism is central to the production of feminist theory; this sense of injustice is a critical impetus for feminist political action" (1989: 7–8).

For many women, this process of truth-telling took the form of ongoing analysis of and commentary upon their experiences, speaking or writing with insight into body politics and the effects of these politics on women's everyday lives throughout the life course. Their self-conscious understandings, what Anthony Giddens calls "practical consciousness" (1979: 5), emerged out of their own personal experiences and bodily histories. Chris, a white working- class mother in her early thirties, shared her story, closing it with an insightful feminist analysis:

I can't remember my first menstrual period exactly, which must have been some time during my twelfth year. I do remember several periods passing without telling my mom, sneaking the appropriate materials from her bathroom, before she caught on. I remember feeling terribly ashamed of the whole thing, and praying that my mother wouldn't want to discuss anything of a sexual nature with me. I completely blocked out the notion that my father would know that I had begun menstruating. I'd wear my winter coat throughout the school day, sweltering but petrified that blood had leaked through, or that people would see the pad through my clothing. I realize now that my feelings had a lot to do with our culture's belief that menstruation is dirty and smelly, that women are somehow unclean while menstruating, and that it's not a subject that should be talked about around men.

Many women used contradictory voices to tell their stories, revealing an interesting form of resistance. Women moved between an anxious, hesitant and fearful style of disclosure, complete with multiple "uhmms," "you knows," and "I don't know," to the staging of their story as a series of adventures, often framing it, in hindsight, as ridiculous. In so doing, they appropriated and claimed control over experiences and events, thereby defusing their pain and anguish. This form of resistance emphasizes the sometimes contradictory ways gender is negotiated, and demonstrates how discourses of resistance are crucial components of this negotiation. Virginia and Vicky illustrate this as they joke about the story of their first periods, laughing and staging the event as a funny experience:

So, I was ten years old and didn't understand any of it. In fact, I misunderstood most of it. What I remember about it from the [Kotex] *book was that somehow the menstrual blood came out on the outside of your lower abdomen, somehow like it seeped through your skin!* (laugh)...*and so, here's the book telling me that these napkins don't show and I'm holding them up to my stomach and saying, yeah, right,* (laugh), *that is going to show, you can't tell me that is not going to show...so I told my mother and it was like "oh", she did seem rather pleased but it wasn't like the kind of pleased where if I got a really good grade or you know, gotten the solo in the school play* (laugh)...*She pulls out the Kotex kit and that is when I begin to connect, this is what it is, it doesn't come out of your stomach!* (laugh) (Virginia).

I also remember the (laugh)—*this is so funny—I do remember the first time, and I used one of those little strip things, and I didn't know, I mean, the sticky strip part, I was like, where do you put the sticky part? It didn't come with instructions in those days, and I ended up sticking parts to me! Like I was so bad! I was like, this is not fun, why do people do this? And of course a little while later I figured it out, oh, it's supposed to go in your underwear! Oh God!* (Vicky).

Another example is from Hannah, who, as a survivor of incest, spoke very poignantly about the anguish associated with her first menses. However, alongside her sadness she told funny stories of menarche, her humor helping her gain control over her pain:

I saw blood in my underwear and it was like I just sat on the toilet (laugh) *and I am like "mom". She comes in and she was like, "what?...well honey, congratulations, you are a little lady now." I am like, say what?!! I was cramping really bad and I was given medication. It was to get me regulated.... I remember lying on the floor and my mom, she used to have bad cramps because she had a tipped uterus, so my grandfather used to buy her a pint of alcohol because they didn't have medication then, and she would drink it and she would pass out and she would be out for a day. So my mom gave me some brandy because she thought it would solve it!* (laugh) *Well, after I had the brandy I just started to york it, I was throwing up left and right, so it seems like after that time every period I ever had I would throw up!* (laugh).

Many of the women with whom we spoke told their first blood stories with clear voices that expressed anger about and resistance to their situations. For example, Julia, white and twenty-two years old, had the following to say about the ridiculous and unjust ways women's bleeding bodies are construed:

But guys always, ooh ick, a period. They just think of it as the commercials on TV. Like I don't see any commercials for jock itch or condoms, or, you know, all those things. You only see commercials for feminine or other not-so-fresh feelings, or the smell, you know, all these things, and, oh wait, it has wings, and it has this and it has that. And it is like, this is something that is a part of us, and you are making a mockery of it. And men always flip the channel, you know, uugghh, disgusting, you know. It is like, what if I put a commercial on about, you know, diapers for men when they are going through puberty, so they can wear those at night [against nocturnal emissions] *or something, so they can be judged.*

I just wish we had some kind of menstrual uprising in society. Women should just be able to say "hey, I've got my period right now and I don't feel like dealing with you." They should be able to say to men, you know, don't label me because of this, because this is something that is a part of me. I mean, I don't label men because they don't have a chest, you know, why don't you have a chest? Women should be able to go to their boss and say "I just got my period, I need to go to the bathroom", rather than saying "can you excuse me for a minute, I need to go into my desk for something and I'll be right back." I mean, that is the way that we are, because the topic is bad and it is wrong, and you know, don't let anybody know about it.

Yvonne, an African-American woman in her thirties, summed-up what she and many other women felt about the situations Julia described so clearly by stating "*I was pissed.*" Another example of the transformative power of anger and resistance is seen in the experiences of Jennifer W., a white woman in her early twenties, who shared a written narrative with us that was very typical of the many stories we heard. She was a "*late bloomer*": "*So, here I was, a sophomore in high school, still waiting to experience cramps, tampons, pads, and all the pleasure involved with bitching about being a female. I felt so left out!*" However, when she actually started menstruating she felt very embarrassed and went to great lengths to hide it. While, like other women, she analyzed her first blood experiences in ways that helped her feel better about them, her story has a unique ending. Jennifer W. recently decided to confront her father about what she saw as inappropriate behavior on his part around the time of her menarche. She felt empowered by this conversation:

My father always left the room or told us to be quiet whenever my mother and I started to discuss any kind of female issue. It was very clear that he didn't want to hear it and it wasn't an appropriate topic of conversation in his opinion. Looking back on my teenage years, I am pretty sure this is why I always hid my tampon boxes in my bedroom so no one would see them. So I decided to confront him...he said "It's a personal thing women ought to keep to themselves—don't tell me about it, I don't want to know." I said "Dad, I want you to know that every female in the world has a period and there is nothing to be embarrassed about. I realize that your family decided that female issues were not to be discussed, but times are changing and in today's society it is okay to talk about menstruation as a healthy part of a woman's life and not a dirty forbidden topic. Growing up, I felt embarrassed about my period because you made it clear we weren't going to talk about it, and I felt like I had done something wrong. I want you to know I have my own family now and am going to talk with our children about every aspect of female issues and let the children know menstruation is a perfectly natural occurrence."

We offer no further analysis or commentary of Jennifer's statement, for what more needs to be said?

Denial, Coping, and Appropriation

We found that, as adolescent girls, many of the women in our project resisted menarche and its accompanying pubertal developments by denying that these changes were occurring to them. This strategy tended to involve a denial of their femininity, not surprising given that femininity is coded with real and perceived restrictions and loss of power and control. Countless women talked and wrote about being "tomboys," and attempting to live their denial by associating mostly with boys and their activities. Of course, for most girls this was ultimately a short-lived strategy, as boys started to reject them once they were marked by the physiological changes associated with an inferior gender. In addition, this strategy also facilitated internalized sexism, as "tomboys" often learned to hate the feminine and all that was labelled feminine in themselves. Nonetheless, it was still a form of resistance, as girls became aware of and began to respond to negative scripts associated with gender. Anne and Gretchen share some memories of their denial of menarche:

I did not want to have my period and I think it is because of—and I don't know whether it is this awareness of what it means to be a fertile female, or what. I have thought a lot about it over the years, for I have always had cramps, bad cramps—and various people have told me it's because I resist being female.... I think the resistance that I felt initially, to the denial of it, are still with me today. There were numbers of years in my adolescence where I wished I was a boy—I didn't see anything about being female around me that would make me embrace this mark of femaleness...All of a sudden I became a sexual being and it pissed me off (Anne).

I think I felt really betrayed by my body because I had walked around before saying, I will not get breasts, it is just not going to happen if I just tell myself I won't get them, my body won't (Gretchen).

For some women, most especially those at mid-life and beyond, there was a general sense of "acceptance" or resignation to the politics of the menstrual career and female embodiment that ran through their narratives. We had not thought of this as a form of "resistance" until we read Emily Martin's discussion of acceptance, lament and non-action as a way of responding to women's reproductive restrictions (Martin 1987: 184–6). These ways of coping and surviving are important; note how they also serve to subvert the masculinist idea of resistance as oppositional action and behavior. Many women, when asked about the specifics of their first blood, responded with such comments as *"people didn't talk about such things back then"*; *"it was just something I had to endure"*; *"that's the way it was back then."* Alex's comments were typical: *"And in those days we didn't have the sanitary napkins we have today, or even now the tampax and so on, but you always had that laundry to do. That was just not very pleasant but it was a thing you did. I mean, that was the way it went."*

The most important point we can make about this form of "acceptance" is that it serves as a survival and coping mechanism. Louie, for example, talked about the hardships associated with menstruation before the widespread availability of commercial sanitary supplies. She recalled being in a tight spot with no menstrual cloths: *"I had a jackknife and I cut up one of my blankets for pads and used those."* Women of all ages reported using toilet paper, tissue, and underwear to help them hide their bleeding and cope with their first menses. Some women hid evidence of their bleeding, some threw the evidence away, and most washed blood out of their undergarments when no one was around. Many worked out ways to avoid going to the grocery store to buy supplies if they might be seen by an acquaintance, and others modified their clothes and activities to avoid embarrassments. Remember Judy, who many years before sanitary pads were created and commercially available actually fashioned her own adhesive-backed pads by using masking tape.

Women learned, quite on their own, to protect themselves from some of the consequences associated with menarche and a sexualized female body. An incest survivor, Jewell writes poignantly about resistance: *"My body insisted on becoming a woman and I wanted absolutely no part of it. So I fought it with every fiber of me—I'm sure that is why I had such terrible cramps most of my life. I just couldn't accept the female part of me that had been so ravaged and that seemed to have betrayed me so much...So each time I got my period, my body would fight itself and I would throw up and have severe diarrhea for twenty-four hours."* Many women of all ages and races wrote and talked about using their bleeding bodies—from menarche onward—as a way to avoid potential unwanted sexual contact. Monica, age twenty-two, and Jennifer L., age sixty-one, share some memories:

I think he actually said "do you want to have sex or something," and I was like, "I am on the rag." And I said it again and I was just like, you know, I wasn't at that point. I wasn't ready to do that right then so I just like—that's an excuse, that one will work, so I used it at that point (Monica).

You could tell them, you know, "I am a virgin," that scares them off. And the other thing was "I have my period," and that would stop them too, it was just a dead-ringer (Jennifer L).

Not all of the women, of course, had negative memories of menarche, although almost all spoke of feeling ambivalence during this time. About a dozen women of different ages remembered feeling proud that they had started their period, and at least a third overall articulated that they appreciated the new grown-up status starting to menstruate implied, even though "womanhood," as they perceived it, might have its drawbacks. This is, in a sense, a form of resistance/appropriation, since their integration of positive aspects of adult female embodiment meant more positive self-perceptions. Even though these positive aspects ultimately tended to be contextualized in traditional ideologies about the glories of impending womanhood, these women were able to feel better about themselves and resist—at some level—the negativities associated with menarche. As Marian remembers:

I rejoiced the day my period started at the age of thirteen years as at last I was a woman! My whole life was devoted to wishing to be an adult, as childhood for me was full of responsibility looking after my two younger brothers and waiting for my mother to come home from work. I had been looking forward to this event since the age of ten years when my mum, over a sink full of washing, informed me of the facts of life.... Going back to the day when I first found blood on my knickers, I was at home after school and I went to find Mum with a face flushed with pleasure and made my pronouncement. She took me up to the bedroom, her bedroom as this was a very special occasion and she made me my first sanitary pad which was huge and uncomfortable as it was made of torn pieces of an old sheet.... I was so thrilled to be one step nearer maturity and could hardly wait for the opportunity to tell my Dad and my brothers. But my Mum was aghast at this news as women didn't mention things like that to men, she said she would tell him when they were alone together.

Such a desire for the perceived benefits of adulthood was also shared by Ivy: *"I knew that it was going to happen some time, and so it just, you know, it would be, I mean I was, in a way I thought it was one more step to growing up so I welcomed it. I wanted to grow older."* As we discussed in chapter 5, some women remembered distinctly the new status they enjoyed among their peers, and this added to their positive experiences of menarche. Remember that Edith, whose story we shared in chapter 3, exclaimed: *"I was glad knowing, simply, that I had caught up with the rest of the class."* She had felt like *"a complete failure"* because she had not yet experienced puberty and achieved the status that goes along with impending womanhood. For her, menarche was a way to gain status and recognition; in this sense, this developmental transition can be used by women to improve certain conditions of their lives. As Barrie Thorne (1993) suggests, the popular girls set the stage; if they are perceived as having started their period, then this development is seen as more desirable. Since such popularity and standing is wound up with their sexual status, this process is complex: girls do not want to start too soon and be seen as too advanced or promiscuous, but then again, they do not want to start last and be branded as less mature and a child. Timing is definitely of the essence.

Appropriation occurs when women take or transform power and reclaim authority surrounding the things their bodies do. This is exhibited by the large number of women who spoke and wrote in the present about *"seeing things different now,"* emphasizing how life-experiences and education had helped them make friends with their bodies and accept, appreciate and even celebrate their monthly cycles and the "power" many felt they now had. While very few women remembered being able to feel this during their adolescent years, many still managed to appropriate menarche for their own convenience and opportunity. A few used and exaggerated stereotypical feminine changes associated with menarche in order to create positive images of femininity for themselves. As an example of this we might remember Judy, whose story we shared earlier, and her discussion of the manipulative powers of her sexuality. Another illustration comes from Jacqueline, a white, working-class woman in her twenties, who remembered clearly the manipulative power of her budding (hetero)sexuality. She writes:

I grew eight inches in the same year [as she started her period], *so I got a waist and everything. You know...I think I learned that to manipulate men, you know, when I started looking more like a woman it was a lot easier to manipulate men, to get what I wanted, and I used this strength I thought I had and so I was, it really had a lot to do with deciding what to show and what not to show of myself, I think it was a time of real game-*

playing. I don't know if it is making any real sense but it is starting to make more sense to me when I talk about it (laugh).

Many women told stories of using menstruation as a way to manipulate and have some control over situations: sex, chores in their family, showering at school and participating in sports and physical education. Gerta, aged seventy-seven, spoke for many when she wrote: *"As far as school was concerned—during Physical Education, we were benched for three days. CLUB members* [those girls who had already started their period] *often considered this a plus as we were not required to wear gym attire."*

A vivid example of resistance/appropriation taking place at the other end of the menstrual career was seen in Louie's and Daisy's decisive acts of self-advocacy in response to the normative medicalization of the menopause. Recall that Louie and Daisy refused to take HRT, against the advice of their doctors, because they didn't like how it made them feel and they were not sure the benefits outweighed the risks. As Daisy proclaimed: *"I flushed the stuff down the toilet. I said I do not need to be a teenager again. I do not need sore breasts, I do not need my face breaking out."* We detect something else going on here, as well: acceptance. In refusing to take HRT, these two women were accepting as normal and natural the physiological and hormonal changes they were experiencing, rather than seeing them as diseases which needed to be medicated or "cured."

Bonding and Solidarity

As we discussed in chapter 5, for many of the women, the experience of menarche helped them identify and bond with other girls, resulting in mutual support and solidarity. As Karin remembers: *"I think it brought me closer to girls in a certain way because when you talk about things that are personal it really kind of strengthens your relationship and makes it more intimate. I felt very close to them."* This form of resistance is especially productive because it offers the opportunity for girls to resist collectively rather than in solitary ways. While many women remembered suffering the embarrassments of menarche alone, some described how they and their girlfriends supported and helped each other. Monica told a story about helping a classmate:

One of my friends did start at school. I remember us being like: "You started? Are you sure?" First of all she like bunched up a bunch of toilet paper because we didn't have anything, and then that was, like, not working. We had those machines and this was a really ancient machine so we had no idea what was going to come out (laugh)*." We actually found some* *money. It didn't even have, like, the adhesive strip yet; it had pins, and so we were like, well, hey, it's a pad, and she took it and used it.*

Women shared how friends and sisters helped them figure out what was happening to their bodies, as well as helped them access and use menstrual products and hide embarrassing leaks and stains. Isabel spoke about the importance of her friends during menarche; her story also demonstrates the solidarity that girls often feel with other girls they perceive as needing help and with whom they can identify:

That was my support system, all of us girls talked and shared among ourselves. We would always tell each other we were having our period. And we talked about if we had cramps or how uncomfortable it was. We talked to each other about the length of our periods because we had varying lengths. We talked like how often we had to change our pads...Once one of our teachers was having her period and somehow her pad became unhooked and it was really obvious, it was just poking, kind of poking way out (laugh), *and she was busy lecturing. Well, she was a teacher who had always seemed to be somewhere else anyway, and she didn't notice it. So one of the girls wrote her a very nice little note and handed it to her.*

Jessica, a fifty-six-year-old white woman who grew up in Germany, also illustrated the ways women help other women in need around these issues. Her story concerned her memory of how difficult it was when she started her period, and an incident in which she received help from a stranger:

And also many times I leaked through and you know, sitting on a train, there was once, I asked a total stranger, a woman of course, if she could just stand there with me a moment so I could just pretend to rearrange things a little bit while she stood there with me, so I didn't have to stand there all by myself, you know...and we just pretended.

Women described over and again how, as girls, they developed camaraderie and solidarity around the issue of menarche through the reappropriation of certain names for menstruation, especially when these names were used to create a "code" that those outside of the group could not understand. For example, several women intentionally used the term "on the rag" as a way to reclaim the term and potentially subvert its misogynous effects. Other stories are shared below:

Sometimes we would call it "Aunt Flo is visiting" (laugh), *or...a couple of people had just random names just because between friends that is what they would call it. They would call it—one would say "the grinch is back"* (laugh). *I mean, they'd just make up words for it like friends would know what it was, but no one else would know* (Sally L.).

Men don't have something to bring them together, where women have this, it's shared, they understand each other...you know, we used to call [tampons] *"spirit sticks" in high school. We were cheer leaders. "Does anyone have a spirit stick?!" You know, because spirit sticks were what we got for cheering the loudest, so it sort of is one of those things, it just had something to do with like, happiness, like, you know, and we would just say it and nobody else knew what it was. With my girlfriends we'd say, we'd think of a name, like Fred, like what that's what we were going to call it* (Julia).

Changing Scripts

I hope that we are all honest and that the younger women can benefit from what we have gone through, and I hope they would not repeat the same mistakes, you know, keeping it such a secret and such a mystery, because it is not a mystery. It is something very natural and I hope that women look for ways to empower other women (Liz).

While many of the women with whom we spoke expressed painful memories of their first period, often because of lack of information and positive role models in their families, there is evidence to suggest that such patterns are being disrupted. Many women who had negative experiences with their mothers at menarche said that they would never want to perpetuate such an experience with their own daughters. Judy M., a Japanese-American in her twenties, shared her desire for a better experience for any future daughters: "*If I have daughters of my own in the future, I will tell them more positive things about periods such as that it's not something you should be ashamed of or something dirty. I would make sure that they'll have some knowledge about menstruation before it starts because, when my period started, I didn't have any knowledge why women have a period or how it starts or anything.*" Similarly, several of the mid-life and older women who are mothers described how they had socialized their adolescent children in more open and instructive ways.

While Sarah K., whose story of shame and contamination we shared in chapter 3, had internalized many feelings of embarrassment and inadequacy about her body, she also showed resistance to the negative discourses surrounding menstruation by vowing to change the scripts for her children. She also wrote about providing her sons with positive, woman-affirming messages. By preparing them with positive messages about women, their bodies and sexuality, Sarah showed active resistance to a culture that aims to control women in part through the scripts of the body:

Every month I felt dirty, until age seventeen when I became pregnant. Five years of feeling humiliated, different and afraid. When I became pregnant I was happy. I was looking forward to a baby—and also nine months of being smell-free "down there." It was only after my child was born that I realized this was a beautiful gift I had. I began to feel better about being a woman! I made a vow that I would explain menstruation to my children—girls or boys. I wouldn't let them become another victim. Along with this positive information, why there is a lack of education, the horror stories and lack of understanding the natural processes of a woman's menstrual periods were explained to both of my children. Two boys!

Ann, a mother of two daughters and grandmother to several children, spoke with regret that she acted very much like her own mother in that she was not able to give information to and help her daughters feel good about their first menses. She emphasized, however, that she was committed to undoing this piece of family history with her granddaughter: "*My mother neglected telling me and I neglected telling my girls and I wouldn't want that to happen to my granddaughter... because I wouldn't want it to come from an outside source like from girls at school. I feel that my daughter really should do this, but like I said, if she doesn't I am prepared to do it for her.*" The decision of Ann and other women to use their own, often negative, experiences to instruct and enlighten the next generation of women is an interesting example of generativity. As Martin has suggested: "At the heart of people's ability to question the social order is their ability to conceive of an alternative kind of regime" (1987: 183). Unfortunately, the creation of a new regime is a slow process; several women who are mothers emphasized that even though they had prepared their children and made menarche a positive experience, their daughters still felt some shame and embarrassment. We must remember that the values of this (and every) culture are strong; children are not raised in a vacuum and thus quickly internalize the negative messages associated with menstruation and female embodiment.

Women's bodies are products of and situated in a sociocultural context that devalues and trivializes women; and yet, while adult woman have internalized the stigma and shame associated with having bodies that bleed, and all that this entails in terms of restrictions on body, mind and soul, they have responded as active agents, and have resisted these discursive regimes through a variety of ingenious means. Women continue to resist the strictures imposed upon them as embodied women living in a patriarchal culture by reminiscing about their first menses, viewing their experiences retrospectively, framing and re-framing them, hopefully neutralizing the pain, perhaps taking back their authority and power. They have dealt with menarche and a life circumscribed by menstruation and reproduction by denying menarche's existence, but also via acceptance and creative coping strategies. They have diluted the negativity surrounding the first blood by framing impending womanhood with status and authority, and they have identified menarche with an ability to manipulate in order to both get what they want and avoid what they do not want. Menarche is also a time when girls experience camaraderie, when resistance to negative scripts takes the form of solidarity and bonding. Finally, some women are changing the sociocultural scripts associated with the menstrual career, hopefully impacting the bodily histories of future generations of women.

Coda

In this book we have focused on menarche as a point of confluence in the female life course and as a central element of body politics. The first blood is a physiological happening, framed by the bio-medical metaphors of current scientific knowledge, yet also a gendered sexualized happening, a transition to womanhood as objectified other. As we have seen, the ways girls experience their bodily selves at the first blood can have a strong impact on how they relate to their bodily selves throughout the life course, and more practically, on how they experience themselves as sexualized beings in day-to-day life. What is crucial here is that this juncture, menarche, is a site where individual girls begin to produce themselves as women and gender relations are re-produced. In this context, such gender relations are too often about loss or absence of power, about dis-embodiment, about shame and ambivalence, about being defined and controlled by others. However, in listening and giving witness to the women's stories we have begun to imagine a different reality in which gender relations are about the authority and power to define one's life, to inhabit one's body fully and with safety, about the power to move through one's lifetime in this world with dignity and respect. May this be in our futures.

figure 7.1

References

Allen, Katherine R., and Robert S. Pickett. 1984. Historical perspective on the life course of elderly women born in 1910. *Journal of Applied Gerontology* 3 (2): 161–70.

———. 1987. Forgotten streams in the family life course: Utilization of qualitative retrospective interviews in the analysis of lifelong single women's family careers. *Journal of Marriage and the Family* 49: 517–26.

American Association of University Women Report (AAUW). 1992. *How schools shortchange girls.* Anapolis Junction, MD: American Association of University Women.

———. 1993. *Hostile hallways: The AAUW survey on sexual harassment in the schools.* Anapolis Junction, MD: American Association of University Women.

Anderson, Kathryn, and Dana C. Jack. 1991. Learning to listen: Interview techniques and analyses. In *Women's words: The feminist practice of oral history,* ed. Sherna Berger Gluck and Daphne Patai, 11–26. New York: Routledge.

Apter, Terri. 1990. *Altered loves: Mothers and daughters during adolescence.* New York: St. Martin's Press.

Bailey, Kenneth D. 1987. *Methods of social research.* New York: The Free Press.

Baltes, Paul G., Hayne W. Reese, and Lewis P. Lipsitt. 1980. Life-span developmental psychology. *Annual Review of Psychology* 31: 65–100.

Banner, Lois W. 1983. *American beauty.* New York: Knopf.

———. 1992. *In full flower: Aging women, power, and sexuality.* New York: Knopf.

Barbre, Joy W. 1993. Meno-boomers and moral guardians: An exploration of the cultural construction of menopause. In *Menopause: A midlife passage,* ed. Joan C. Callahan, 23–35. Bloomington: Indiana University Press.

Bardwick, Judith M., and Elizabeth Douvan. 1987. Ambivalence: The socialization of women. In *Growing up in America: Historial experiences,* ed. Harvey J. Graff, 569–79. Detroit: Wayne State University Press.

Barnett, Rosalind C. 1984. The anxiety of the unknown—Choice, risk, responsibility. In *Women in midlife,* ed. Grace Baruch and Jeanne Brooks-Gunn, 341–57. New York: Basic Books.

Bartky, Sandra Lee. 1990. *Femininity and domination: Studies in the phenomenology of oppression.* New York: Routledge.

———. 1992. Foucault, femininity, and the modernization of patriarchal power. In *Feminist philosophies: Problems, theories and applications,* ed. Janet A. Kourany, James P. Sterba and Rosemary Tong, 103–118. Englewood Cliffs, NJ: Prentice Hall.

Belenky, Mary F., Blythe M. Clinchy, Nancy R. Goldberger, and Jill M. Tarule. 1986. *Women's ways of knowing.* New York: Basic Books.

Bell, Susan Groag, and Marilyn Yalom. 1990. *Revealing lives: Autobiography, biography and gender.* New York: State University of New York Press.

Benner, Patricia. 1994. *Interpretive phenomenology: Embodiment, caring, and ethics in health and illness.* Newbury Park, CA: Sage Publications.

Berger, Peter. L., and Thomas Luckman. 1966. *The social construction of reality.* New York: Doubleday.

Berkun, Cleo S. 1985. Changing appearances for women in the middle years: Trauma? In *Older women: Issues and prospects*, ed. Elizabeth Warren Marson, 11–35. Lexington, MA: Lexington Books.

Berman, Morris. 1989. *Coming to our senses.* New York: Bantam.

Bertaux, Daniel. 1981. *Biography and society: The life history approach in the social sciences.* Newbury Park, CA: Sage Publications.

Birren, James E., and Betty A. Birren. 1990. The concepts, models, and history of the psychology of aging. In *Handbook of the psychology of aging.* 3rd edition, ed. James E. Birren and K. Warner Schaie, 3–20. New York: Academic Press.

Blank, Thomas O. 1989. Social psychology, contexts of aging, and a contextual world view. *International Journal of Aging and Human Development* 26 (3): 225–39.

Block, Jeanne H. 1978. Another look at sex differentiation in the socialization behaviors of mothers and fathers. In *Psychology of women: Future directions of research,* ed. Julia Ann Sherman and Florence Denmark, 29–87. New York: Psychological Dimensions.

Block, Marilyn R., Janice L. Davidson, and Jean D. Grambs. 1981. *Women over forty: Visions and realities.* New York: Springer.

Blume, Judy. 1970. *Are you there God? It's me Margaret.* New York: Dell Publishing.

Bordo, Susan R. 1989. The body and the reproduction of femininity: A feminist appropriation of Foucault. In *Gender/Body/Knowledge: A feminist reconstruction of being and knowing,* ed. Alison M. Jaggar and Susan R. Bordo, 13–33. New Brunswick, NJ: Rutgers University Press.

———. 1993. *Unbearable weight: Feminism, western culture, and the body.* Berkeley: University of California Press.

Bowles, Cheryl. 1986. Measure of attitude toward menopause using the semantic differential model. *Nursing Research* 35(2): 81–85.

Broch-Due, Anne-Katherine. 1992. Reflections on subjectivism in biographical interviewing: A process of change. In *All sides of the subject: Women and biography,* ed. Teresa Iles, 93–101. New York: Columbia University Teachers College Press.

Brooks-Gunn, Jeanne, and Barbara Kirsh. 1984. Life events and the boundaries of midlife for women. In *Women in midlife,* ed. Grace Baruch and Jeanne Brooks-Gunn, 31–68. New York: Basic Books.

Brooks-Gunn, Jeanne, and Anne C. Petersen. 1983. The experience of menarche from a developmental perspective. In *Girls at puberty: Biological and psychosocial perspectives,* ed. Jeanne Brooks-Gunn and Anne C. Petersen, 155–77. New York: Plenum Press.

Brooks-Gunn, Jeanne, and Diane Ruble. 1980. The interaction of physiological, cultural, and social factors. In *The menstrual cycle*, vol. 1, ed. Alice J. Dan,

Effie A. Graham, and Carol P. Beecher, 141–59. New York: Springer.
———. 1982. The development of menstrual-related beliefs and behaviors during early adolescence. *Child Development* 53: 1567–77.
———. 1983. Dysmenorrhea in adolescence. In *Menarche,* ed. Sharon Golub, 251–61. Lexington, MA: D.C. Heath.
Brown, Catrina, and Karin Jasper, eds. 1993. *Consuming passions: Feminist approaches to weight preoccupation and eating disorders.* Toronto: Second Story Press.
Brown, Lynn Mikel, and Carol Gilligan. 1992. *Meeting at the crossroads: Women's psychology and girls' development.* Cambridge: Harvard University Press.
Brown, Roger, and James Kulik. 1977. Flashbulb memories. *Cognition* 5: 73–99
Brownmiller, Susan. 1984. *Femininity.* New York: Ballantine.
Bruner, Jerome. 1986. *Actual minds: Possible worlds.* Cambridge: Harvard University Press.
———. 1990. Acts of meaning. Cambridge, Mass.: Harvard University Press.
Buchanan, Kim Shayo. 1993. Creating beauty in blackness. In *Consuming Passions,* ed. Catrina Brown and Karin Jasper, 36–52. Toronto: Second Story Press.
Buckley, Thomas, and Alma, Gottlieb. 1988. *Blood magic: The anthropology of menstruation.* Berkeley: University of California Press.
Bullough, Bonnie. 1974. *The subordinate sex: A history of attitudes toward women.* New York: Penguin.
Bullough, Vern. 1975. Sex and the medical model. *The Journal of Sex Research* 11 (4): 291–303.
———. 1983. Menarche and teenage pregnancy: A misuse of historical data. In *Menarche,* ed. Sharon Golub, 187–94. Lexington, MA: D.C. Heath.
Butler, Judith. 1993. *Bodies that matter: On the discourse of sex.* New York: Routledge.
Butler, Robert. 1963. The life-review: An interpretation of reminiscence in the aged. *Psychiatry* 26: 65–76.
Callahan, Joan C., ed. 1993. *Menopause: A midlife passage.* Bloomington: Indiana University Press.
Cavanaugh, Eunice. 1989. *Understanding shame: Why it hurts, how it helps, how you can use it to transform your life.* Minneapolis: Johnson Institute.
Cayleff, Susan E. 1992. She was rendered incapacitated by menstrual difficulties: Historical perspectives on perceived intellectual and physiological impairment among menstruating women. In *Menstrual health in women's lives,* ed. Alice J. Dan and Linda L. Lewis, 229–35. Urbana: University of Illinois Press.
Cicirelli, Victor G. 1980. A comparison of college women's feelings toward their siblings and parents. *Journal of Marriage and the Family* 78: 111–18.
Chanfrault-Duchet, Marie-Francoise. 1991. Narrative structures, social models and symbolic representations in the life story. In *Women's words: The feminist practice of oral history,* ed. Sherna B. Gluck and Daphne Patai. New York: Routledge.
Chapkis, Wendy. 1986. *Beauty secrets: Women and the politics of appearance.* Boston: South End Press.

Chernin, Kim. 1981. *The obsession: Reflections on the tyranny of slenderness.* New York: Harper and Row.

Clark, Anne E., and Diane N. Ruble. 1978. Young adolescents' beliefs concerning menstruation. *Child Development* 49: 201–234.

Clausen, John A. 1975. The social meaning of differential physical and sexual maturation. In *Adolescence in the life cycle,* ed. Sigmund E. Dragastin and Glen H. Elder, 25–47. New York: Wiley.

Clifford, James. 1983. On ethnographic authority. *Representations* 1 (2): 118–46.

Collins, Patricia Hill. 1990. *Black feminist thought: Knowledge, consciousness, and the politics of empowerment.* New York: Routledge.

Copper, Baba. 1988. *Over the hill: Reflections on ageism between women.* Freedom, Cal.: The Crossing Press.

Covey, Herbert C. 1985. Qualitative research of older people: Some considerations. *Gerontology and Geriatrics Education* 5 (3): 41–50.

Coward, Rosalind. 1985. *Female desires: How they are sought, bought and packaged.* New York: Grove Press.

Cutler, Winnifred B., and Celso-Ramon Garcia. 1992. *Menopause: A guide for women and the men who love them.* New York: W.W. Norton.

Damon, Albert, and Carl J. Bajema. 1974. Age at menarche: Accuracy of recall after thirty-nine years. *Human Biology* 46 (3): 381–84.

Dan, Alice J., and Linda L. Lewis, eds. 1992. *Menstrual health in women's lives.* Urbana: University of Illinois Press.

Dan, Alice, J., Effie, A. Graham, and Carol P. Beecher, eds. 1980. *The menstrual cycle*, vol. 1. New York: Springer.

Danza, Roberta. 1983. Menarche: It's effects on mother-daughter and father-daughter interactions. In *Menarche,* ed. Sharon Golub, 99–105. Lexington, MA: D.C. Heath.

de Beauvoir, Simone. 1952. *The second sex.* New York: Vintage Books.

Debold, Elizabeth. 1991. The body at play. In *Women, girls and psychotherapy: Reframing resistance,* ed. Annie C. Rogers and Deborah L. Tolman, 169–83. New York: Harrington Park Press.

Debold, Elizabeth, Marie Wilson, and Idelisse Malave. 1993. *Mother Daughter revolution: From betrayal to power.* New York: Addison-Wesley.

Delaney, Janice, Mary Jane Lupton, and Emily Toth. 1988. *The curse: The cultural history of menstruation.* Urbana: University of Illinois Press.

D'Emilio, John, and Estelle B. Freedman. 1988. *Intimate matters: A history of sexuality in America.* New York: Harper and Row.

Demos, John, and Virginia Demos. 1969. Adolescence in historical perspective. *Journal of Marriage and the Family*: 632–638.

Denzin, Norman K. 1989. *Interpretive interactionism.* Newbury Park, CA: Sage Publications.

Deutsch, Helen. 1944. *The psychology of women: A psychoanalytic interpretation.* vol. 1. New York: Grune and Stratton.

de Waal, Mieke. 1993. Teenage daughters on their mothers. In *Daughtering and mothering: Female subjectivity reanalyzed,* ed. Janneke van Mens-Verhulst, Karlein Scheurs and Lisbeth Woertman, 125–34. London: Routledge.

Diamond, Irene, and Lee Quinby, eds. 1988. *Feminism and Foucault: Reflections on resistance.* Boston: Northeastern University Press.

Dickson, Geri L. 1993. Metaphors of menopause: The metalanguage of menopause research. In *Menopause: A midlife passage*, ed. Joan C. Callahan, 36–58. Bloomington: Indiana University Press.
Dinnerstein, Dorothy. 1976. *The mermaid and the minotaur: Sexual arrangements and human malaise.* New York: Harper and Row.
Diprose, Rosalyn. 1995. *The bodies of women: Ethics, embodiment and sexual difference.* New York: Routledge.
Douglas, Mary. 1966. *Purity and danger: An analysis of concepts of pollution and taboo.* London: Routledge and Kegan Paul.
Duck, Steve. 1983. *Friends for life: The psychology of close relationships.* New York: St. Martin's Press.
Eagleton, Terry. 1991. *Ideology: An introduction*. New York: Verso.
Edelman, Hope. 1994. *Motherless daughters: The legacy of loss.* New York: Bantam, Doubleday, and Dell.
Eichenbaum, Luise, and Susie Orbach. 1987. *Between women: Love, envy and competition in women's friendships.* New York: Penguin.
Elder, Glen H. 1974. *Children of the Great Depression.* Chicago: The University of Chicago Press.
———. 1987. Adolescence in historical perspective. In *Growing up in America: Historical experiences*, ed. Harvey J. Graff, 5–47. Detroit: Wayne State University Press.
Elkind, David. 1978. Understanding the young adolescent. *Adolescence* 13: 127–34.
Elshtain, Jean Bethke. 1981. *Public man, private woman.* Princeton: Princeton University Press.
Engel, Nancy S. 1987. Menopausal stage, current life change, attitude toward women's roles, and perceived health status. *Nursing Research* 36 (6): 353–57.
Epston, David and Michael White. 1992. *Experience, contradiction, narrative and imagination*. Adelaide, Australia: Dulwich Centre Publications.
Erikson, Erik H. 1968. *Identity: Youth and crisis.* New York: W.W. Norton.
Ernster, Virginia L. 1975. American menstrual expressions. *Sex Roles* 1: 3–13.
Esposito, Joseph L. 1987. *The obsolete self: Philosophical dimensions of aging.* Berkeley: University of California Press.
Etter-Lewis, Gwendolyn. 1991. Black women's life stories: Reclaiming self in narrative texts. In *Women's words: Feminist practice in oral history,* ed. Sherna B. Gluck and Daphne Patai, 43–58. New York: Routledge.
Faust, Margaret S. 1983. Alternative constructions of adolescent growth. In *Girls at puberty: Biological and psychological perspectives,* ed. Jeanne Brooks-Gunn and Anne C. Petersen, 105–25. New York: Plenum Press.
Fausto-Sterling, Anne. 1985. *Myths of gender: Biological theories about women and men.* New York: Basic Books.
Fenichel, Otto. 1945. *The psychoanalytic theory of neuroses.* New York: Norton.
Fine, Michelle. 1988. Sexuality, schooling and adolescent females: The missing discourse of desire. *Harvard Educational Review* 58: 29–53.
———. 1992. *Disruptive voices: The possibilities of feminist research.* Ann Arbor: University of Michigan Press.
Fine, Michelle, and Pat MacPherson. 1992. Over dinner: Feminism and adolescent female bodies. In *Disruptive voices: The possibilities of feminist research,*

ed. Michelle Fine, 75–203. Ann Arbor: University of Michigan Press.
Flaake, Karin. 1993. A body of one's own: Sexual development of the female body in the mother-daughter relationship. In *Daughtering and mothering: Female subjectivity reanalyzed,* ed. Janneke van Mens-Verhulst, Karlein Schreurs and Liesbeth Woertman, 7–14. London: Routledge.
Foster, Patricia, ed. 1994. *Minding the body: Women writers on body and soul.* New York: Anchor.
Foucault, Michel. 1977. *Discipline and Punish: The birth of the prison.* Trans. A. Sheridan. Harmondsworth U.K.: Peregrine.
———. 1978. *The history of sexuality: An introduction.* Trans. R. Hurley. Harmondsworth U.K.: Peregrine.
———. 1980. *Power/Knowledge: Selected interviews and other writings, 1972–1977.* New York: Pantheon Books.
Frank, Gelya. 1980. Life histories in gerontology: The subjective side to aging. In *New methods for old age research: Anthropological alternatives*, ed. Christine L. Fry and Jennie Keith, 155–176. Chicago: Center for Urban Policy.
Freire, Paulo. 1986. *Pedagogy of the opressed.* New York: The Continuum Publishing Company.
Freud, Sigmund. 1954. *Collected works: Standard edition.* London: Hogarth Press.
Friedan, Betty. 1974. *The Feminine mystique.* New York: Dell.
Fry, Christine L., and Jennie Keith. 1980. *New methods for old age research.* Chicago: Center for Urban Policy.
Gadow, Sally. 1983. Frailty and strength: The dialectic in aging. *The Gerontologist* 23 (2): 144–46.
Gavey, Nicola. 1989. Feminist poststructuralism and discourse analysis. *Psychology of Women Quarterly* 13: 459–75.
Gerike, Ann E. 1990. On gray hair and oppressed brains. In *Women, aging and ageism,* ed. Evelyn R. Rosenthal, 35–46. New York: Harrington Park Press.
Giddens, Anthony. 1979. *Central problems in social theory.* Berkeley: University of California Press.
Gilligan, Carol. 1982. *In a different voice.* Cambridge: Harvard University Press.
Gilligan, Carol, Nona P. Lyons, and Trudy J. Hanmer, eds. 1990. *Making connections: The relational worlds of adolescent girls at the Emma Willard School.* Cambridge: Harvard University Press.
Gilligan, Carol, Annie G. Rogers, and Deborah L. Tolman, eds. 1991. *Women, girls and psychotherapy: Reframing resistance.* Harrington Park, NY: Haworth Press.
Gilligan, Carol and Annie Rogers. 1993. Reframing daughtering and mothering: A paradigm shift in psychology. In *Daughtering and mothering: Female subjectivity reanalyzed,* ed. Janneke van Mens-Verhulst, Karlein Scheurs and Lisbeth Woertman, 125–34. London: Routledge.
Glasser, Barney G., and Anselm L. Strauss. 1967. *The discovery of grounded theory: Strategies for qualitative research.* Chicago: Aldine Publishing Company.
Gluck, Sherna Berger, and Daphne Patai, eds. 1991. *Women's words: The feminist practice of oral history.* New York: Routledge, Chapman, Hall.
* Golub, Sharon, ed. 1983. *Menarche: The transition from girl to woman.* Lexington, MA: D.C. Heath.

———, ed. 1983a. *Lifting the curse of menstruation: A feminist appraisal of the influence of menstruation in women's lives.* New York: Haworth Press.
———, ed. 1992. *Periods: From menarche to menopause.* Newbury Park, CA: Sage Publications.
Golub, Sharon, and Joan Catalano. 1983. Recollections of menarche and women's subsequent experiences with menstruation. *Women and Health* 8 (1): 49–61.
Grahn, Judy. 1982. From sacred blood to the curse and beyond. In *The politics of women's spirituality,* ed. Charlene Spretnak, 265–79. New York: Anchor.
———. 1993. *Blood, bread, and roses: How menstruation created the world.* Boston: Beacon Press.
Greer, Germaine. 1991. *The change: Women, aging and the menopause.* London: Hamish Hamilton.
Grief, Esther B., and Kathleen J. Ulman. 1982. The psychological impact of menarche on early adolescent females: A review of the literature. *Child Development* 53: 1413–30.
Griffin, Susan. 1978. *Women and nature.* New York: Harper and Row.
Grosz, Elizabeth. 1991. Introduction. *Hypatia* 6 (3): 1–3.
———. 1993. Bodies and knowledges: feminism and the crisis of reason. In *Feminist epistemologies*, ed. Linda Alcoff and Elizabeth Potter, 187–215. New York: Routledge.
———. 1994. *Volatile bodies: Toward a corporeal feminism.* Bloomington: Indiana University Press.
Gunn, John C. 1901. *Gunn's household physician.* Philadelphia: W.B. Saunders.
Haight, Barbara K. 1993. Reminiscence and life review. In *Encyclopedia of adult development,* ed. Robert Kastenbaum, 401–405. Phoenix: Oryx Press.
Hall, G. Stanley. 1904. *Adolescence.* New York: Appleton.
Hancock, Emily. 1989. *The girl within.* New York: Random House.
Haraven, Tamara K. 1978. *Transitions: The family and the life course in historical perspective.* New York: Academic Press.
Haraway, Donna. 1988. Situated knowledges. *Feminist Studies* 14: 575–99.
Harding, Sandra. 1991. *Whose science? Whose knowledge? Thinking from women's lives.* Ithaca, NY: Cornell University Press.
Hart, M., and Charles Sarnoff. 1971. The impact of the menarche: A study of two stages of organization. *Journal of the American Academy of Child Psychology* 10: 257–71.
Haug, Frigga, and others. 1987. *Female sexualization.* London: Verso.
Hays, Terence. 1987. Menstrual expressions and menstrual attitudes. *Sex Roles* 16: 605–14.
Heilbrun, Carolyn G. 1988. *Writing a woman's life.* New York: Ballantine.
Hernadez-Avila, Ines. 1995. To other women who were ugly once. In *Women, images and realities: A multicultural anthology,* ed. Amy Kesselman, Lily D. McNair, and Nancy Schneidewind, 98. Mountain View, Cal.: Mayfield.
Hetherington, E. Mavis. 1989. Coping with family transitions: Winners, losers and survivors. *Child Development* 60: 1–14.
Highwater, Jamake. 1991. *Myth and sexuality.* New York: Meridian.
Hill, John P., and Grayson N. Holmbeck. 1987. Familial adaptation to biological change during adolescence. In *Biological-psychological interactions of early*

adolescence, ed. Richard M. Lerner and Terryl T. Foch, 207–23. Hillsdale, NJ: Erlbaum Press.

Hill, John P., and Mary Ellen Lynch. 1983. The intensification of gender-related role expectations during early adolescence. In *Girls at Puberty: Biological and psychosocial perspectives,* ed. Jeanne Brooks-Gunn and Anne C. Petersen, 201–208. New York: Plenum Press.

Hinds, Pamela S., Doris E. Chaves, and Sandra M. Cypess. 1992. Context as a source of meaning and understanding. In *Qualitative health research*, ed. Janice M. Morse, 31–42. Newbury Park, CA: Sage Publications.

Hite, Shere. 1981. *Hite report on male sexuality.* London: MacDonald.

———. 1994. *The Hite report on the family: Growing up under patriarchy.* New York: Grove Press.

hooks, bell. 1992. *Black looks: Race and representation.* Boston: South End Press.

———. 1993. *Sisters of the yam: Black women and self recovery.* Boston: South End Press.

Horney, Karen. 1967. *Feminine psychology.* New York: Norton.

Iles, Teresa. 1992. *All sides of the subject: Women and biography.* New York: Teachers College Press.

Irigaray, Luce. 1985. *Speculum of the other woman.* Trans. G. C. Gill. Ithaca, NY: Cornell University Press.

Jackson, Beryl. 1992. Black women's responses to menarche and menopause. In *Menstrual health in women's lives,* ed. Alice J. Dan and Linda L. Lewis, 178–90. Urbana: University of Illinois Press.

Jaffe, Dale J., and Eleanor M. Miller. 1994. Problematizing meaning. In *Qualitative methods in aging research*, ed. Jaber F. Gubrium and Andrea Sankar, 51–64. Newbury Park, CA: Sage Publications.

Jayaratne, Toby E., and Abigail J. Stewart. 1991. Quantitative and qualitative methods in the social sciences: Current feminist issues and practical strategies. In *Beyond methodology: Feminist scholarship as lived research,* ed. Margaret Fonow and Judith A. Cook, 85–106. Bloomington: Indiana University Press.

Jenkins, Renee R. 1983. Future directions in research. In *Girls at Puberty: Biological and psychosocial perspectives,* ed. Jeanne Brooks-Gunn and Anne C. Petersen, 325–38. New York: Plenum Press.

Kahana, Eve E., Asuman A. Kiyak, and Jersey Liang. 1981. Menopause in the context of other life events. In *The menstrual cycle*, vol. 1., ed. Alice J. Dan, Effie A. Graham, and Carol P. Beecher, 167–77. New York: Springer.

Kaminsky, Marc. 1984. *The Uses of reminiscence: New ways of working with older adults.* New York: Hawthorne Press.

Karp, David A. 1988. A decade of reminders: Changing age consciousness between fifty and sixty years old. *The Gerontologist* 28 (6): 727–38.

Kaufert, Patricia A. 1986. Menstruation and menstrual change: Women in midlife. *Health Care for Women International* 7 (1–2): 63–70.

Kaufman, Sharon R. 1986. *The ageless self: Sources of meaning in late-life.* Madison: University of Wisconsin Press.

———. 1994. In-depth interviewing. In *Qualitative methods in aging research,* ed. Jabar F. Gubrium and Andrea A. Sankar, 122–36. Newbury Park, CA: Sage Publications.

Kerber, Linda D., and Jane De Hart Mathews. 1982. *Women's America: Refocusing the past.* New York: Oxford University Press.

Kestenberg, Judith. 1964. Menarche. In *Adolescents: A psychoanalytic approach to problems and therapy,* ed. Sandor Lorand and Henry Schneer, 19–50. New York: Harper and Row.

———. 1967. Phases of adolescence: Parts 1 and 2. *Journal of the American Academy of Child Psychiatry* 6: 426–63.

Kett, Joseph F. 1977. *Rites of passage.* New York: Basic Books.

Koff, Elissa. 1983. Through the looking glass of menarche: What the adolescent girl sees. In *Menarche*, ed. Sharon Golub, 77–86. Lexington, MA: D.C. Health.

Koff, Elissa, Jill Rierdan, and Ellen Silverstone. 1978. Changes in representation of body image as a function of menarcheal status. *Developmental Psychology* 14 (6): 635–42.

Koff, Elissa, Jill Rierdan, and S. Jacobson. 1981. The personal and interpersonal significance of menarche. *Journal of the American Academy of Child Psychiatry* 20: 148–58.

Komnenich, Pauline, McSweeney, Maryellen, and Novack, Janice. 1981. *The menstrual cycle*, vol.2: *Research and implications for women's health.* New York: Springer.

Kramer, Deirdre A. 1987. Cognition and aging: The emergence of a new tradition. In *The elderly as modern pioneers,* ed. Philip Silverman, 114–132. Bloomington: Indiana University Press.

Lachman, Margie E. 1984. Methods for a life-span developmental approach to women in the middle years. In *Women in midlife*, ed. Jeanne Brooks-Gunn and Barbara Kirsh, 11–30. New York: Basic Books.

Ladd, Rosalind E. 1993. Medical decision making: Issues concerning menopause. In *Menopause: A midlife passage,* ed. Joan C. Callahan, 145–59. Bloomington: Indiana University Press.

Lakoff, George. 1987. *Women, fire, and other dangerous things*. Chicago: University of Chicago Press.

Lander, Louise. 1988. *Images of bleeding: Menstruation as ideology.* New York: Orlando Press.

Lander, Nedhera. 1983. There's nothing to compare with how you feel when you're cut cold by your own.... In *Shadow on a tightrope: Writings by women on fat oppression,* ed. Lisa Schoenfielder and Barb Wieser, 223–26. San Francisco: Aunt Lute Books.

Laquer, Thomas. 1986. Female orgasm, generation, and the politics of reproductive biology. *Representations* 14 (spring): 1–82.

LaRocco, Susan A., and Denise F. Polit. 1980. Women's knowledge about the menopause. *Nursing Research* 29 (1): 10–13.

Laws, Sophie. 1990. *Issues of Blood: The Politics of Menstruation.* London: MacMillan.

Lee, Janet. 1994. Menarche and the (hetero)sexualization of the female body. *Gender and Society* 8 (3): 343–62.

Lee, Janet, and Jennifer Sasser-Coen. 1996. Memories of menarche: Older women remember their first menstrual period. *Journal of Aging Studies* 10 (2) [in press].

Lees, Sue. 1993. *Sugar and spice: Sexuality in adolescent girls.* London: Penguin Books.

Leiblum, Sandra R., and Leora C. Swartzman. 1986. Women's attitudes toward the menopause: An update. *Maturitas* 8: 47–56.

Lempers, Jacques D., and Dania S. Clark-Lempers. 1993. A functional comparison of same-sex and opposite-sex friendships during adolescence. *Journal of Adolescent Research* 8: 89–108.

Lloyd, Genevieve. 1989. The man of reason. In *Women, knowledge, and reality: Explorations in feminist philosophy*, ed. Ann Garry and Marilyn Pearsall, 111–28. Boston: Unwin Hyman.

Logan, Deana Dorman. 1980. The menarche experience in twenty-three foreign countries. *Adolescence* 15 (58): 247–56.

Lorde, Audre. 1984. *Sister outsider: Essays and speeches by Audre Lorde.* Freedom, Cal.: Crossing Press.

Lott, Bernice. 1994. *Women's lives: Themes and variations in gender learning.* Belmont, CA: Brooks/Cole.

Luborsky, Mark R. 1990. Alchemists' visions: Cultural norms in eliciting and analyzing life history narratives. *Journal of Aging Studies* 4 (1): 17–29.

———. 1994. The identification and analysis of themes and patterns. In *Qualitative methods in aging research*, ed. Jaber F. Gubrium and Andrea Sankar, 189–210. Newbury Park, CA: Sage Publications.

MacDonald, Barbara, and Cynthia Rich. 1983. *Look me in the eye: Old women, aging and ageism.* San Francisco: Spinsters/Aunt Lute.

MacPherson, Kathleen I. 1993. The false promises of hormone replacement therapy and current delimmas. In *Menopause: A midlife passage,* ed. Joan C. Callahan, 145–59. Bloomington: Indiana University Press.

MacQuarrie, Margaret A., and Barbara Keddy. 1992. Women and aging: Directions for research. *Journal of Women and Aging* 4 (2): 21–32.

Maguire, Patricia. 1987. *Doing participatory research: A feminist approach.* Amherst, Mass.: The Center for International Education.

Mankowitz, Ann. 1991. The neglected crisis. In *Women of the fourteenth moon: Writings on menopause,* ed. Dena Taylor and Amber Coverdale Sumrall, 20–24. Freedom, CA: The Crossing Press.

Martin, Biddy. 1988. Feminism, criticism and Foucault. In *Feminism and Foucault,* ed. Irene Diamond and Lee Quinby, 3–19. Boston: Northeastern University Press.

Martin, Emily. 1987. *The woman in the body: A cultural analysis of reproduction.* Boston: Beacon.

———. 1990. Science and women's bodies: Forms of anthropological knowledge. In *Body/Politics: Women and the discourses of science,* ed. Mary Jacobus, Evelyn Fox-Keller, and Sally Shuttleworth, 69–82. New York: Routledge.

Marx, Karl. 1964. *The economic and philosophic manuscripts of 1844.* Trans. M. Mulligan. New York: International Publishers.

———. 1970. *Preface to a contribution to the critique of political economy.* Trans. M. Mulligan. New York: International Publishers.

McCain, Marian Van Eyk. 1991. *Transformation through menopause.* New York: Bergin and Garvey.

McGoldrick, Monica. 1989. Sisters. In *Women in families: A framework for fam-*

ily therapy, ed. Monica McGoldrick, Carol M. Anderson, and Froma Walsh, 244–66. New York: W.W. Norton.
McNay, Lois. 1992. *Foucault and feminism: Power, gender and the self.* Boston: Northeastern University Press.
Mead, Margaret. 1949. *Male and female.* New York: Morrow.
———. 1952. Adolescence in primitive society. In *Readings in social psychology,* ed. Theodore Mead Newcomb and Eugene L. Hartley, 76–82. New York: Holt.
Meggitt, Mervyn J. 1964. Male-female relationships in the highlands of Australian New Guinea. *American Anthropologist* 66 (4): 204–24.
Miller, Ann C. 1990. The mother-daughter relationship and the distortion of reality in childhood sexual abuse. In *Gender and power in families,* ed. Rosine Jozef Perelberg and Ann C. Miller, 137–48. London: Tavistock/Routledge.
Modell, John. 1989. *Into one's own: From youth to adulthood in the United States, 1920–1975.* Berkeley: University of California Press.
Moore, Henrietta L. 1994. *A passion for difference: Essays in anthropology and gender*. Bloomington: Indiana University Press
Morgan, Gareth. 1983. *Beyond method: Strategies for social science research.* Newbury Park, Cal.: Sage Publications.
Morgan, Robin. 1982. *The anatomy of freedom: Feminism, physics, and global politics.* New York: Anchor Press.
Morrison, Toni. 1970. *The bluest eye.* New York: Pocket Books.
Moss, Zoe. 1970. It hurts to be alive and obsolete: The ageing woman. In *Sisterhood is powerful,* ed. Robin Morgan, 188–94. New York: Vintage Books.
Nathanson, Constance A. 1991. *Dangerous passage: The social control of sexuality in women's adolescence.* Philadelphia: Temple University Press.
Neugarten, Bernice L., Vivian Wood, Ruth J. Kraines, and Barbara Loomis. 1963. Women's attitudes toward the menopause. In *Middle age and aging,* ed. Bernice L. Neugarten, 195–200. Chicago: The University of Chicago Press.
Nielsen, Joyce McCarl. 1990. *Feminist research methodologies: Exemplary readings in the social sciences.* San Francisco: Westview.
*Olesen, Virginia L., and Nancy Fugate Woods. 1986. *Culture, society and menstruation.* Seattle: Hemisphere Publishing.
Ollman, Bertell. 1971. *Alienation: Marx's concept of man in capitalist society.* Cambridge: Cambridge University Press.
Orbach, Susie. 1978. *Fat is a feminist issue.* New York: Berkely Books.
———. 1986. *Hunger strike.* London: Faber and Faber.
Orenstein, Peggy. 1994. *Schoolgirls: Young women, self-esteem and the confidence gap.* New York: Doubleday.
*Owen, Lara. 1993. *Her blood is gold.* San Francisco: Harper San Francisco.
Parker, Jeffrey G., and John M. Gottman. 1989. Social and emotional development in a relational context. In *Peer relationships in child development*, ed. Thomas J. Berndt and Gary W. Ladd, 95–131. New York: Wiley.
Parlee, Mary Brown. 1978. Psychological aspects of menstruation, childbirth, and menopause. In *The psychology of women: Future directions in research,* ed. Julia A. Sherman and Florence L. Denmark, 179–226. New York: Psychological Dimensions, Inc.

Patterson, Ellen T., and Elwynn S. Hale. 1985. Making sure: Integrating menstrual care practices into activities of everyday living. *Advances in Nursing Science* 7: 18–31.

Personal Narratives Group. 1989. *Interpreting women's lives: Feminist theory and personal narratives.* Bloomington: Indiana University Press.

Petchesky, Rosalind. 1984. *Abortion and women's choice.* New York: Longman.

Petersen, Anne C. 1980. Puberty and its psychological significance in girls. In *The Menstrual cycle*, vol. 1, ed. Alice J. Dan, Effie A. Graham, and Carol P. Beecher, 45–55. New York: Springer.

———. 1983. Menarche: Meaning of measures and measuring meaning. In *Menarche,* ed. Sharon Golub, 63–76. Lexington, MA: Lexington Books.

Phelps, Linda. 1979. Female sexual alienation. In *Women: A feminist perspective*, ed. Jo Freeman, 18–26. Palo Alto, CA: Mayfield.

Piaget, Jean. 1954. *The construction of reality in the child.* New York: Basic Books.

Pillemer, David B., Elissa Koff, Elizabeth D. Rhinehart, and Jill Rierdan. 1987. Flashbulb memories of menarche and adult menstrual distress. *Journal of Adolescence* 10: 187–99.

Pipher, Mary. 1994. *Reviving Ophelia: Saving the selves of adolescent girls.* New York: Ballantine.

Pliner, Patricia, Shelly Chaiken, and Gordan L. Flett. 1990. Gender differences in concern with body weight and physical appearance over the life span. *Personality and Social Psychology Bulletin* 15 (2): 263–73.

Power, T. 1981. Sex-typing in infancy: The role of the father. *Infant Mental Health Journal* 2: 226–40.

Raymond, Janice. 1986. *A passion for friends: Toward a philosophy of female affection.* Boston: Beacon.

Reinharz, Shulamit. 1992. *Feminist methods in social research.* New York: Oxford University Press.

Rich, Adrienne. 1986. *Of woman born: Motherhood as experience and institution.* New York: Norton.

Rierdan, Jill, and Elissa Koff. 1980. Representation of the female body by early and late adolescent girls. *Journal of Youth and Adolescence* 9: 339–96.

———. 1991. Depression symptomology among very early maturing girls. *Journal of Youth and Adolescence* 20 (4): 415–25.

Rierdan, Jill, Elissa Koff, and Margaret L. Stubbs. 1989. Timing of menarche, preparation, and initial menstrual experience: replication and further analyses in a prospective study. *Journal of Youth and Adolescence* 18 (5): 413–26.

Romanyshyn, Robert D. 1992. The human body as historical matter and cultural symptom. In *Giving the body its due,* ed. Maxine Sheets-Johnstone, 159–79. New York: State University of New York Press.

Rosenthal, Evelyn R. 1990. Women and varieties of ageism. In *Women, aging and ageism,* ed. Evelyn R. Rosenthal, 1–6. New York: Harrington Park Press.

Rowles, Graham D., and Shulamit Reinharz. 1988. Qualitative gerontology: Themes and challenges. In *Qualitative gerontology,* ed. Shulamit Reinharz and Graham D. Rowles, 3–33. New York: Springer.

Rubin, Gayle. 1984. Thinking sex: Notes for a radical theory of the politics of sexuality. In *Pleasure and danger: Exploring female sexuality,* ed. Carole S. Vance, 267–319. Boston: Routledge and Kegan Paul.

Rubin, Lillian. 1979. *Women of a certain age: The midlife search for self.* New York: Harper and Row.
———. 1985. *Just friends: The role of friendship in our lives.* New York: Harper and Row.
Rubinstein, Robert L. 1988. Stories told: In-depth interviewing and the structure of its insights. In *Qualitative Gerontology*, ed. Shulamit Reinharz and Graham D. Rowles, 128–46. New York: Springer.
Ruble, Diane N., and Jeanne Brooks-Gunn. 1982. The experience of menarche. *Child Development* 53: 1557–66.
Sankar, Andrea, and Jabar F. Gubrium. 1994. *Qualtative methods in aging research.* Newbury Park, Cal.: Sage Publications.
Sasser-Coen, Jennifer. 1991. Musings on the mind/body split and the problematic nature of embodiment. Unpublished manuscript. Oregon State University, Corvallis.
———. 1996. The point of confluence: A qualitative study of the life-span developmental importance of menarche in the bodily histories of older women. Unpublished dissertation. Oregon State University, Corvallis.
Sault, Nicole, ed. 1994. *Many mirrors: Body image and social relations.* New Brunswick, NJ: Rutgers University Press.
Schaef, Anne Wilson. 1985. *Women's reality: An emerging female system in a white male society.* San Francisco: Harper and Row.
Schoenfielder, Lisa and Barb Wieser. 1983. Shadow on a Tightrope: Writings by Women on Far Oppression. San Francisco: Aunt Lute.
Schreurs, Karlein. 1993. Daughtering: The development of female subjectivity. In *Daughtering and mothering: Female subjectivity reanalysed,* ed. Janneke van Mens-Verhulst, Karlein Schreurs, and Liesbeth Woertman, 3–6. London: Routledge.
Scott, Joan Wallach. 1992. Experience. In *Feminists theorize the political*, ed. Judith Butler and Joan Wallach Scott, 22–40. New York: Routledge.
Selman, Robert L. 1980. *The growth of interpersonal understanding: Developmental and clinical analyses.* New York: Academic Press.
Shainess, Natalie. 1961. A re-evaluation of some aspects of femininity through a study of menstruation: A preliminary report. *Comprehensive Psychiatry* 2: 24.
Sheets-Johnstone, Maxine. 1992. Charting the interdisciplinary course. In *Giving the body its due*, ed. Maxine Sheets-Johnstone, 1–15. New York: State University of New York Press.
x Shuttle, Penelope, and Peter Redgrove. 1986. *The wise wound: Myths, realities, and meanings of menstruation.* New York: Bantam Books.
Silverman, Philip. 1987. The life course perspective. In *The elderly as modern pioneers,* ed. Philip Silverman, 1–16. Bloomington: Indiana University Press.
Simmons, Roberta G., and Dale A. Blyth. 1987. *Moving into adolescence.* New York: Aldine de Gruyter.
Simons, Margaret A., and Jessica Benjamin. 1979. Simone de Beauvoir: An interview. *Feminist Studies* 5 (2): 330–45.
Smith, Dorothy. 1992. Sociology from women's experience: A reaffirmation. *Sociological Theory* 10 (1): 88–98.
Smith-Rosenberg, Carroll. 1974. Puberty to menopause: The cycle of feminin-

ity in nineteenth-century America. In *Clio's consciousness raised,* ed. Mary Hartman and Lois Banner, 23–37. New York: Harper and Row.
Sontag, Susan. 1972. The double standard of aging. *Saturday Review* 55: 29–38.
Spretnak, Charlene, ed. 1982. *The politics of women's spirituality: Essays on the rise of spiritual power within the feminist movement.* New York: Anchor.
Stacey, Judith. 1988. Can there be a feminist ethnography? *Women's Studies International Forum* 11 (1): 21–27.
Steele, Robert S. 1989. A critical hermeneutics for psychology: Beyond positivism to an exploration of the textual unconscious. In *Entering the circle: Hermeneutic investigation in psychology,* ed. Martin J. Packer and Richard B. Addison, 223–37. New York: State University of New York Press.
Steinem, Gloria. 1983. If men could menstruate. In *Feminist Frontiers: Rethinking sex, gender and society,* ed. Laurel Richardson and Verta Taylor, 349–50. New York: Random House.
Stern, Lori. 1990. Conceptions of separation and connection in female adolescents. In *Making Connections*, ed. Carol Gilligan, Nona P. Lyons and Trudy J. Hanmer, 73–87. Cambridge: Harvard University Press.
Stoltenberg, John. 1989. *Refusing to be a man: Essays on sex and justice.* New York: Penguin.
Stoltzman, S. M. 1986. Menstrual attitudes, beliefs, and symptom experiences of adolescent females, their peers, and their mothers. *Health Care for Women International* 7: 97–114.
Tarnas, Richard. 1991. *The passion of the western mind: Understanding the ideas that have shaped our world view.* New York: Ballantine Books.
Taylor, Dena. 1988. *Red flower: Rethinking menstruation.* Freedom, Cal.: Crossing Press.
Taylor, Dena, and Amber Coverdale Sumrall. 1991. *Women of the fourteenth moon: Writings on menopause.* Freedom, CA: The Crossing Press.
Thompson, Clara. 1942. Cultural pressures in the psychology of women. *Journal of Comparative Psychology* 23: 439–55.
Thorne, Barrie. 1993. *Gender play: Girls and boys in school.* New Brunswick, NJ: Rutgers University Press.
Tobin-Richards, Maryse H., Andrew M. Boxer, and Anne C. Petersen. 1983. The psychological significance of pubertal change: Sex differences in perceptions of self during early adolescence. In *Girls at Puberty: Biological and psychosocial perspectives,* ed. Jeanne Brooks Gunn and Anne C. Petersen, 127–54. New York: Plenum Press.
Tolman, Deborah L. 1991. Adolescent girls, women and sexuality: Discerning dilemmas of desire. In *Women, girls and psychotherapy: Reframing resistance,* ed. Carol Gilligan, Annie G. Rogers and Deborah L. Tolman, 55–69. New York: Haworth Press.
Tolman, Deborah L. 1994. Doing desire: Adolescent girls' struggles for/with sexuality. *Gender and Society* 8 (3): 324–42.
Tolman, Deborah L., and Elizabeth Debold. 1994. Conflicts of body and image: Female adolescents, desire, and the no-body body. In *Feminist perspectives on eating disorders,* ed. Paricia Fallon, Melanie A. Katzman, and Susan C. Wooley, 301–17. New York: Guilford Press.

Tong, Rosemary. 1989. *Feminist thought: A comprehensive introduction.* Boulder, CO: Westview Press.

Turner, Kay. 1982. Contemporary feminist rituals. In *The politics of women's spirituality,* ed. Charlene Spretnak, 219–33. New York: Anchor.

Ulman, Kathleen H. 1992. The impact of menarche on family relationships. In *Menstrual health in women's lives,* ed. Alice J. Dan and Linda L. Lewis, 236–45. Urbana: University of Illinois Press.

Ussher, Jane. 1989. *The psychology of the female body.* New York: Routledge.

Uttal, David H., and Marion Perlmutter. 1989. Toward a broader conceptualization of development: The roles of gains and losses across the life span. *Developmental Review* 9 (2):101–32.

Voda, Ann M. 1993. A journey to the center of the cell: Understanding the physiology and endocrinology of menopause. In *Menopause: A midlife passage,* ed. Joan C. Callahan, 160–193. Bloomington: University of Indiana Press.

Wallace, J. Brandon. 1994. Life-stories. In *Qualitative methods in aging research,* ed. Jabar F. Gubrium and Andrea Sankar, 137–54. Newbury Park, Cal.: Sage Publications.

Weedon, Chris. 1987. *Feminist practice and poststructuralist theory.* Cambridge,: Blackwell.

*Weideger, Paula. 1976. *Menstruation and menopause: The physiology and psychology, the myth and reality.* New York: Knopf.

Whisnant, Lynn, and Leonard Zegans. 1975. A study of attitudes towards menarche in white, middle-class american adolescent girls. *American Journal of Psychiatry* 132: 809–14.

Whisnant, Lynn, Elizabeth Brett, and Leonard Zegans. 1975. Implicit messages concerning menstruation in commercial educational materials prepared for young adolescent girls. *American Journal of Psychiatry* 132: 815–20.

White, Michael. 1995. *Re-authoring lives: Interviews and essays*. Adelaide, Australia: Dulwich Centre Publications.

——— and David Epston. 1990. *Narrative means to therapeutic ends*. Adelaide, Australia: Dulwich Centre Publications.

Williams, Lenore. 1983. Beliefs and attitudes of young girls regarding menstruation. In *Menarche,* ed. Sharon Golub, 133–37. Boston: Lexington Books.

Wilshire, Donna. 1989. The uses of myth, image, and the female body in revisioning knowledge. In *Gender/Body/Knowledge*, ed. Alison M. Jaggar and Susan R. Bordo, 92–114. New Brunswick, NJ: Rutger University Press.

Wilson, Robert. 1966. *Feminine Forever.* New York: M. Evans.

Wolf, Naomi. 1991. *The beauty myth: How images of beauty are used against women.* New York: Doubleday.

Wong, Nellie. 1995. When I was growing up. In *Women, images and realities: A multicultural anthology,* ed. Amy Kesselman, Lily D. McNair, and Nancy Schneidewind, 97. Mountain View, CA: Mayfield.

Woods, Nancy F., Gretchen D. Dery, and Ada Most. 1982. Recollections of menarche, current menstrual attitudes, and perimenstrual symptoms. *Psychosomatic Medicine* 44 (3): 285–93.

Young, Iris. 1990. *Throwing like a girl and other essays in feminist philosophy.* Bloomington: Indiana University Press.

Zita, Jacqueline N. 1993. Heresy in the female body: The rhetoric of menopause. In *Menopause: A midlife passage*, ed. Joan C. Callahan, 59–114. Bloomington: Indiana University Press.

Index